INNO DEVELOPMENT

Emerging Worldviews and Systems Change

Tom Christensen, Editor

Integral Publishers
Tucson, AZ

Integral Publishers
4845E. 2nd St.
Tucson, AZ 85711

ISBN: 978-1-4951-5908-4

Cover by QTPunque.

DEDICATION

Feeling gratitude and not expressing it is like wrapping a present and not giving it.
— William Arthur Ward

Thank you Professor Clare W. Graves.

The efforts of the many brilliant and skilled professionals documented in these volumes would not be here if it were not for the diligent and long term efforts of the first Gravesian, Professor Clare W. Graves (1914 – 1986). As the classic metaphor says, these authors would not have risen to this level of competence and visibility without the broad and tall shoulders of Professor Graves to stand upon.

There are a few who knew "Clare" personally, and all reports indicate he was a personable, caring, and artful researcher, theorist, educator, family man and friend. This would be legacy enough for many of us. Graves, however, left us with even more; he embodied the leading edge of human development that he discovered. He was captured by a vision of how all the apparently limited perspectives on a healthy psychology could be lined up so as to address the contexts they pertain to. His approach was not constrained by either/or thinking, but had the scope to integrate truths into a larger vision where all well-founded truths had their place.

Graves level of cognitive complexity could not be served by linear thinking or models. He had to reach to what is still the most complex template for organizing information, General Systems Theory, in order to be able to account for feedback loops between capacity and context. Systems Theory was necessary to describe the emergence of more complex and unpredictable measures out of the less complex and predictable; to give theoretical consistency to the levels of maturation he noted as deriving from changes of equilibrium and disequilibrium; to account for change occasioned by perturbations from excessive energy deriving from solved challenges; to include the relevance of an array of subsystems, including human biology, physiology, neurology, as well as culture, education and management. If you had any trouble comprehending those past few sentences, then you have gotten a sense of how complex Grave's cognition might have been and what understanding may yet lie ahead for you.

Graves was a path finder. He struggled with the concepts of his time and left us with a map that resolved many of the developmental conundrums of his time; a map that may well drive creative thinking about humans and human systems for ages to come. For those whose curiosity about human nature is insatiable, Graves has provided answers, directions, milestones, insights, and nudges towards what is still unknown. From the stories that follow, it should be clear that we now have new degrees of freedom for engaging humanity's problems.

At the leading edge of Grave's model, we find a humanity that has left selfish behavior behind, that cares for planetary well-being as its own well-being, that has integrated love and compassion, and gone beyond this with artful, collaborative, action. For all the effort, enjoyment, records, ideas, and trail-making that Graves left behind, gratitude is a natural, as well as deserved response. For his vision of what else is possible for humanity, he deserves much more than gratitude. Perhaps living his highest vision for humanity is what comes after gratitude. May he be honored in such a way… until what is beyond even this appears.

TABLE OF CONTENTS

REVALUING PURPLE, RED AND BLUE 328

By Jasper Rienstra

AUTHORS...339

PUBLISHER'S PREFACE

The chapters in the book, *Innovative Development: Emerging Worldviews and Systems Change,* and in its companion, *Developmental Innovation: Emerging Worldviews and Individual Learning,* represent the conjunction of many streams of thought and practice. Each chapter is influenced by one or more of the following conceptual frameworks.

First is adult development psychology. This is a young field with several frameworks and approaches to understanding how we develop as individuals. Theorists and researchers such as Clare W. Graves, Michael Commons, Michael Basseches, Jane Loevenger, William Perry, Jean Gebser, Susann Cook-Greuter, Robert Kegan, Bill Torbert and others have laid foundations for better understanding how we as individuals develop and evolve cognitively, emotionally, psychologically and even spiritually.

Another is integral theory. This is based on the work of theorists such as Ervin Laszlo and Ken Wilber. While not all authors or all of their offerings give attention to integral theory, the relationship between adult development psychology and integral theory is an interesting one in that it provides a way of understanding how our development as individuals cannot be fully understood without attention to our psychology and our biology. In addition, we cannot understand our development without attention to the cultural and systemic Life Conditions we have encountered and created. Integral theory supports the integration of monological views of individual psychology in which the focus is on the internal dynamics of each individual with a dialogical view. The dialogical approach requires that we understand individual psychology in terms of the interactive processes of individuals with their contexts and Life Conditions.

A central concern of both adult development psychology and integral theory is how we create meaning and make sense of ourselves and our world. We cannot achieve that by focusing on individuals and their human relationships. We also need to attend to the cultures, systems, technologies, structures, processes, and artifacts of that world, those contexts. In the case of the chapters found in these two books, this contextual perspective is underscored by Clare Graves' attention to the importance of Life Conditions to the worldview we bring to making sense and meaning out of our selves and our world.As a growing interest in transdisciplinarity suggests, we are recognizing that we cannot effectively address the complex and critical challenges we face with simplistic solutions. Scientism and spirituality are in need of integration. This requires the integration of diverse worldviews and ways of making meaning. The authors in these volumes have been influenced by many elements of this diversity.

In these volumes we will find work that seeks to integrate our understandings from the labors of Clare W. Graves and the extension of his research by others, particularly Don E. Beck and his colleagues and students, with theories and models drawn from systems theory, cognitive science, cultural theory, organization development, learning theory and a myriad of other influences. These two volumes represent a step along the path toward more transdisciplinary engagement with the development of human systems and of individuals. The editor, Tom Christensen, has organized this material around the two themes of systems, on the one hand, and individuals, on the other. Keep in mind that this separation is an organizing device. It would be a mistake to think of these as two independent domains.

The reader is encouraged to review the material in both volumes as a way to build an appreciation of the depth and scope of the work of Clare W. Graves and his followers, as well as promoting an integration of how we make sense and meaning out of the complex dynamics facing us in the world, today. The fourth dimension of time is playing a more and more limiting role on the choices we make and how we go about implementing them. Until we can more effectively integrate our individual learning and development with how we develop and evolve our systems and relationships with cultural and developmental diversity in the world we will likely continue down a path that seems to be leading to the destruction of the world as we know it.

This is a time in which it is increasingly difficult to muster up a sense of optimism for the world and our selves. We require a critical mass of individuals around the world building the capacity for engaging with diversity and realigning our systems to embrace that diversity in ways that help us build more constructive allocation of resources and addressing the critical challenges of our day. There are not many signs for optimism in this era of the clash of civilizations, the leveraging of technology to build and to destroy, the inequities that exist not just in the distribution of wealth within developed nations, but between nations and within cultures that span national boundaries. The construction of boundaries in all aspects of human being in the world underlies much of our sense of identity, as well as the ways in which we engage with each other – and seek to destroy each other.

Daily headlines expose us to barbarism and destruction as individuals seek to protect these boundaries designed to defend the status quo, the distribution of resources, the growing economic and political power of the oligarchies, the freedoms enjoyed by the military-industrial complex at the expense of millions of human lives, the aggressive defense of the past by religious fanatics, the barbaric destruction of human life and cultural artifacts by those seeking to dominate in the face of power vacuums and inequities, the ongoing destruction of the environment, the loss of species due to greed and environmental degradation, and so on.

It seems an overwhelming challenge to find a path that will lead us out of this self-destructive chaos. Today, as I write this in my office in Tucson, Arizona the world seems peaceful and delightful. We have been blessed with cooler than usual temperatures for a few days. Birds are chirping – I can see sparrows, desert doves, woodpeckers and blackbirds taking turns enjoying the water filled birdbath outside my office window. For this rare moment – a period of ongoing challenges in our lives – peace and contentment seem possible. But I know this is just a moment in an ongoing process of development and destruction. I can enjoy this moment of peace and personal contentment, yet the threats of our collective challenges in the world are all around me.

While I may find it difficult to see generative paths ahead, I am convinced that it is the work of people like the authors in these two volumes that holds out hope for the development of such paths. Theirs are not quick fixes, nor simplistic solutions. Instead, their work helps us understand the necessity to shift our ways of meaning making so that our views are less static, are open to seeing dynamic processes of being and living and creating. It is my intention that bringing these two volumes to you will contribute to the design and implementation of a generative path for us, individually and collectively, in support of life on this planet for the natural evolution of species and systems.

Russ Volckmann, PhD
Publisher, Integral Publishers
May 25, 2015

FOREWORD

Laura Frey Horn

More than sixty years ago, Dr. Clare W. Graves began his research and quest to develop a fuller, more complex understanding and theory of human development, or as he described it "the psychology of the mature human being". He continued his work until his death in 1986. With the work of others, including initially Dr. Don E. Beck and those in this book, Graves' work lives on.

Dr. Graves was keenly aware of the limitations of other theories of adult development. His research was carried out over decades. My understanding was that he conducted research within organizations in addition to his research at the individual levels of development. He was also extremely well versed in all of the current and past theories of adult development and current scientific, sociological and other research that could impact human development. However, an area of research of which I am certain I was a part that did occur at Union and involved students was the assignment in one of the upper class courses he taught. One major paper was to address our own theory of adult development. My later understanding (from Don E. Beck in one of our many conversations about Clare) was that this was a part of his research.

Dr. Graves was, in my opinion, a constant observer. On one of my trips to Union's Library and the special archives, I found pages of his notes where he had made observations about different individuals' behaviors, actions, comments or words. At the top of pages, he would denote a level (i.e. D-Q, F-S, G-T, etc.). It was clear that comments had been added over time and the comments could have been made by different individuals.

As Graves moved more deeply into his research, he recognized that all aspects of human development needed to include our understanding of whole systems. His research focused on the complete spectrum of the adult human being, including the psychological, sociological, physical, cultural, biological and developmental impacts of systems changes in the development of human beings. Although other psychologists had developed hierarchal developmental models and theories, Graves' work was the first to include a holistic or whole systems approach.

Gravesian theory is deeply and widely complex simply because human development is deeply and widely complex. The deeper Graves' research took him, the more he found connections to complementary systems that impacted the psychology of the mature human being. Graves also uncovered how individuals' collective growth and development could impact sociological systems at the tribal, community, organizational and cultural levels. Graves identified the significant impact of open and closed systems as well as effective/ineffective (healthy/unhealthy) traits or behaviors. Hence, Gravesian theory was known, at least for a time at Union College, as the Gravesian "Bio-Psycho-Social-Double Helix Model of Emergent Adult Development". (I believe that it went through several name changes over time.) Dr. Graves had recognized that the levels of human development he had been researching also applied to organizational levels of adult psychology. He recognized that biology, psychology, sociology and other areas – including culture – impacted human development. He was the first psychologist to acknowledge the critical importance of all of these parameters. And, yet, many of his peers did not understand his theory and its importance.

By the time I arrived at Union College in the early 1970s (the second class of women admitted to the college), Graves had already spent two decades of his life extensively researching and developing his theory. Clare Graves was an iconic figure on Union College's campus. He was tall, strong and rarely spoke to students when he strode across campus. (I do believe that he had already experienced health issues by the time I came to Union, but doubt many students knew.) He was admired, but certainly misunderstood by many students.

There were certainly many students, including psychology majors at Union, who resisted taking Graves' courses because they knew the theory was challenging and difficult to follow. I often wondered if other psychologists resisted or resented his work because his theory was difficult to understand. Dr. Don E. Beck once told me that Clare held off publishing results of his studies until he felt his research was incontrovertible because his colleague, Abraham Maslow, warned him that he would be attacked for such a remarkably different theory of human development, as had been Maslow's experience in presenting his theory of motivation.

It was well known that Dr. Graves had a "ranch" outside the town of Schenectady, New York where he trained and rode horses. The rumor was that he "broke wild stallions with his bare hands" in his spare time – when he wasn't teaching or doing his research. The role of "stallion tamer" only added to his reputation. And, the fact that he was developing a complex, new theory that few, including psychology majors, could understand created an image even larger than life. I think Clare knew that many students were reticent to talk to him and he used it to his advantage. I also often thought that he used it as a test, even as a piece of his own research. In fact, it seemed many students were afraid of him. He was a legend on and off campus. If the man could "break" wild stallions, what would he do if you challenged that gruff demeanor?

I learned just how strong this iconic image of Dr. Graves was within the first days of arrival at Union. During Freshman Orientation, the few women (fewer than 100 women in the 1500 student body) were offered considerable guidance by the upperclassmen. A senior psychology major offered to provide a tour of the Psychology Department and building, with a complete run down of my advisor and the other professors. When told my advisor was Dr. Clare W. Graves, he immediately said, "Oh no! Tomorrow morning, first thing you MUST go to the registrar's office and request a new advisor. Tell the registrar anything! Just tell her you have got to have a different advisor! I mean it! First thing, before anyone else puts in their request!" There was fear in his voice. I don't scare easily, so I asked, "Really? How bad can SHE be?!" Needless to say, I did not request a change. Graves' deep voice and focus on his research may have contributed to the sense that he seemed aloof and hard to reach to those who didn't know him well. In fact, more than a large number of students were wary of him and willing to avoid him. I think Dr. Graves was quite aware of his reputation and probably found it humorous.

When I first met him I was exposed to his gruff persona. As my advisor, Dr. Graves had to approve and sign off on my course selection. He also required that students come to him in person for the sign off, while many advisors were delighted to have students leave the form under the door. Dr. Graves only taught upper class courses, but as his advisee, I had the opportunity to meet him as a freshman. Although most faculty members – especially full professors like Dr. Graves – chose the more spacious offices on the second floor of the "Psych Department" building, he chose the quieter, smaller third floor "attic" office. Although I don't scare easily, I did hear and heed the legendary stories of Dr. Clare W. Graves, and proceeded with caution. When I reached his office, he was deep in thought and writing. I paused outside his office for a moment and waited. I knew he had heard and seen me, but there was no response. Finally, I said quietly, "Dr. Graves?" "YES!" with a bit of a BOOM! I was a bit taken aback and considered the options – run or stay. Before I could decide, I noticed it… the small square of beautiful blue sky behind Dr. Graves! There, behind him, the legend, the man who "…breaks wild stallions with his bare hands…" sitting in a tiny office… with boxes surrounding him and a pile of papers on his desk! Shouldn't he be outside right this moment on a horse… racing across the mountains?!

"Dr. Graves, WHAT are you doing inside right now?! It is so beautiful outside! Shouldn't you be outside now?" With that Dr. Graves startled and looked at me. Oh no, I am really in for it now!

"WELL, IF YOU DAMN STUDENTS DIDN'T GIVE US DAMN PROFESSORS SO MUCH DAMN WORK, I COULD BE OUTSIDE!"

And, a glare. Do I stay or run… Hmmph… Two can play this game! "Well (A TINY bit more quietly than his BOOM), IF YOU DAMN PROFESSORS DIDN"T GIVE US DAMN STUDENTS SO DAMN MUCH WORK, YOU COULD BE OUTSIDE RIGHT NOW! (Quick now, SMILE!! BIG SMILE!)

Then, suddenly a huge smile from Dr. Graves, "What can I do for you, Teri?" He knew my family/friend nickname! That was the start of Dr. Graves truly becoming my professor, my advisor, and whether he ever realized it or not my mentor. I was fortunate to work in the Psychology Department the rest of my time at Union in addition to my full time jobs. It allowed more time for short conversations for me and for my dog, Dutch, to visit Dr. Graves in his office.

Dr. Graves had his softer side, too. When I was taking his classes it was not uncommon for students to bring their dogs onto campus and into classrooms. This I did with Dutch. He would go to Dr. Graves' classes with me and lie down under the table next to where Dr. Graves was lecturing. Dr. Graves had much to say, and sometime lectured a bit longer than the allotted class time. One day the class went way past the end time. Dutch got up, strode to the door, turned around, sat down and quizzically looked at Dr. Graves. Some of my fellow students became nervous. Students might challenge other professors, but never Dr. Graves. Dr. Graves finally looked up and noticed Dutch at the door. As students looked my way and wondered what wrath would befall my pet and me, Dr. Graves looked at Dutch and said in his gruff voice, "I guess Dutch thinks class must be over! And it is." As I was leaving, Dr. Graves gave me a brief smile.

He knew I had figured out that his gruff persona was a ruse and that I kept his secret.

Dr. Graves, as a full professor, was able to spend most of his time at Union focused on his research. He taught two courses for upper class students. I remember the titles as "Theories of Personalities" and "Organizational Psychology." The first half of the course, "Theories of Personalities" was similar to the college textbook I had read years before coming to Union. It was the reason I wanted to become a psychologist. However, in Graves' course, only the first half of the course covered the theories the textbook covered, while the second half of the course covered Gravesian theory. I knew then I was exactly where I belonged. The second of Clare Graves' courses, "Organizational Psychology" was pure application of Gravesian theory in organizations. From our first encounter, when I called his bluff on gruffness, I knew I was at Union to meet and learn from him. From the moment I stepped into his first class session, I knew this was the critically important theory missing from the textbook I had read years earlier. Between the two courses, Gravesian theory not only became easily applicable, but I could immediately see the relevance in everyday life – in my work, studies, and social encounters.

When I was his student and he was my mentor and advisor, Clare Graves never told me what to do. He might ask me a question or two, but would then indicate that I would know just what needed to be done. And, he was right! In fact, our conversations were always short. (Probably surprising for those who know me and not at all surprising for those who knew Clare.) He gave me advice only once and then only after I had returned to Union – more than a year after graduating – for a stint as an administrator. He welcomed me and asked about events since we had last seen each other. He then told me not to stay too long. I promised I would not. He smiled and told me he knew I wouldn't. And, when I called him "Dr. Graves," he acknowledged my new position and reminded me, "It's Clare now, Laura." It was the last time we had the opportunity to speak.

Dr. Clare W. Graves was probably at least 40 years ahead of his time. He told our mutual dear friend, Dr. Don E. Beck, that he should continue to develop the theory, which Don has continued to do with Spiral Dynamics & Spiral Dynamics integral. I have used Gravesian and Spiral Dynamics integral in all areas of my life and work. I believe that my beloved mentor and professor would be thrilled that this book is filled with examples of applications by authors who are actively using Gravesian theory in their work. Several of the authors in this volume are dear friends and colleagues whose work I know and admire. There are others whose work I do not yet know. May they all shine as well in honoring Dr. Clare W. Graves with their works.

INTRODUCTION

This book is intended for:

1) Those who are hungry. Worms, mold, and other micro organisms will turn it into healthy soil, which grows healthy food.

2) Those two leggeds who need a physical embodiment of sacred wisdom, a book that sits in a sacred place, silently guides one's clan, and holds the sacred stories of those who were possessed by its special spirit.

3) Those who want power over people, places and things and can use the knowledge herein to establish their territories of unquestionable expertise.

4) Those who are looking for THE answers, and know learning them will, one day, provide a reward that fulfills the purpose of human life.

5) Those who wish to be more effective in their efforts, who have a vision of personal goals, and are doing all they can to achieve these ends.

6) Those who know nothing will work until everyone is included, understood, cared for and about.

7) Those who have found loving fully is not enough to fix the world. Artful action is required. Resources, capacities and

abilities must be aligned to satisfy the existential needs of all of those in categories 1–6.

8) Those who have realized their integral presence in the collective of all of life, and live so as to foster the health and wellbeing of the whole planet.

The reader who can see themselves in all these categories will find the most value in this book. Consider one ideal situation: A person recognizes they are a system of many systems (8), and sees that artful action is necessary to foster healthy living in all their systems (7), they respect all points of view (6), have personal goals they are striving to achieve (5), know the conventional purpose and rules of life (4), have a territory where their presence is respected (3), appreciate the magical in their lives (2), and make sure their basic survival needs are reliably addressed. This could very well describe you, dear reader. And the fact that one frame of reference could suggest the life story of any reader here, is a measure of the value of the work of Professor Clare W. Graves, who first created this framework from the years of research data he had collected.

What you will read in the following chapters is a reiteration of the 8 perspectives above, framed in a multiple of contexts. There are nuances you will find in the reports to follow, and there are individual spins on the body of Gravesian knowledge represented here. But all the stories told here are built around the same developmental trajectory, the same path of maturation, the same line of increasing cognitive complexity.

We all begin with a need to resolve the demands of survival. If we transcend and include our survival needs we enter the path of increasing cognitive complexity. We don't all mature to the maximum available to humans. Sometimes capacity is not there for further maturation. Sometimes Life Conditions argue against further maturation. The end of this maturation line is unknown. Graves noted this ever unfolding human nature as the "Never ending Quest."

What the following advises is that there is a path of existential development; it is knowable; knowing it can reduce suffering and foster health and well-being. Some of you will note this is not a unique claim. What follows, however, is a unique formulation, perhaps retold in an idiom perfect for our time.

Orienting Details

Graves, being the research scientist that he was, designated the developmental levels he asserted, with a two letter indicator. The first letter pertains to individual capacity, the second to context, showing that any level is a combination of these two. Thus Graves would call the first level, A-N, the second B-O, and so on. Don Beck, who has done more than anyone to popularize Graves' work, has provided a nomenclature for these levels based on colors (Beck & Cowan, *Spiral Dynamics.* (1996) Blackwell. Malden, MA, USA) . AN is Beige. BO is Purple. CP is Red. DQ is Blue. ER is Orange. FS is Green. GT is Yellow. HU is Turquoise.

Cowan has since presented his work as "Spiral Dynamics". Beck presents his work as "Spiral Dynamics Integral" (SDi) All the authors in both volumes have studied in the lineage of Don Beck, and thus you will find the Beck and Cowan colors, and "SDi" used throughout…except for academic researcher and author John Cook, who uses the alpha nomenclature in his chapter.

This book presumes a basic knowledge of SDi, such as that available in the following: *Spiral Dynamics, The Never Ending Quest,* or your editor's Second Tier tutorial here http://www.academia.edu/6716201/An_Introduction_To_and_Tutorial_For_Spiral_Dynamics_Integral_SDi_. Most of the SDi related books noted in Appendix 1 have excellent introductory material in them. Both Beck and Cowan, separately, continue to market their versions of Graves' work through their own trainings, and you may find attending these periodic offerings of value. If you are a newbie to Graves' work, there is sufficient content and context provided in the chapters ahead that you will soon get a grasp of the framework.

What follows are reports from the field, the complement to the theory sources mentioned above. Volume 1 is focused on professional practitioners' experiences with larger scale systems. Volume 2 focuses on reports from people who apply Graves' insights to themselves, their relationships, and to others thru self-study, therapy, counseling and coaching. In short we can say that Volume 1 focuses on Ken Wilber's lower right quadrant, while Volume 2 focuses either on the introjection of the theory, the upper left quadrant, or relationships, the lower left quadrant (Wilber, *Integral Psychology*, 2000). Together the two volumes present a foundation for understanding the wide range of application of Graves' work.

The chapters presented here are, in sum, the voices of Third Generation Gravesians. There could be no third without a second and that debt is honored by all here.

Thank you to my parents, Harry and Gladys, and wife Stephanie. Without them these volumes would not have occurred.

Tom Christensen, Editor

SDi IN THE INTEGRAL CITY

By Marilyn Hamilton, PhD, CGA, CSP

The core ideas in this chapter have been drawn from the book by Marilyn Hamilton (2008) *Integral City: Evolutionary Intelligences for the Human Hive, New Society, Gabriola Island, BC, Canada.*

In The Beginning

In the early 2000's I was inspired to look at a new paradigm for the city, one that is complex, integral evolutionary and adaptively alive. In my coming to terms with this calling, I have been deeply influenced by the field work, writing and personal guidance of Dr. Don Beck and his frameworks for values, culture and change at the scales of individual, organizational and societal development.

My book, *Integral City: Evolutionary Intelligences for the Human Hive* is liberally pollinated with the nectar of SDi, as it helps to explain the emergence, coherence and resonance of human systems at the scale of city systems. This chapter will condense the nectar into a honey pot, so readers can taste test and hopefully appreciate more concisely how SDi can be applied to understanding, enacting, designing and evolving human systems in the city, with the city and as the city.

Understanding Values In The City

Several decades earlier than either Bloom or Holling conceived the complexity and resilience systems (described in chapter 2 of *Integral City*),

Graves (2003) in the 1960's and 1970's conducted an 18-year study, whose conclusions came to be known as the "evolutionary complex levels of human existence." Graves' research showed that human behaviors arising out of one set of conditions created problems of existence that could not be solved at that level (echoing Einstein's proposition of the same nature).

As a result new adaptive behaviors are called into existence. Graves identified a group-centric cluster of behaviors he called "sacrifice self" values and an individual centric cluster of behaviors he called "express self" values. Moreover, his research showed that these behaviors adapted and alternated with one another at an ever-increasing level of complexity, as Life Conditions changed. Graves used a set of identifiers to represent Life Conditions (designated by letters from the first half of the alphabet) and bio-psycho-cultural-social human development (designated by letters from the second half of the alphabet).

Beck and Linscott (2006), Beck and Cowan (1996) and Beck (2002) have devised a system of color codes to identify each level of complexity. Beige, Red, Orange and Yellow (i.e., warm colours) relate to "express self" versions of existence. Purple, Blue, Green and Turquoise (i.e., cool colours) relate to "sacrifice self" versions of existence.

Because the dominant behaviors arise in response to Life Conditions, as one would expect from any complex adaptive system (Capra, 1996; Holling, 2001; Stevenson & Hamilton, 2001), each level of existence behaves with increasing levels of complexity in order to maximize the organizing principle or value of the current Life Condition. This behavior results in a tendency to protect the status quo at its current level of complexity (Hamilton 2007). In Bloom's terms[1], this could be interpreted as conformity enforcement of the organizing principle or value.

Thus a tension in favor of the values and behavior that are most coherent with the current Life Conditions will be demonstrated by people in the city as conformity enforcement. The flip side of this behavior is that the dominant culture will also protect itself against diversity generation. This protection will continue until such time as Life Conditions require the solutions that diversity generation can offer. These solutions will solve the problems created by maximizing the values and organizing principles in

---

1   Bloom (2000) identified 4 roles in the bee hive: Conformity Enforcers, Diversity Generators, Resource Allocators and Inner Judges. These appear to be fractal and used by other systems such as Adizes' Producers, Entrepreneurs, Administrators and Integrators and at the city scale. Hamilton (website) identifies them as Cityzens, Civic Managers, Civil Society and Business Developers.

play at the presenting level of existence. Moreover, in the city, we can see the natural evolutionary cycles emerge at all levels of scale: individual, family, organization, society.

Figure x.1. Levels Of Complexity

Source: Hamilton, 2008, p. 86, Adapted from Beck, 2002.

EXPRESS SELF STAGE	ORGANIZING PRINCIPLE OF LIFE CONDITIONS	SACRIFICE SELF STAGE	ORGANIZING PRINCIPLE OF LIFE CONDITIONS
AN – Beige	Survival	BO – Purple	Safety/Belonging
CP – Red	Command & Control	DQ – Blue	Authoritarian Structure
ER – Orange	Economic Success	FS – Green	Humanitarian Equality
GT – Yellow	Systemic Flex & Flow	HU – Turquoise	Planetary Commons

How To Apply Values Mapping In The City

Being able to map the values of any given city neighborhood (or household or street even) informs strategic decision making related to resource allocation. In the map below one can see different sets of values mapped onto the city's neighborhoods. I have been told by Police Chiefs, Fire Marshalls and Social Service providers that this makes all the difference in how they deliver services to specific areas, because they better understand differing values and therefore cultures in the city.

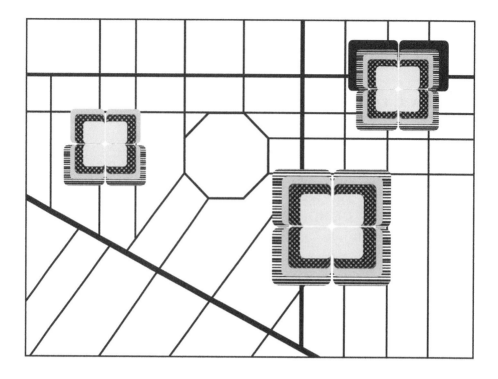

Values Mapped onto City Streets (from Integral City: Evolutionary Intelligences for the Human Hive, p. 70)

Creating Organizational Structures In The City

Graves' systemic model proposed that the Life Conditions that stimulated our bodies and brains to adapt and survive were accompanied by an evolving consciousness that enabled the evolution of what it means to be human. It is precisely those Life Conditions that contribute to the evolution and the state of well-being of our cities today. Like our physical bodies and habitat structures, our individual human life cycles bear witness to the developmental nature of the human system. Clare Graves provides this fractal list that demonstrates the historical development of human consciousness as well as potential individual development:

1)   Beige. 100,000 years ago.

2)   Purple. 40,000 years ago.

3)   Red. 10,000 years ago.

4) Blue. 4,000 years ago.

5) Orange. 1400 years ago.

6) Green. 80 years ago.

7) Yellow. 30 years ago.

8) Turquoise. Emerging.

Superimposing this time line on the AQAL map below shows the approximate historical emergence of these levels of consciousness as homo sapiens sapiens has developed.

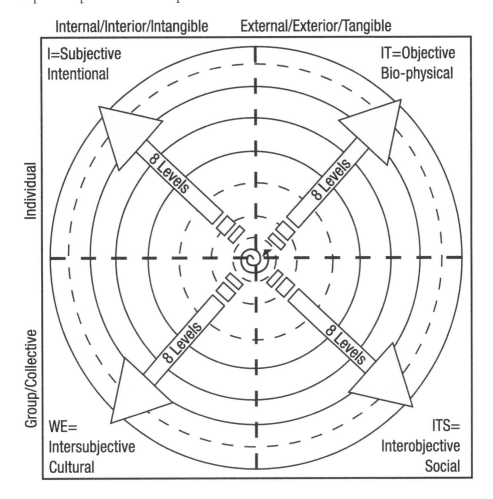

Four Quadrant Map of Integral City (from Integral City: Evolutionary Intelligences for the Human Hive, p. 62)

In support of individual human systems, we mirror the nested hierarchies and fractal patterns of life that show up in our bodies into the structures of our cities where they emerge through the four quadrants and eight levels of development shown above. Whether conceived in the womb or the test tube, we are born helpless and dependent on our parents (or pseudo-parents). They in turn are massively interconnected and both inter- and intra-dependent on the system of friends, work, health, school and community, who are likewise multiply dependent on the social systems of city, state and nation, who are multiply dependent on the cultural norms, who are multiply dependent on the relationships with friendly and hostile cultures and states, who are multiply dependent on the natural ecology of their geography, which is integrated with the global system of climate and energy flow (Barnett, 2005; Diamond, 2005).

The structural complexities of human systems increase as we move from the hearth-based circle of family survival (Beige), through the bonding systems of clan and tribe (Purple), to the power struggles of chief and king (Red), to the ordering authorities of state and place of worship (Blue), to the strategic economies of material exchange (Orange), to the accepting embrace of diverse peoples (Green), to the flex and flow of global systems (Yellow), to a Gaia honoring of all life (Turquoise). (This is discussed in more detail in *Integral City*, chapters 6 and 7.) With each of these levels of historical complexity, we have created new artefacts, habitats, structures and forms to contain our human systems. We call the most concentrated and complex of these containers cities.

A modern city in the developed world contains all of these structures functioning simultaneously, often at cross purposes. When we have inappropriate role relationships, embedded in organization structures and processes and individual values and capabilities, human systems are misconstrued, misconstructed and performance is suboptimal. Nevertheless SDi shows us the potential and logic of the meta system of the city.

An alignment of infrastructure and human organizational structure optimizes intelligence. The exploration of Graves' research through Spiral Dynamics (Beck & Cowan, 1996) has identified eight natural structures of human organizing systems that illustrate the correlation of human structures to human values. The basic shape of those structures is almost a leaf out of Buckminster Fuller's exploration of the natural system of crystals or Bennett's systematics as an exploration of increasing complexity in form.

The structures can be described as follows:
- Beige – Hearth circle.
- Purple – Tribal gathering circle.
- Red – Power-based hierarchy.
- Blue – Authority-based hierarchy.
- Orange – Strategic hierarchical system.
- Green – Social network.
- Yellow – Self-organizing system.
- Turquoise – Global noetic field.

How To Apply Structural Alignment In The City

In a similar (fractal) manner, every organizational agency and/or sector of the city can be analysed through the Spiral levels of complexity: City Hall, Education, Health Care, Justice, Emergency Response, etc. Using the Education Sector in the city as an example, we can discern that its purpose should be for optimizing collective as well as individual knowledge, skills and abilities. It should focus on lifelong learning and capacity development. It should teach people how to think and learn, not just what to think and learn. It should encourage individuals to develop competency not only for individual performance, but for team, management and leadership. It should help people discover personal purpose and enable them to utilize their natural intelligence for creativity and innovation for the five bottom lines in the city: purpose, principles, profit, people and planet (Beck, 2004).

The education system should discover and implement the structures for educators to create the conditions for all citizens to be lifelong learners. The education system needs to integrate education across the span of the human levels of thinking complexity in all four quadrants and eight levels (and whatever evolves beyond that). The education system needs to understand the intentions of city leaders and create the conditions for new leaders to think ever-more deeply and creatively not just on their own but together in dialogue and consortia.

The education system needs to be reframed to embrace not just institutional delivery but on-the-job delivery in all the other sectors of workplace, health and governance systems. In short, people in workplace systems should be working in conjunction with people in city governance, health systems and education systems to clearly understand how the systems contribute to the well-being of the city.

Adapting To Change In The City

In order to make sense of the behavior of any complex living system like the city, a theory of change inevitably emerges. The fundamentals of change have their roots in the self-organizing nature of the universe, i.e., what has emerged since the big bang? And how is it changing?

At this stage of evolution we know that order does emerge from chaos, and that the universe has stabilized patterns of change so that the litho/geo/biospheres (Eddy, 2005; Hamilton 2013) have produced beings conscious of their own consciousness. However, stability is a relative term and can be used as a measure of change at multiple levels of the Spiral and multiple scales of systems in the city.

Selecting a model for change in the city is very scale dependent, bringing into play the relationships between individuals and groups. Thus the effectiveness of any model will be related to what change we want to notice. We need to identify the degree of granularity or resolution that we need, to notice the change amongst different elements. On a fundamental basis, in a living self-organizing system, change must be marked in relationship to the system's survival, connection to its environment/Life Conditions and its capacity to regenerate life (Capra, 1996).

Reporting change requires that we track data that is relevant to any or all of these elements. Graves proposed from his research fundamental stages of change, which SDi has adapted to a weather model (for ease of understanding). Since, on Earth weather is one of the most fundamental Life Conditions that affects human existence, and therefore city existence, this provides an apt metaphor for change in the city. Constantly changing, weather is a visible reminder of our sensitivity to its key states: stable, stormy/unsettled, turbulent, clear. These descriptions, with which we are so familiar that we use them as constant reference points in our conversations, turn out to be useful general descriptors about the change state of any city system.

As complex adaptive systems, humans in cities are constantly attempting to adjust their individual circumstances to survive in the conditions of the city. We could call this complex adaptiveness "learning." We are constantly learning how to adapt and survive under all possible Life Conditions: stable, stormy/unsettled, turbulent, clear.

Using semantic differential and structural differential approaches, Don Beck has developed surveys asking respondents to rate their observations of local "cultural weather" conditions on scales of polar opposites that particularize the general conditions as stable, stormy/unsettled, turbulent, clear. In an Integral City, we can map these responses, combining them with values-based levels of complexity, and reveal the tensions between values, change states and neighborhoods in the city. The tensions reveal the areas most ready and/or resistant to change as people attempt to adapt their inner experience to optimally match outer conditions.

Thus, both our inner ways of knowing (phenomenology) and outer ways of knowing (structuralism) create the mental models and maps of our subjective experience of life in the city. They are, in fact, integral aspects of the individual and collective fabric in the Integral City.

Stages Of Change In The Integral City

The evolutionary structural view of the city can be seen in its archaeological cross-section but within the vertical context of its geo-bio-region across time. This can demonstrate how coherent the city's use of information is in relation to the sources of its matter and energy.

The dynamics of change are best pictured as vectors that expand the four quadrants of the whole city outward from the seminal center as it adapts to the provocations in its Life Conditions. These vectors are the outward pointing arrows on Map 1, above. Beck and Eddy deconstruct these vectors from the geographer's perspective where they map out the city's complexifying structures over time. Historical examples provide apocryphal tales of the most chaotic states of change of city life and its attendant "ill being": the oceanic submergence of Atlantis, the volcanic burial of Pompeii, the misery of London during the Plague.

It may be that the cities most able to demonstrate adaptive capacity and therefore resilience are the actual city states like Singapore (and laterally Hong Kong), where the orders of government don't dilute the governance strength needed to bind the fabric of mixed cultures, but instead encourage and manage them (Beck, 2007; United Nations Human Settlements, 2005, p. 85).

Change Wizards

In the midst of city change scenarios, move change Wizards like global sustainability activist Peter Merry, Founder of the Hague Center for Peace; cultural Meshworker Elza Maalouf, Founder of Center for Human Emergence, Middle East; and human emergence pioneer Don Beck (Beck & Cowan, 1996; Beck & Linscott, 2006). Each is adept at adaptation, flexing and flowing, designing and disturbing systems so that exchanges occur that shift and metamorphose organizations across levels, strata and paradigms. They focus on "what is important" around here, enabling exchanges across multiple stakeholders. They ask, "How are people different?" They notice what sorts of change is ongoing and what kind of exchanges occur between people in the system. And they inquire about people's dreams for the future. Thus they learn about the complex adaptive behaviors of citizens and focus on designing habitats that are historically informed and future inspired, but are also the next natural developmental stage for these people in this place.

SDi offers a fractal framework for understanding the emergence of structural change in the city. In their article "The Futures of Cities," Beck and Cowan (1994; 1997, p. 1) explore three dynamics of cities:

- **Horizontal Dynamic**: This dynamic addresses all the possible demographics through categories and classifications of Groups, Types, Norms and Traits.
- **Vertical Dynamic**: This dynamic reflects the evolutionary, developmental Value Systems and value system vMemes that produce them. They are represented by the Spiral of emergent, unfolding ranges of paradigms, worldviews, mindsets and organizing principles.
- **Diagonal Dynamic**: This is the dynamic of Change which reveals the shifting patterns of transition, transformation and the sequences of complexity through which they unfold.

It is very difficult to keep aware of all these dynamics when considering the city. Only when we picture them as fractal dynamics that exist at every level of scale, can we start to see the effects of dynamic patterns in operation. This is a starting point for understanding the complexity of collections of human social holons in the city, such as families, special interest groups, professions, governments, corporations, non-government organizations, social networks, consortia and self-organizing webs.

From a fractal perspective we can recognize that vertical stages have stage cycles within them. Each one of the social holons has its own criteria for maintaining or advancing such cycles. As Grave speculated, most specialized areas of humanities studies, e.g. psychology, sociology, archaeology and palaeontology, have revealed the patterns of stage evolution and their effects on individual performance. Furthermore, what SDi's concise description frames for us is that each of the collective structures has different life endurance expectations related to their orientation:

- **Family.** Reproduction, care, maintenance of biologically and/or culturally related people. Multiples of generations every 20 years.
- **Teams.** Project and/or process oriented. Days or weeks to years.
- **Groups.** Purpose oriented. Weeks to years
- **Consortia.** Contract for project completion.
- **Professions.** Standards/quality/practices oriented. Decades.
- **Private Organizations.** Process oriented. Years to decades
- **NFP/NGO.** Project or cause oriented. Years to decades
- **Social networks.** Purpose or cause oriented. Years to decades
- **Governments/Justice.** Governance delivery. Decades to centuries
- **Self-organizing webs.** Relationship oriented. Years

If Life Conditions did not change, then the change stage cycle in the city might be expected to continue indefinitely as the living systems in the city would be well matched to the Life Conditions that supports its life cycle. But, as SDi proposes, when Life Conditions shift, the living city system changes or adapts to match it, and thus the diagonal dynamic of change comes into play. Through the diagonal dynamic of change, the living city system recalibrates its internal energies to permit people to survive in the Life Conditions. Organizational and structural form and alignment shift upwards or downwards on the scale of complexity until a match is found that allows it to survive.

Another revelation from the archaeological record arises from vertical evidence of a city's life or death, and its related collective worldview and city paradigm. Cities have a habit of building upon the rubble of past paradigms, where archaeological digs from Troy to London, Pompeii to Los Angeles and Xian to New Orleans reveal the demographics of how the city survived at each horizontal layer. While it is tempting to interpret that each layer contains only one paradigm, in fact each layer probably contains at least three. Using SDi reference points, each layer would represent the center of gravity of the dominant worldview at any given time in history. But that center of gravity would include evidence of its ancestral roots and leading edge future aspirations.

Those manifestations will reveal how the political objectives were accomplished through the allocation of resources. Beck and Cowan (1994, 1997) suggest that political objectives translate across a spectrum of complexity in ways that optimize what the leaders value, i.e. the leaders are conformity enforcers, directed and resourced by inner judges and resource allocators (1996, pp. 4-13). vMeme orientation and resource allocation formulas:

1) Beige. This level of complexity is apolitical. Physical survival takes full energy.

2) Purple. At this level, the group has primacy (either Ethnic or Extended Family or both). The group shares the spoils, jointly owns assets and lives together.

3) Red. At this level, the powerful elite(s) in charge demand the spoils. Everyone else takes second place.

4) Blue. At this level, the righteous earn the spoils they deserve. Everyone else earns by merit of some kind.

5) Orange. At this level, the successful competitors win the spoils. Everyone competes.

6) Green. At this level, everyone shares equally in the process of dividing the spoils.

7) Yellow. At this level, the natural, functional needs present in the Life Conditions determine and distribute energy of all kinds.

8) Turquoise. At this level, collective individualism preserves all life.

Anthropologists tell us that our political decisions reveal what was important to people at that time, i.e. what they invested valuable resources to eat, wear and build, as well as what was not important, i.e. what they wasted, discarded and trashed. If you want to understand what a city values, look at the bio-psycho-cultural-social connections through which it supports its children's education, youths' coming of age, adults' health and elders' wisdom.

Conclusion

Since we developed the research and practices behind *Integral City*, a capability network has emerged to help cities implement these SDi informed ideas. We use Integral City Systems (ICS) as a value management and development framework for Meshworking in the human hive. ICS offers decision-making systems for the built environment and quality of life, utilizing human values systems and engineering techniques that optimize available resources for strategic outcomes.

We apply Integral City systems to six scales: Region, City, Community/ Neighborhood, Organization, Team/Group and Leader. The key work we perform includes:

- **Visioning.** Imagining tomorrow. Facilitating dialogue. Discovering leaders.
- **Assessing.** Culture scans. Capacities for change. States of change. Preferences for change. Priorities for change. Risk.
- **Mapping.** Leadership development. Community values. Social capital. Asset mapping.
- **Capacity Building.** Competencies. Performance. Resilience. Collaboration. Social Responsibility.
- **Facilitating.** Appropriate change. Information Flow. Branding. Relationships. Processes. Structures.
- **Planning.** Strategic. Scenario. Complex adaptive. Official community plan (OCP) alignment.
- **Tracking.** Integral dashboards. Well-being indicators. Vital signs monitors. Organization health. Community wellness.

SDi provides a common language for stakeholder participation, professional expertise and dynamic urban change. While there is much more covered in Integral City, in this chapter we have limited our discussion to the use of SDi in understanding the city through values, organizational structures, and stages of change. If we wanted to summarize the SDi-inspired advantages of using an Integral City approach, we would say it:

- Reflects natural patterns of change.
- Reframes and integrates hierarchies of complexity.
- Provides a meta-framework for other frameworks.
- Builds physical, intellectual, social, cultural capacity.
- Is based on research.
- Enables natural design.
- Uses four lenses, i.e. bio/psycho/cultural/social.
- Embraces multiple and diverse perspectives.
- Responds to horizontal, vertical, diagonal and relational adaptive conditions.
- Offers a multidisciplinary platform for organizing resources, expanding capacity and improving effectiveness at all levels of scale.

We have been very pleased with the outcomes we have seen from ICS involvement in City level change. The impact of using SDi in this way owes much to the generous sharing and mentoring of Dr. Beck. We are grateful for his introduction to the SDi model; Clare Graves' research; Meshworks™ alignment; "Bloom's Pentad" and the work and wonderful bee story of Howard Bloom. We are further grateful to the constellation of Spiral Wizards catalyzing global emergence. Those directly impacting our work included Lorraine Laubscher, Dr. Bruce Gibb, Cherie Beck, Peter Merry, Elza Maalouf; and Steve McIntosh.

Bibliography

Barnett, T. P. M. (2005). *The Pentagon's New Map: War and Peace in the Twenty-First Century* (trade paperback ed.). New York: The Berkley Publishing Group.

Beck, D. (2002). "Spiral Dynamics in the Integral Age." Paper presented at the Spiral Dynamics Integral, Level 1.

Beck, D. (2004). "Natural Designs and Meshworks: Creating our Region's Tomorrow through Second Tier Leadership, Organizational Foresight and Integral Alliances." Paper presented at the Spiral Dynamics Integral, Level 2, Natural Designs.

Beck, D. (2006). *Spiral Dynamics Integral, Level 1 Course Manual*. Denton, TX: Spiral Dynamics Group.

Beck, D. (2007). Personal communication. In M. Hamilton (Ed.), *Messaging for Change*. Winnipeg, MB.

Beck, D. (2007). The Meshworks Foundation: A New Approach to Philanthropy (Electronic Version). Retrieved January 15, 2008 from www.humanemergencemiddleeast.org/Meshworks-foundation-philanthropy.html.

Beck, D. (January, 2008). A Spiral Full of Foundations. *Sense in the City, 3.1*.

Beck, D. & C. Cowan (1994, 1997). "The Future of Cities." Unpublished article. The National Values Center.

Beck, D. & C. Cowan (1996). *Spiral Dynamics: Mastering Values, Leadership and Change*. Malden, MA: Blackwell.

Beck, D. & G. Linscott (2006). *The Crucible: Forging South Africa's Future*. Columbia, MD: Center for Human Emergence.

Bloom, H. (2000). *The Global Brain: The Evolution of Mass Mind from the Big Bang to the 21st Century*. New York: John Wiley & Son Inc.

Capra, F. (1996). *The Web of Life: A New Scientific Understanding of Living Systems*. New York: Anchor Books, Doubleday.

Diamond, J. (2005). *Collapse: How societies choose to fail or succeed* (first ed.). New York: Penguin Group.

Eddy, B. (2005). "Place, Space and Perspective." *World Futures, 61*, 151-163.

Gunderson, L. C., & Holling, C. S. (Eds.). (2002). *Panarchy: Understanding Transformations in Human and Natural Systems* Washington, DC: Island Press.

Hamilton, M. (2008). *Integral City: Evolutionary Intelligences for the Human Hive.* Gabriola Island BC: New Society Publishers.

Hamilton, M. (2007). "Approaching Homelessness: An Integral Reframe." [Philosophy]. *World Futures: The Journal of General Evolution, Volume 63*(2), 107-126.

Hamilton, M. (2013). "Meta Security in the Human Hive: Integrally Aligning Sustainability Responses." Paper presented at the International Society of Systems Sciences, Haiphong, Vietnam.

Stevenson, B., & Hamilton, M. (2001). "How Does Complexity Inform Community? How does Community Inform Complexity?" *Emergence, 3*(No. 2), pp.57 – 77.

USING SDi TO CREATE NEW ORGANIZATIONS

By Bruce Gibb

Introduction

This case study is a retrospective SDi analysis of the establishment of six manufacturing plants outside of the United States. In March 1986, a supplier to one of the major Blue/Orange US automobile companies engaged me to advise on the development of a Greenfield plant in Chihuahua, Mexico. During the rest of the 1980s and the 1990's I advised on this and additional plants in Spain, Portugal, Hungary, Thailand and India for the same company using the same methodology. However, I only became acquainted with *Spiral Dynamics integral* (SDi) in 2001. In the stories of these development projects, however, I find that I was intuitively using SDi concepts in designing and building them; I was designing both structures and processes from a Yellow perspective. The timing of events differed in each plant startup, but roughly followed the same sequence. Some of the techniques described in this story were discovered in later projects but are included here to give a complete development process.

The Story

The plant manager[1] responsible for the development of the Mexican plant asked me to advise him because of my experience and reputation in retrofitting classical Blue/Orange organizations with Green Socio-Technical Systems (STS).[2] This type of organization is also referred to as one having "self-directed teams" or more precisely as "semi-autonomous teams." In my first working session with him, he revealed his vision for the plant. He wanted to move from the traditional Blue/Orange culture and organization of the parent company to an Orange/Green culture and organization. More specifically he wanted to create a manufacturing plant that differed from the parent company in the following ways:

1) From a Blue hierarchical driven to Orange customer (internal and external) driven;

2) From a Blue hierarchical concept of organization to Yellow process flows.

3) From Blue manager and supervisor-directed operating units to semi-autonomous Green team-directed production units.

4) From Orange technical staffs which dictate to operating teams to staffs that would train and serve Yellow operating teams as their internal customers.

5) From Blue tightly held information by management to Yellow open information sharing data about production, quality, waste, finances, all visually displayed (personnel records would be private).

6) From Orange information about production and performance going to Blue supervisors and managers to information going also to Orange operators to use to control their work.

---

1   To maintain their privacy, I refer to the individuals involved by their positions rather than their names.
2   See Wikipedia article at: http://en.wikipedia.org/wiki/Sociotechnical_systems

7) From Blue supervision and direction by supervisors and managers to Green development of people and processes for current production and development for future strategy consistent with the xyz templates (referred to as Operating, Developmental, and Strategic general functions).

8) From Blue requirement that operators follow formal quality processes to Orange holding supervisors, managers and executives accountable to follow formal processes as well.

9) From Blue hierarchically directed meetings to adding Green bimodal structures[3] and processes.

10) From Blue identification of a person by role to Green total person including multiple roles.

11) From Orange job descriptions to Yellow role descriptions using systems model.[4]

12) From Blue pay by position to Orange pay by position, competencies, and profit.

13) From Orange shareholder primacy to Green including all stakeholders.

14) From Blue traditional operating system to Orange quality operating system.

The plant manager then hired directors for each of the functional units using as a major criterion that they be amenable to his vision for the plant. The first round of this process produced candidates that other directors and managers did not want and the plant manager then had to aggressively target and recruit people he needed. The result was mixed in terms of competence and confidence but strong on commitment.

---

3   See appendix A for diagram of the bimodal structure and processes. For a detailed exposition on the concept, contact the author at blgibb@aol.com to obtain a copy of the paper, "SDi Version of the Organizational Leadership Structure", 2001.

4   See appendix B for diagram of the systems model; this format was used for design of teams, departments, and the total organization.

In June of 1986 the new plant leadership/management team (LMT) met at a hotel in Chihuahua for the first of many Leadership Conferences (LCs)[5]. The time between these LCs varied from one to four months. The objectives of this first meeting were: to begin to build them as a Purple team; to empower and energize them (Red) to act; to create Blue values and guiding principles which would be used in designing and operating the plant; and to draft an Orange mission statement.

To create a Purple LMT we used Bruce Tuckman's group development sequence:[6] forming, storming, norming, and performing. However in retrospect the questions the members answered were more aligned to the SDi development sequence. In the forming phase, we asked them to introduce themselves to each other by telling about their families of origin and their contemporary families (Purple). In the storming phase, they talked about the process of their becoming independent from the families, how they preferred to be managed and what their "hot buttons" were (Red). They shared their personal religious/philosophical beliefs (Blue) and how they applied them at work during the norming phase. They reported on their major achievements and failures (Orange) for the performing phase. They spoke of the most productive and unproductive and the most creative and repressive work environments they had experienced (mixtures of first 6 vMeme levels).

The group then examined in detail the expectations of their parent and customer organizations including the time, quality, and financial targets they had to meet for building the physical plant, the human organization, and the supplier relationships. To become more familiar with the Mexican milieu they held conversations with visitors from other US manufacturing plants (maquiladoras) in Mexico and from Mexican organizations to determine the success factors they had discovered.

After these seeding events, the group developed an Orange mission statement (who they serve, what products and services they provide, and the standards they would meet in providing them). Further, they drafted a set of Blue core values (what they would invest in) and guiding principles they would use to design and operate the plant (MVGP). They developed a common Yellow vision for the plant and drafted an initial system design consistent with it.[7]

---

5 These LCs were the Leadership or Camp mode of the bimodal structure.

6 http://en.wikipedia.org/wiki/Tuckman's_stages_of_group_development

7 The final plant MVGP is presented in Appendix C.

Finally, at this LC, the team prepared to reenter the management/ performance mode. Each person listed what they were going to achieve in the next three months, the time of the next LC meeting, and the support they would need from each other. Among these objectives was the hiring of the next level of the staff mostly from the Mexican population. Several of the leadership team planned to attended workshops on STS during the three-month interim period. They established a review and planning meeting process and format (RPM) that they would each use for one-on-one meetings with the plant manager to track progress, obtain resources, and get support during the three-month period. Let me add at this point that I am reporting on the activities in which I was directly involved. To design, build, and operate the plant required a tremendous amount of work in the management mode which is not included in this story.

The second LC took place as planned approximately three months after the first. This was also a Purple "camp" or circle-type meeting, the leadership mode of the bimodal system. As such, it included all employees that at this juncture consisted of the plant manager, department heads and their newly-hired direct reports, in total about 35 people. We used the Keirsey-Bates personality indicator[8] to build understanding of each other and establish the Green value of welcoming diversity.

To break the bands of Blue culture the whole group engaged in a simulation named the Moonbeam Company. In the first round of the simulation, the traditional Blue structure and processes are used to build small circuit boards that power a light. Measurements are taken of the quality, quantity and cost of the product as well as the satisfaction of the participants. Before the second round, the participants are asked to make suggestions to improve production and satisfaction and their suggestions are used to restructure the physical and social layout. Production and satisfaction improve marginally in this round. Before the third round, the participants are reorganized into three groups, they set production targets, and they plan their production processes. Production increases about four-fold during the third round and satisfaction maxes out. It is obvious to all that this Green team structure is more satisfying and productive than the Blue first round, and the Orange second round. During the simulation debrief, the leadership team affirmed that the Green team concept would

8   David Keirsey and Marilyn Bates, *Please Understand Me: Character and Temperament Types (Del Mar California: Prometheus Nemesis), 1984.*

be used in the design and operation of the plant and that the structures and processes would be shaped accordingly.

To build ownership and commitment to the MVGP, they reviewed the previous draft that the Leadership Team had created and had everyone in mixed groups analyze, critique and suggest modifications which were debated and some included in the next draft of the MVGP. Finally, the work to be done during the next three months was anticipated and plans were made by departments to get it accomplished. Significant was the Green redesign of the plant blueprints to provide spaces to accommodate team meetings. Also, the traditional Blue wall dividing the office staff and the plant operators was eliminated and the staff offices were located in disbursed locations on the production floor. The plant manager and facilities manager contacted the local university to have their architecture department submit a Purple design for the exterior of the building.

During the interim period, I travelled with the LMT members to an electronics plant in Idaho that employed STS principles. They were able to see their application in detail in each of the functional departments. The consultant that advised them during their design and startup was also present to give the theory and backstory.

The next LC included the leadership teams of each of the departments that had been hired and organized during the interim. Participants were seated in mixed groups (each group having members from each department to assure a total organization perspective) and no one was seated with his/her immediate supervisor. One of the reasons for doing so is that we wanted people to feel free to express with Red honesty what they experienced and thought. In addition to the review and modification of the MVGP based on input from everyone, these groups each took one of the guiding principles and described the specific behaviors that would be consistent with it and those which would be in violation of it. These Blue principles in application were then shared and debated with the whole gathering and the principles were modified accordingly.

The major organizational advancement established in this Conference was the agreements to Orange interdepartmental contracts. These specified missions of each of the departments as well as the products, services and expectations they provided to and received from other departments, including the LMT. Actual external customers and suppliers attended the Conference. The overall structure constituted a Yellow integrated "flow" with feedback mechanisms for the whole system and suprasystem.[9] Again, plans were made for the interim period.

During the interim period, they began to hire and train operators for production teams. A Training Center was established to train operators in both social and technical skills. All trainees participated in the Moonbeam simulation to develop an understanding of the core concepts upon which the plant was organized and would be operated. The Center had a production line that potential operators used for both diagnosing their skills and improving them to the requisite standards. The Center provided operators with specialized courses in electronics, hydraulics and mechanics. A major innovation for Mexico was the inclusion of training in social skills: team problem-solving, decision-making, giving and receiving feedback, conflict utilization, etc. As operators were working on the simulated production line, problems would be inserted which required the operating team to use these skills. All operators hired after training were proficient in both technical and social skills as measured by their scores on final tests at or above the 75th percentile.

Many of the core concepts used by the plant such as the quality operating system were illustrated by Orange/Green experiential activities at the training center. For example, a volleyball game was used to demonstrate the incentives and responses to quality issues, the ball hitting the ground being a quality problem. There were three rounds of play each with different conditions. There was a debrief after each round to garner what the participants had learned.

The first round was played with the standard volleyball rules and the winning team shared a monetary prize (the Orange competitive team condition). The second round was played with the rule that the person who knocked the ball over the net the most times would win the prize (the Red individualistic competitive condition). The final round was played in which the prize money was shared among all the members but the amount was based on the number of times the ball crossed the net without hitting the ground during a specified time period (the Green organization winning condition). The way the participants slowed down the game, helped each other on both sides, and became very accurate in their shots illustrated the ideal behavior operators should exhibit when a quality problem arose in the plant.

---

9   See Suprasystem diagram in Appendix E.

The next leadership conference included operators and numbered in the hundreds. As usual, the MVGP was reviewed and modified with input from the new attendees. Performance on interdepartmental contracts were evaluated and celebrated by each department sending a "love letter" to every other department appreciating what they provided to them and asking them to make the changes they needed to perform better.

The semi-autonomous production teams were structured with each team member having two roles, a team service role and a production role. The five service roles on each production team were: quality, human resources, safety, finance (and scrap), and external (supplier and customer) relations.

Team members in their service roles were connected to the service staff units who trained them in the performance of these roles. These team service roles were rotated among team members periodically so that all would be proficient in all service roles. In some STS plants, these service roles are called "star" roles, symbolically indicated by a five-pointed star.

Since the team members were expected to be able to perform all the production processes, the production roles were also rotated among team members until all were proficient in doing all processes. After all could perform all the production processes, the team could decide by individual preference or necessity how to organize themselves to produce their products. The teams were supported by a team facilitator (the transformed supervisor role) who considered the team as his or her customers. As a supplier to the team, the facilitator was expected to provide everything that the team needed to perform to the quality, quantity, cost and timing standards of their internal and external customers.

Production teams operated at first slowly until their processes were under control, then up to normal speed, then they "pulsed" them at higher speeds to find potential glitches. Test products had been sent to customers who provided feedback to the plant and the operators. When customers sent back products with quality problems, some of the operators actually wept from shame.

To give employees in all functions and all levels an understanding of the Orange significance and Blue meaning that their products had for the end users, the LMT commissioned the making of a videotape which showed the benefits and potential problems which their products—in this case the car radio—would have for consumers. The video showed a group of teenagers dancing to the music of their car radio in a parking lot; a family enjoying radio programs as they traveled; and a family while traveling in a downpour who hear from their car radio that a bridge ahead of them had been washed out. The video was featured at one of the LCs.

The physical facility, the organization, the relationships as designed and built began operations in July of 1987. The plant went formally on line having met its quality, cost, and timing targets.

The last Leadership Conference I organized was attended by 700 people. To manage this large number, we created seven groups of 100 each with 10 subgroups of 10. Regular Leadership Conferences continued with product-line meetings every six months, department meetings monthly, and short start-up team meetings daily and longer meetings weekly. The format for these meetings roughly followed the change formula: DVF>R (the product of D = Dissatisfaction [and Satisfaction], V = Vision [and Goals], F = First action steps, must be greater than R = Resistance to Change).

These Leadership Conferences had the effect of making employees Purple members of the organization; employees did not work "for them" but "for us." Although they were not in fact shareholders, they had a strong Orange feeling of ownership. They demonstrated high levels of commitment to the plant and the product they produced because they had participated in all aspects of its development. They were empowered, they could speak freely and be heard, they did not suffer the fear that typifies unhealthy Blue and Orange organizations.

As the plant continued operating, the manager observed that there were regressions to the traditional Blue parent company culture. He and his team asked me to organize a special seminar for "cultural philosophers", people in normal roles who would be available to respond to "Why?" questions, advise teams, spot violations of the MVGP, and be the go-to people for plant members to understand the foundational philosophy of the plant. We (myself and the human resources director) organized and conducted a week-long, intensive, in-depth seminar at a local hotel to educate and prepare this group of 24 philosophers. The methodologies included lectures, simulations, readings, case studies, and team problem solving. Many of the LMT participated as presenters in the course.

While the narrative to this point has been focused on the development of the plant, there were other initiatives which were targeted on the needs and values of the members. Free, nourishing, plentiful food was available at mealtimes. Recreation and exercising facilities were provided for all members of the plant community. Both of these satisfied Beige needs.

An impact of the parent organization was in the compensation system (read Beige). People were hired with competencies at or above the 75th percentile. The parent company insisted that they be compensated at the average salary for comparable positions in the area, that is at the 50th percentile. Some of the professionally educated left the plant and obtained higher compensation in organizations in the area. Subsequently, they reached high levels of management in part due to the training they had received at the plant. To some extent the plant became a training ground for other organizations in the region and in Mexico; an expression of the third value of the plant.

Unexpectedly, there were conflicts between the culture of the plant and the local Mexican culture. The human resource department began to notice that the divorce rate among operators was increasing dramatically over the norm. The LMT hired a sociologist from the local university to study the issue. She found that since most of the operators in the plant were women and they had become proficient and empowered to use social skills at work, they were also using them at home. Both the traditional Blue spouses who believed in fixed male-female roles and other Red power-oriented, macho husbands did not appreciate their wives' changed attitudes and behaviors. When the women refused to return to their subservient roles, divorce resulted. To correct the problem, all married candidates and their spouses were required to attend a one-day experiential workshop in which the social techniques were demonstrated and their impact on the family were shared. If the couple agreed that they could live with the change to Orange/Green relationships, the candidate could be trained. With this innovation, the divorce rate returned to normal.

When the plant manager returned to the US, he was replaced by a manager who was driven by the Orange "bottom line". He centralized decision-making, he ignored the culture, quality suffered and the morale of the plant sank. The Green culture went underground but it was successfully resurrected four years later when he was replaced by an engineer who had been involved since the beginning and had been one of the "philosophers." The plant eventually received the highest honor for organizations from the Mexican government, the equivalent of the US Baldrige award.

Lessons From Other Startups

Similar concepts and processes were used to develop manufacturing plants in five other countries: Spain, Portugal, Hungary, Thailand, and India. I will present just a paragraph about an important lesson learned in each of these countries.

In Spain, we had a problem with the engineers whose Blue/Orange culture considered the operators to be beneath them in class and status. They were formally responsible for helping operators maintain and repair the equipment at their work stations but only did so haphazardly. To correct this behavior, we had the operators contribute to the performance appraisals of the engineers. One engineer resigned in disgust, the rest became very diligent in serving the operators.

In Portugal, the LMT took a course about local culture from a vendor who specialized in cultural training for expats. The vendor basically painted Portuguese culture as traditional Blue. However, the young candidates who were attracted to work at the plant had a strong center of gravity at Orange. We learned to determine the local culture from the candidates rather than from the "cultural specialists."

Hungary presented a unique problem. The plant was established not long after the communist regime was ousted. When work teams were told they were to be empowered to make decisions they laughed and said that they had been told this many times during the communist period. They only believed and acted empowered when they had real decisions to make, when they could exercise healthy Red/Orange.

In Thailand at the second Leadership Conference to develop the guiding principles for the plant the participants were divided into two groups, one of Thais, the other of expats. Each group was asked to identify the characteristics of plants in Thailand that were both successful and a great place to work. They were then to craft a set of no-more-than ten guiding principles that could be used to guide the development and operations of the plant. The expat group was puzzled when the Thai group's list had five which used the term "heart." In response to the expats queries about what "heart" meant, the Thais just kept repeating, "you know, act with heart." To concretize the discussion, I asked the Thais how they would deal with a person who was not performing using a "heart" approach. They responded that the facilitator (supervisor) would talk to the person privately and humbly tell them what they expected them to do. The employee would see that they were not doing it correctly and change their behavior. In response to how the expats would deal with the situation, they said that they would confront the person and tell them they were not doing the job correctly. The Thais were aghast at this method saying that in Thailand the person would "lose face" and resign. The expats finally agreed that using "heart" would be the better method and the term remained in the final set of principles.

India was rich in cultural vMemes. First, villages had a long tradition of people meeting after work in a Purple communal space to share experiences, learn from each other, build and maintain relationships. The Purple Leadership Conference was "natural" for them. The status and dynamics of Blue bureaucratic structures was deep and the necessity of the Green work teams had to be continually reinforced. Finally, we learned that Red freedom to make decisions cannot be turned over to teams unless and until they feel a strong sense of Purple identity with, ownership of and commitment to the whole organization.[10]

Conclusion

In the design and building of a new Green organization, all levels of the spiral need to be addressed.[11] Establishing purple Leadership Conferences in the startup phase gradually expanded the individual's identity to include the system community and the larger suprasystem including all stakeholders. It also allowed people to experience and exercise their healthy Red voice free from fear. Continuing to use these conferences at the dyadic, team, department and total organization scale when the plant is in operation produces the forum for making quick adjustments to changes in the external environment.

A formal and shared Blue conceptual framework (the Systems Model) is essential to keep everyone on the same page. The Blue values and principles owned by all members are critical both in the design and operation of quality processes.

---

10   See "A Framework for Describing Organizational Models and A Path of Transformation" by Raghu Ananthanarayanan and Bruce L. Gibb in the *Organization Development Journal*; Winter 2002.

11   For a description of organizations at each level of the spiral see "Primer for Spiral Dynamics in Organizations," 2007, by Bruce Gibb at: blgibb@aol.com.

Orange efficient and effective performance processes and measures within the overall flow of the production from suppliers to end-users are essential. Explicit Orange processes[12] such as the RPM for leading and managing the organization need to be specified.

To the greatest extent possible Green self- and team leadership and management need to be vested in the operating teams. The responsibilities and authority of the three general functions, i.e. strategic, developmental, and operating, need to be understood and enacted. The number and structure of the management ranks should be minimal, limited to the number required to support the operating teams and develop people and processes to implement long-term strategy.

During the startup phase, the work done at each LC needs to be reviewed and modified with input from new attendees to develop the experience of belonging, ownership and commitment.

The design and development of the venture are best done from a Yellow perspective which recognizes and values the contribution of each Spiral level.

---

12   For example a list of these processes would include: communication, decision-making, planning, problem-solving, evaluation, celebration, policy creation, continuous improvement, etc.

MODES OF OPERATION

**LEADERSHIP MODE
("CAMP" STRUCTURE)**

**MANAGEMENT MODE
("WORK" STRUCTURE)**

EXAMPLES OF PROCESSES
PERFORMED WITHIN EACH MODE:

- INFORM, SHARE INFORMATION
- THINK AND DECIDE
- PLAN ACTIONS TO BE TAKEN
- CELEBRATE ACHIEVEMENTS
- LEARN FROM EXPERIENCE

- DISCIPLINED PERFORMANCE
- ACT AND MONITOR ACTION
- IMPLEMENT ACTION PLANS
- CONTRIBUTE
- DEVELOP SKILLS AND ABILITIES

IMPACT ON THE INDIVIDUAL OF
PARTICIPATING IN EACH MODE:

- COMMITMENT TO ORGANIZATION
- FEELING OF IDENTITY, BELONGING
- FEELING OF MEMBERSHIP

- COMPETENCE AND CONFIDENCE
- SELF-ESTEEM, SELF-WORTH
- SECURITY BASED ON ADDING VALUE

EFFECT ON THE ORGANIZATION OF
USING EACH MODE:

- EFFECTIVENESS
  (DO THE RIGHT THING)

- EFFICIENCY
  (DO THE THING RIGHT)

Appendix B.

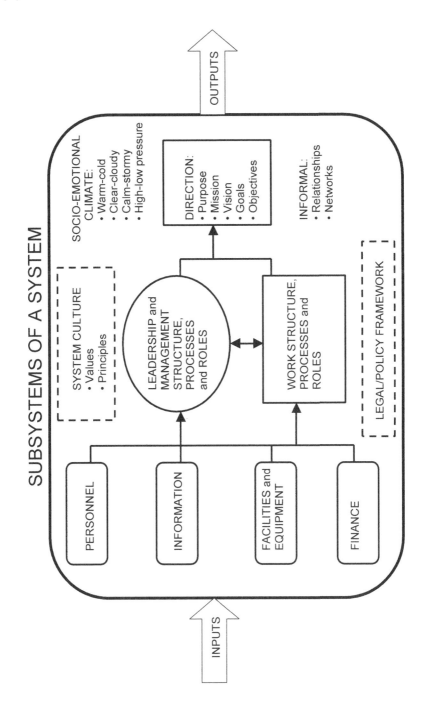

Appendix C.

Plant Mission Statement:

A customer driven supplier of automotive products at world-class quality and cost.

Values:

- People are the source of our strength.
- Suppliers are an extension of ourselves and vital to our existence.
- We strive to be a responsible social force in the community and with its governments.

Guiding Principles:

- Product quality reflects the quality of our effort.
- We use teamwork to obtain our common mission.
- We encourage two way communication to eliminate barriers and reach a common understanding.
- We give and receive objective and timely feedback.
- Cooperation and service enhance our value.
- Those affected by problems together seek long and short term solutions.
- We recognize achievements.
- We encourage and provide the means for people to reach their professional, technical, and organizational goals.
- We all share the responsibility, risk and success.
- We maintain a clean and orderly plant to achieve safety and well-being.

Appendix D.

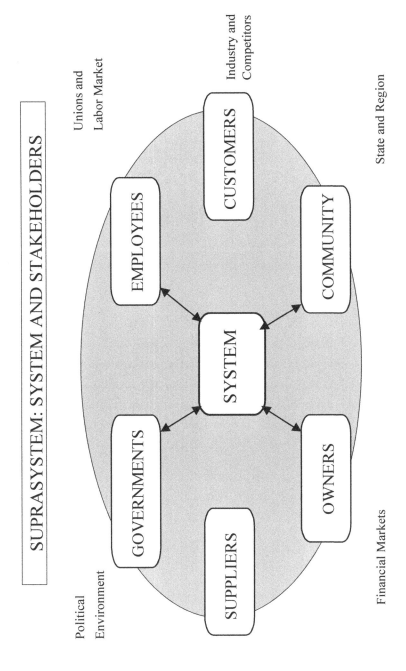

SUPRASYSTEM: SYSTEM AND STAKEHOLDERS

Political Environment

Unions and Labor Market

Industry and Competitors

State and Region

Financial Markets

EMPLOYEES

CUSTOMERS

GOVERNMENTS

SYSTEM

COMMUNITY

SUPPLIERS

OWNERS

SOLONIC PRACTICE: STANDING ON THE OTHER SIDE OF THE LINE

By Christopher and Sheila Cooke

Synopsis

A 5 Deep[1] project, delivered between April to December 2013, used SDi as the main theoretical template, within an approach known as Solonic Practice[2]. Whilst the primary client requirement focused on the development of an Integral Curriculum for a soccer training organisation in the USA, the project serves as a case study to demonstrate three principles of application:

1) Understand your Kosmic Address[3], and that of your client.

2) Consciously absorb information, like a Kosmic Sponge, that gives you insight into the overall inner and outer change dynamics of self, client, and Life Conditions.

3) Be Integral[4], and when appropriate, support your client to be the same.

---

1   5 Deep is an experiment established in April 2001, by Christopher Cooke, to demonstrate the application of Spiral Dynamics Integral.
2   Solonic Practice is the art and science of human emergence.
3   Kosmic Address is a term used by Ken Wilber to identify a person's unique evolutionary developmental point in time.
4   The term Integral, as used here, refers to a new stage of development that when active within an individual, creates a stance or perspective that possesses the capacity to lead through the complex Life Conditions that have emerged over the past 150 years.

The chapter provides background on the client, Future Captain Sports, and its founders, and uses mentoring, culture scanning, facilitation and advisory examples to demonstrate the three principles of Solonic Practice.

The Intended Audience

This chapter is written for those who wish to further their application of an Integral Perspective regardless of their preferred stage development theoretical base. Ken Wilber (Wilber 2000) maps numerous primary-researched frameworks in his work Integral Psychology. The authors' preferred theoretical base is derived from the work of Clare W. Graves (*The Graves Technology*, 1978). Following extensive field trials in South Africa from 1974 to 1995 the work became known as Spiral Dynamics (Beck and Cowan, 1996). In 1998 through a synthesis of Spiral Dynamics and Integral Theory (Wilber, 1998) it was further developed as Spiral Dynamics Integral (SDi) (Beck and Wilber, 1998). This lineage is the only framework that offers a primary-researched model that shows the interrelationship between the stages of development and Life Conditions. Additionally, sixteen years of international application have demonstrated the theory to be valid in any human setting.

Spiral Dynamics Integral In Summary

Primary research has mapped clear stages of human development emerging over the past 120,000 years. Each stage carries its own unique range of biological, psychological, cultural and societal attributes. These stages, or complex adaptive coping mechanisms, equip an individual to adapt to changing Life Conditions.

In 1974, Graves identified a Major Leap for Mankind, a transition from *human doing*, where humans are largely instinctually driven, to *human being*, where new forms of awareness equip the individual with greater behavioural freedom. Jean Gebser (1949) named this new awareness "Integral-aperspectival" and Graves identified this new awareness as the start of a Second Tier of human consciousness. The transition into Second Tier is a significant singularity, one that is not yet appreciated by society, nor by many of the professions that support human development.

The Three Principles Of Working
With An Emergent Kosmos

Becoming a fully-fledged Solonic Practitioner takes time. "Practitioner" is used in a broad sense to include advisors, catalysts, change agents, coaches, consultants, facilitators, mentors, trainers, etc. There is much to learn. Even when one has mastery of all aspects of our present understanding of humanness, specifically the emergent nature of all bio-psycho-cultural-social holons and holarchies, the ability to use this knowledge fluently and meaningfully in front of a client may still be lacking. Why? Because, talking about the attributes of Integral thinking may neither be necessary nor enough. Being Integral is the key. It is not what you do; it is who you are that makes the difference.

The place in which you stand as a practitioner as you listen, observe, think, design, and deliver has a dramatic effect on the outcome of your work. Stance matters. Stance matters so much that we believe it is the essence of gaining mastery of a practice we term, "Solonic Practice," where the primary purpose is the emergence of the solon ("soul" + "holon" = "solon"). The term holon is used to describe a discreet intelligence, in this context, a human being, that is a "whole" unto itself, and forms "part" of a holarchy. The soul, which is also a discreet intelligence, is like the expression of a song in a Kosmic song line, creating a bridge between holon and spirit, where Spirit is both the original song and the invitation to sing. Solonics is the art and science of humanness. Solonics equips the practitioner with an unfolding wisdom of how to create the Life Conditions that enable human emergence.

Solonic Practice is derived from an ever-unfolding scientific and philosophical understanding of humanness, and is positioned as an Integral technology for the transition to "the other side of the line." (The line is a metaphor we use to identify the demarcation between First Tier and Second Tier stages of development; a transition from Post Conventional to Post-Post Conventional thinking.) Equally important is the need to understand the capacities of your participants, students or clients, in order to ensure that your interaction with them is coherent and aligned with their dominant coping mechanisms.

In essence, this work is not about types of people. It is not about Red People, Green People, or even Integral People. It is about creating the Life

Conditions in which the real-time adaptation of the autonomous human holon, as part of a social holarchy, occurs. The models and theories of stage development, which are based on The Graves Technology, provide insights into the dynamics and attributes of emergence of the human holon, and cultural/social holarchies. Since 2001, we have found that when the stage development theory is explicitly set in a Kosmological metaphorical context, it provides a profoundly meaningful insight into the deeper dynamics of the emergence of all life.

As practitioners, we have developed a practice called "Solonic Practice" that forms the basis of our interaction with clients, and of our teaching that includes SDi. The practice focuses on working with the core dynamics of the vMeme[5] codes through the creation of Life Conditions that enable the client's next natural emergence.

What distinguishes the Solonic Practitioner is the ability to hold open a psychological space, in a chameleon-like manner, that is half a step ahead for both self and client; a space where both client and practitioner are perpetually in flow, each surfing on the edge of his or her own open wave. Essentially, a Solonic Practitioner is acting as-if, or is an Integral being. Very few people on the planet today, the authors of this chapter included, have fully emerged into Second Tier. It is known, however, that the process of learning and applying the body of Integral knowledge may create the Life Conditions for one's own emergence into Second Tier.

So, what is a curious and aspiring Solonic Practitioner to do? In this chapter, we offer several insights that underpin a developmental pathway towards mastery. To start with, we have found it helpful to imagine that your client is not the primary client. Engage the evolutionary impulse that flows through the entire Kosmos as your real client. We use the term "evolutionary impulse" to describe an organising dynamic that has the capacity to create and sustain new forms of matter, life, and consciousness. And, we use the term "Kosmos", rather than "cosmos", to signify the Greek definition, which includes all aspects of the workings of the physical and metaphysical universe(s). In making this shift, your function is to amplify the emergence of both yourself and your client, in service to your primary client, an emergent Kosmos. This reframe creates a larger context for your work, and the Life Conditions for your own emergence.

---

5   vMeme codes are fundamental structures of the mind that emerged over human history, to equip our species with increasing behavioural flexibility to survive and create new meaning.

Within the reframe of, "working with an emergent Kosmos," we offer three important principles, or fundamental concepts and assumptions, that when woven together, prepare you to apply Solonic theory and practice in any context.

1) Understand your Kosmic Address, and that of your client.

2) Consciously absorb information, like a Kosmic Sponge, that gives you insight into the overall inner and outer change dynamics of self, client, and Life Conditions.

3) Be Integral, and when appropriate, stimulate your client to be the same.

What Is Kosmic Address?

Working with "Kosmic Address" goes right to the heart of the practice. One of the core competencies of Solonic Practice is to be fully aware of one's own vMeme profile, as an indication of the core dynamics of one's holon, in order to ensure that one is as clean and unfettered by personal preferences and biases as possible, as one listens to and observes the client. These Kosmic systems, or vMemes, speak through us. The aim here is to take the stance of a hollow bamboo that allows a free flow of information through its core. In 2006, in his book, *Integral Spirituality: A Startling New Role for Religion in the Modern and Postmodern World*, Ken Wilber coined the phrase, "Kosmic Address", to describe the unique expression of an individual, the core dynamics of one's holon, defined as a function of his or her stage of development (or the centre of gravity of the active vMemes, to use SDi vernacular), and the perspective that he or she holds in a given moment, either first, second or third person.

It is important to understand that Kosmic Address is not a type. It is the centre of gravity of the musical chord-like range of core intelligences that equip the individual to flex and adapt in a given situation; and it is in effect the first attempt of characterising the essence of a human holon that lifts one above a conventional conversation about "type". The Kosmic Address can be likened to your personal mobile phone. It has a dial-up number, which is yours, and yours alone, the device communicates and receives information, whilst also permitting your geo-spatial location to be pinpointed.

As a principle, the individual's centre of gravity is typically defined by the characteristics of the three dominant adjacent vMemes: the one that is fading into the past, the one that is currently dominant, and the one that is emerging on the horizon. Adaptation can take three primary forms: an up-stretch towards more complex thinking, a down-stretch to earlier thinking, or a refinement and polishing of the centre of gravity intelligence.

With the emergence of Second Tier consciousness, an individual develops greater behavioural freedom and the ability to morph and utilise the full range of signatures of his or her vMeme repertoire. The ability to step outside one's vMeme profile is a capability that is only possible for an individual making a Second Tier transition beyond nodal Green. This natural ability is like looking back in from the balcony of an Integral awareness to experience and utilize all the vMemes active within self and others. In essence, one becomes a Kosmic Sponge.

The metaphor of Kosmic Address, when interpreted using the emergent cyclical double-helix metaphor of Graves, and the Integral template of Wilber, becomes an Alice-through-the-looking-glass opportunity for the practitioner to step through the membrane of the Second Tier transition, to accelerate the conscious utilization of latent Integral capacities. The Kosmic Address is effectively a mesh of adaptive responses that draw upon the available repertoire of all active vMemes to bring to utilisation the necessary intelligences and behaviours that provide the best chance of survival.

Case Study: Applying The Three Principles

Applying the *Three Principles* creates the Life Conditions to enhance your own flexibility and psychological openness, and enables you to deliver the best possible client outcome. Let us elaborate these principles of mastery by weaving them through a real case with Future Captains Sports, in Media, Pennsylvania, USA, that included individual, cultural and Life Conditions, scanning, mentoring, facilitating, and advising. In order to give a context in which to apply the *Three Principles*, we provide a brief background on the project, and then we present the transcript of mentoring session two with David Brown, which is useful for demonstrating Principles 1 and 2.

Developing An Integral Curriculum With Future Captains Sports

David Brown and Scott Spangler, professional soccer players and business partners, run a soccer training school, named Future Captains Sports, for youngsters who are aged 18 months to 20+ years. Their core motive is child and teenage development. Here is the story of how we met.

David Brown, co-owner of Future Captains Sports, had studied many sources that led him to Ken Wilber and then to SDi. In seeking an SDi mentor David found Christopher and Sheila Cooke in April 2013, through an Internet key word search for "Spiral Dynamics coach." Virtual mentoring of David, by Christopher and Sheila Cooke, included the use of stage of development, change readiness and cultural online assessment instruments. By August, co-owner Scott Spangler became engaged in the mentoring process, which later led to David and Scott's additional request for support in the development of an integral curriculum and the refinement of their business administration. The project activity timeline is outlined below.

Integral Curriculum Project Timeline 2013

- **19th April - 12th July** Four one-hour virtual mentoring sessions with David Brown.
- **8th August** Mentoring session with Scott Spangler and David Brown.
- **19th August** Proposal for an Integral Curriculum to Future Captains Sports.
- **9th September** Virtual meeting to design and align the delivery plan for the project using an NLP-based facilitation method known as "Chain of States".
- **10th September – 26th September** Survey the Future Captains Sports leadership team using online SDi instruments, virtual interviews and Life Conditions assessment, submission of recommended approach based on survey findings.
- **14 – 18th & 22nd October** Creation of Integral Curriculum (on-site).
- **24th October** Integral Curriculum document published.
- **13th December** Project review with Future Captains Sports leadership team (virtual).

Integral Curriculum

Curriculum is derived from the Latin – it literally means the race or the course of a race. An integral curriculum sustains a total learning program designed with "Integral Awareness" to support the healthy emergence of human beings in the context of the society in which they reside.

My interest and aspirations with an Integral Perspective are wide-ranging. At first, I saw an opportunity for myself personally. I thought that if I could understand the four quadrants and the various levels and lines that run through them then I could have a heck of a lot more freedom for myself! And, I knew this freedom would eventually turn into power. A few months after I first read Ken Wilber and Spiral Dynamics my best friend offered to partner up with me to grow Future Captains Sports into a global brand. Immediately, I sensed an opportunity for others. I imagined children playing, bursting with enthusiasm, all within structures designed from an Integral Perspective. Of course, I said yes. I knew I had the opportunity of a lifetime.

– David Brown, December 2013

Principle 1: Understand Your Kosmic Address, And That Of Your Client

Mentoring A Client On Kosmic Address

Because we were in the UK, and Future Captains Sports was in the USA, we needed to rely upon virtual collaboration tools for our mentoring of David. One of the challenges of virtual mentoring is that you are not in the presence of the individual, so calibration of stage development may be constrained because of distance and the narrow scope of information that comes through the visual and auditory virtual channels. Our support tools that allowed us to extend our senses and information gathering were the reports from the online instruments, a slideshow, and GoToMeeting, which allowed us to share the documents and to see each other with webcams.

David's data from the online instruments indicated that he was going through a significant Orange-Green-Yellow transition. Following Session 1, which set the baseline for our mentoring relationship, we spent Mentoring Session 2 helping David understand the significance of his Kosmic Address.

Virtual Mentoring Session Number Two
7 May 2013

David: When I got off the last call, I was overwhelmed with positive emotions. I felt the need to acknowledge Scott for being part of this journey. I stood in front of Scott and in that moment found that words were not enough. Only tears of joy came out. Scott was happy. Yes! Something shifted. I have more clarity about emergence through the various levels of the Spiral, and how to work with the levels myself in my business and with my clients. I don't have confidence to recognise the levels of the Spiral.

Christopher: Let's work on recognising stages. The moments you described in Scott's office were meaning-making moments where you struggled to bring words to something you have never expressed before. The answer is within yourself. Our work is to help you understand your inner change process. We're in a transition as a species where for a short period of time we can't self-inspect and become aware of the new schema emerging within us. [Referring to the slide pack] Starting with Orange, which words jump out for you?

David: Strategic, materialistic, motivation.

Christopher: What memories come up for you of your life so far?

David: Scoring a goal on the soccer field, the crowd roars.

Christopher: What was your knowing?

David: That may be a little bit empty, shallow. The high can't last forever.

Christopher: Looking at the exiting transition from Orange on the slide, you'll see the words, "creates loneliness". How does that relate to what you just described?

David: There are not a lot of people who can share the feeling of the crowd roaring for you when you score a goal. It's only about me in that moment.

Christopher: All of our lives are about a series of transitions. For the transition you are in, from Orange to Green and beyond, the exiting signature is loneliness. The individual has succeeded, but gets a sense that there is something more, as the sense of loneliness starts to cut in. It's part of the adaptive schema emerging within you. You can start to track the journey out of Orange that leads you to an emotion-rich experience, one that you described with your colleague, Scott, a few moments ago. Let's turn to Green. What stands out for you on this slide?

David: Sacrifice now to obtain now, love, ideal society, egalitarian, stuckness, cloying.

Christopher: Notice the memories that come up with this slide, and which word is triggering it?

David: Community. I never felt community much. My family felt like a unit for a while. The Jewish community turned their back on me when I was younger. The word "community."

Christopher: Remember the goal-scoring experience and the sense of emptiness. This transition to Green is the search inward for community. We reach inward for a new, deeper understanding of self. In all of these conversations there is an inner and outer dynamic. Green is the stage of development that is integrative. It integrates all of the earlier stages and experiences, and equips our neurobiology for what's coming next naturally, if we can complete that integrative process. Tears signal the completion of a process. We spend so much of our lives working with the outer world, with a scientific-materialistic perspective, and many ignore their inner world. Green enables us to step inside and become a whole human. Last time you talked about your new sense of purpose that is coming to you from higher up the Spiral, and this is a vacuum into which you are learning to grow.

David: That resonates, transitioning from Orange to Green. I thought about what I said last session about my purpose, "bringing life into this world." So many people in my culture are not feeling life inside them.

Christopher: Do you have a sense as to why that is happening?

David: Some type of fear, they might lose their identity, they might not have a foundation for sustaining it.

Christopher: Trust your own awareness. What's coming next in the transition from Green to Yellow is a change of identity. The strength of the myth of civilisation that pervades our culture constricts the transition from Green to Yellow.

David: Our culture is very Orange. I see a lot of materialism in advertisements.

Christopher: It's a bit of a shock that material wealth does not bring happiness or peace. You focused on stuckness and cloying. What are you experiencing around that?

David: I was speaking with my cousin, JJ, on Friday. That's a stage he is in [stuckness]. My cousin had a great surge 3-4 years ago. He's the lead singer of a touring band. But, he's feeling really stuck now. You would think he has the life that our culture tells us to have. He's not feeling great now. He had to tell a person in the band to leave. I spoke with him about this work and he's buying Ken Wilber's book. I told him about, "being stuck in treacle" [molasses] and it resonated with him. He's past the materialism stage and that really resonated with him too.

Christopher: Is there anything else about this Green transition?

David: Egalitarian?

Christopher: Everybody is equal.

David: That is hard for me to believe. I feel a little weakness. It doesn't resonate with me.

Christopher: What is the state that the word, "egalitarian," triggers within you?

David: It's like a little kid saying, "Yeah! Everyone's equal." It's naive.

Christopher: Let's move to Yellow. What stands out?

David: Systemic flow, flexible flow. Accept the inevitability of nature's flow. Functionality. Flex-flow. Flexibility. Spontaneity.

Christopher: Notice the preponderance around the word "flex". How does that link to what your needs are today?

David: I've always been an athlete and flexibility has always been a strength of mine, relative to other athletes. Being able to adapt to the situation. My competitors couldn't do it as quickly as me. I know the advantage of flexibility and how that translates into business, and to succeeding in worlds outside of sports. I've been thinking about systems lately. I've been reading about Yellow. You can save yourself from becoming emotional about surface-level manifestations, and you can understand more about the underlying causes of a chain of events. How do I do this more efficiently?

Christopher: When you look at the word "flexibility", what is really important to you?

David: It triggers within me joy. I've been able to use my flexibility in sports my whole life, and it's a great confidence builder. Your competition treats you with respect. I do yoga as well. I love the practice, which helps me respect flexibility even more.

Christopher: You are your own best teacher. The word in italics, "existence," is the dominant value and motivational system for Yellow. The joy of existence is exactly as you've described it. The process by which you get there is through acceptance. In this moment, we touch all life. This is the signature of this stage of development. It's not to experience life as "out there." It's to experience life through an explosion of our capacities to sense life in its entirety. Having those tears was a process of integration of something that was happening over a long time.

David: It makes a lot of sense.

Christopher: A lot of the work is learning to utilise every piece of information. If it were true that every aspect of your being was in touch with everything that is, what are the implications of that for you personally?

David: Expressing the joy of existence much more consistently.

Christopher: Allow yourself to follow that. What business are you really in then?

David: Inspiring, touching, moving, joy, enthusiasm, peace, creativity, wisdom.

Christopher: What's the one label that brings all those words together?

David: Growth. That's not it.

Christopher: What's the one word?

David: Mentoring

Christopher: Where is freedom in this?

David: Freedom is such a big part of it. That word means a lot to me. I'm in the business of freeing others from a life that doesn't have enough life.

Christopher: What additional freedom do you need to take for yourself?

David: The freedom to experience joy, enthusiasm, peace. I'm feeling like I know what business I'm in, but it's hard to articulate.

Christopher: When you most experience love, joy, peace, as you describe it, what will be the consequences for you personally?

David: Freedom, power, responsibility. Leading groups of people.

Christopher: What will be the consequences on your business partner?

David: Thriving on a financial level. Therefore having the flexibility to create contacts for my team to thrive and thereby giving them the power to create the context in which others can thrive. Becoming a beacon of hope and freedom and being an entity, a system where people can come and feel alive.

Christopher: Imagine as you do this, what is the likely consequence on the United States, as people experience this release of being alive?

David: They'll have a place and an organisation and a system to look to that is inspiring to them and is not only inspiring, but it is not naive. There will be a force that people in the USA can look to grow into, a nation that is once again leading the world, going forth courageously to solve not only our problems, but to help solve the various problems around the world.

Christopher: *Notice the difference between knowing the truth and experiencing the truth.* This capacity to experience the truth in Yellow gives us a new compass heading: to choose to no longer exploit the planet; to recover the Life Conditions that enable us to truly thrive; a heading that allows us to regenerate the vitality of life that we have lost over the last 300 years. All indicators suggest the human immune system is being compromised.

David: "Knowing vs. experiencing the truth," made me think of competitors of ours who are talking negatively about my company. It's a new experience. I've had people talk negatively about me, but not about my company. There's no reason to do that. We're a very positive company. We work with kids. There is courage involved in being the truth vs. knowing the truth. The opposition will test you.

Christopher: Remember that in terms of new thinking, nature has a wonderful way of testing out the new thinking to make sure it will really work. Notice the exiting signature from Yellow to Turquoise. The individual comes up with questions that he or she alone cannot answer, which leads to confusion. How did that lead you to contact us in the first place?

David: I felt I needed a guide to understand the new thoughts that I was having, and the way I was making sense of the world. I got to a point where it was very obvious that I needed help. I have had a great experience with my family's therapist to understand my world over the last seven years. But this work (of SDi) was a whole new way of thinking. I never talked about this type of stuff with the therapist. When I keep reading and testing it in the world it makes so much sense. I started with Eckhart Tolle, then David Hawkins, then Ken Wilber, then Spiral Dynamics. It was matter-of-fact that now I need a teacher to help me, because I'm hitting a ceiling. I'm not enough anymore to understand this work in this world.

Christopher: Remember that the questions that arise within us are a consequence of this vacuum that invites us to expand. The questions come up because of the consciousness reaching out and expanding, but it does not yet know itself. This takes you to the work of Gregory Bateson. Let's go next to Turquoise. What jumps out on Turquoise?

David: Holistic, Gaia, spirituality, energy fields, fluidity, cosmic, holographic, experiential.

Christopher: Notice the means and ends values. The means value is experiencing, learning to experience everything at once before acting. Don't expect quick responses from yourself, and accept that others won't always give you the time to develop an answer that is aligned with all life. The end value is the communion with life. The individual experiences the "I am that I am."

David: There's a song that I love and, "I am that I am," is the name of the song.

Christopher: It's about being in truth. A collective wisdom based on the collective experience. The emergence of this collective mind is part of what is happening on this call.

David: What about the word "freedom?"

Christopher: My intuitive self heard the word freedom coming through you. But, it's also the freedom to be in Yellow. Yellow is the knowing of the individual. Turquoise is the knowing of the knowers.

David: I listened to the recording of the last call twice. I got chills listening to my responses. I got so much more out of it.

Christopher: We're aiming to release the freedom of this Integral intelligence within you. A thought that keeps coming up—have you read, *A Theory of Everything*, by Ken Wilber?

David: I'm reading *Grace and Grit* now.

Christopher: A whole series of books came out by Ken after he discovered Graves. When you review this tape, ponder, "What was your experience?" We're uncovering your own vMeme repertoire. Every time someone speaks, they speak from their own vMeme centre of gravity. Draw a Spiral on paper, and then trace your finger along that journey, and your body will tell you where your centre of gravity is. It's close to freedom and confusion, based on what you've said this morning.

David: In the David Hawkins work I identified the emotions I was working with and I could name them. I remember in Green you talked about getting in touch with the life inside of you. I've been more able to connect with how I'm feeling inside. Is that the Green developing inside of me?

Christopher: When you become aware of it, that transition has served its purpose. You become the observer of your knowing. It's the characteristic of Yellow and beyond. Know that the Kosmos is speaking through you.

David took responsibility for his own emergence once he had the necessary insights and could explore, and accept guidance on overcoming historic and present barriers. As with many in this Second Tier awakening he now knew he was not alone. He took risks and discovered new pathways for his soul.

Applying Principle 1 To Self (the Practitioner): Understanding Your Kosmic Address

The ability to be aware of, and unfettered by one's biases is the essence of "response-ability" of the Solonic Practitioner. Being aware ensures a clean interpretation of the prevailing Life Conditions and the active vMemes of one's client, client organisation and organisational systems. Being aware also positions one's thinking into an Integral frame allowing one to be able to choose and utilise methods and approaches that are no more than half a step ahead of the client situation, or the practitioner's capability. Thus, the Solonic Practitioner, through effective communications, relationship and mutual agency, is aligning self and client with the natural process of emergence. In reflecting on the transcript of Virtual Mentoring Session Two with David (above), Christopher stated:

> I don't find it easy to talk about my Kosmic Address, because there is something like a built-in humility filter. As long as I know for myself that I am mentoring from the other side of the line, that is all I need to know, and I don't really need to communicate it to others. But, if you ask me questions in this case study context, I'll answer them the best I can.

I know when I am in the mentoring space it is as clean as I am going to be. When I am in the mentoring zone, I have heightened awareness of my vMeme profile, and yet, there is little awareness of self. There is no thought, only a responsiveness that follows the stream of consciousness of the mentee. There is also part of me that is tracking for exceptions, spotting my inner reactions, as they arise. There's me, and the meta-me, and the meta-me runs the show.

Having the theoretical prompts on the screen are important in virtual mentoring, because it allows me as the mentor to be largely free of the content. I am using the images and words without any real awareness of the point of view.

I simultaneously calibrate the results from the vMeme and change state scanning instruments that we use against the conversation I hear and the Life Conditions expressed by the mentee, whilst also using the musical chord-like results to shine a torch into otherwise hidden aspects of the mentee's Kosmic Address.

While "in the zone" I experience an almost ecstatic state of heightened awareness, with total recall of this and all previous sessions, nothing is missed. Ironically, I remember what the client says, but little of what I say.

When I review the notes of this session with David, I notice the language I use is rich in metaphor and simile, which is the optimum story-telling mode. It creates safety and security, and in this case, the Life Conditions for the transition from Yellow to Turquoise. What jumps out through this gentle nudging of words is how the questions one asks and the affirmations one makes create an open space for the mentee to be drawn into like a vacuum.

Every interaction with a client elicits heightened awareness of one's own Kosmic Address. A core competency for the Solonic Practitioner is to know when to get out of the way, and when to send in a firefly to shine a light on unexplored areas. "Getting out of the way" means catching your own down-stretch reactions, so you can keep the information flow in your bamboo pipe clean. Notice the times when you up-stretch, because these moments provide "in-flight instructions" on where to send the firefly.

Applying Principle 1 To Client: Understanding The Client's Kosmic Address

Effectively, the Solonic Practitioner is required to become as closely acquainted with the Kosmic Address of the client or mentee as possible. This process of resonance, coherence and alignment creates a springboard from which the practitioner can choose to remain at least half a step ahead in all situations. In all interactions, the practitioner is perpetually triangulating and processing information that is received from three primary sources: the words and expressions of the mentee, the Life Conditions demonstrated and explained by the mentee, and the results from the survey instrument(s). The purpose of the triangulation process is to calibrate the adaptation characteristics of the mentee's Kosmic Address, when in flow or under duress.

In reflecting on the transcript of Virtual Mentoring Session Two with David, Christopher observes how he calibrated David's Kosmic Address.

> I am aware that the mentee is expressing his or her journey through multiple existential states, and I frequently ask questions to probe the vMeme source behind the unprompted words used by the mentee. For example, in the exchange below, I probe for the vMeme that triggered David to highlight the word "egalitarian". In doing so, I discover that he is <u>looking back-in</u> from a Kosmic Address that is somewhere between exiting Green towards Yellow. He responds by looking back in at what does not resonate, calibrating the meaning against his previous meaning-making mechanism of Green. He comments on the naiveté of the belief, "everyone is equal," and willingly moves into an enthusiastic exploration of the attributes of Yellow.

Christopher: Is there anything else about this Green transition?

David: Egalitarian?

Christopher: Everybody is equal.

David: That is hard for me to believe. I feel a little weakness. It doesn't resonate with me.

Christopher: What is the state that the word, "egalitarian," triggers within you?

David: It's like a little kid saying, "Yeah! Everyone's equal." It's naive.

Christopher: Let's move to Yellow. What stands out?

David: Systemic flow, flexible flow. Accept the inevitability of nature's flow. Functionality. Flexibility. Spontaneity.

Every time we speak our Kosmic Address speaks through us. Ultimately, in all contact with David, we were consistently hearing the pursuit of an Integral freedom, a characteristic signature of a Kosmic Address exiting from Green towards Yellow. Below is a quote from David upon completion of our project.

> At first, I saw an opportunity for myself personally. I thought that if I could understand the four quadrants and the various levels and lines that run through them then I could have a heck of a lot more freedom for myself! And, I knew this freedom would eventually turn into power.
>
> – David Brown, December 2013

Principle 2: Consciously Absorb Information, Like A Kosmic Sponge, That Gives You Insight Into The Change Dynamics Of The vMemes.

We use the metaphor of being like a Kosmic Sponge, to refer to the intentional high bandwidth information exchange capacities that emerge in the transition to Second Tier. The adoption of a Second Tier theory, model, metaphor and practice seems to encourage the consolidation and acceleration of the utilisation of this new capacity for information exchange, allowing one, over time and with practice, to accurately bring new meaning to all experience and observation, and to identify the Kosmic Address of self and client.

Each stage of development carries differing capacities to sense and process inner and outer experience. In conventional thinking, there is a focus on the five senses: sight, sound, smell, taste and touch; and a limited range of associated intelligences. What has been shown through the primary and secondary research around The Graves Technology is that the journey from Beige through to Orange shows a steady decline in the range and scope of the sensory awareness and associated intelligences of the human being. Sensory competencies in Beige and Purple extend well beyond the five senses. Visit any indigenous setting to discover the greatly enhanced acuity and diversity of sensory capabilities. In such settings, it might be the injured little toe of the animal in the herd that is observed from a great distance by the hunter, who possesses a greater visual acuity than we do today, that provides an example of the natural capabilities of earlier stages of development that are no longer active due to our modern lifestyle.

The transition from Orange to Green triggers the re-emergence of previously dormant intelligences. Track the bookshelves over the last twenty years to observe the emergence of writing and practices that focus on emotional intelligence, and latterly, spiritual intelligence, as we strive to articulate and utilise heightened senses of feeling and subtle energies. The transition through Green is probably the most significant transition on the Spiral to date, where there is a revisiting and re-alignment of all previous stages to create the platform for the transition to Second Tier.

The emergence into Yellow is literally the start of a mutation of the brain and central nervous system, whereby the neurobiological capacities of Beige become re-used in new ways, and the holographic brain starts to emerge. For example, the neurobiological capacity for fear diminishes. The neurobiology, that had been utilised for fear, with its innate, heightened, sensory capacities, is released to assume a new role that contributes to a more complex mind; but the mind does not know how to utilise it. The unconscious instinctual response of the individual mutates to become a new stance of, "I choose to," as the individual "leaps," over a period of years, into an innate awareness of the subtle interconnectedness of all life, and strives to make sense of, define the meaning of, utilise, and communicate this new information. The individual effectively unfolds into the Second Tier, and becomes intentionally able to sense, absorb and process inner and outer information in radically new ways.

Truly Integral metaphors, models and theories, such as *The Graves Technology*, provide practitioners or clients, who are experiencing a Second Tier transition, with support in the accelerated interpretation and utilisation of their new capacities, by providing a context and meaning reframe. Over the past sixteen years, we commonly hear individuals who are in a Second Tier transition, following exposure to *The Graves Technology*, express a deep sense of relief with words like, "Thank God I am not going mad." "It was like having a veil lifted from my eyes." "It is so obvious. Why have I not thought of this before?" The difference that makes the difference is how closely the theory, model or metaphor reflects the natural dynamics of human emergence. For Solonic Practice, it is the intentional use of a bio-psycho-cultural-social systems perspective that is the dominant criteria. *The Graves Technology* and its later manifestations are the *syat*, a Native American word, which literally means, "to the best of our present knowledge."

Applying Principle 2 To Client: Consciously Absorb Information, Like A Kosmic Sponge, That Gives You Insight Into The Change Dynamics Of The vMemes.

As stated earlier, in all interactions, the practitioner is perpetually triangulating and processing all information that is received from three primary sources: 1) the results from the survey instrument(s) that assess the Kosmic Address of both individual and group, 2) the Life Conditions demonstrated and explained by the client(s), and 3) the words and expressions of the client(s). In the case of Future Captains Sports, the focus of the triangulation process was to assess the readiness and ability of the team to co-create an Integral curriculum.

Triangulation Step 1: Survey The Whole Team.

The online instruments used to survey the whole team during the design phase of the project were as follows:

1) An instrument that provides an indication of Kosmic Address through the assessment of the individual's active vMeme profile, from Purple to Turquoise, including acceptance and rejection, by eliciting responses from a range of perspectives (self, work, and world.)

2) A general-focus instrument that brings additional awareness to the Kosmic Address by offering information

about the predominant change states, change order (first and second order change), readiness for change, and change preference.

3) A work-focused instrument that assesses the degree of inner and outer alignment, or fit, of individuals in their work context with their Kosmic Address, indicated by: their vMeme profile (Purple to Yellow); their change state and predominant order of change (first or second order); their dominant executive intelligences; and the range of analogue to digital mind-brain processing capabilities. It also provides insight into the operation of their organisation by assessing the current and necessary-for-success organising codes and principles.

When the results of a group are collated, it results in an indication of the cultural/social Kosmic Address of the group, which is an expression of the core dynamics of the social holon. Figure 1 provides an example of a cultural/social measurement of the organisation.

PRESENT: Choose the one that best describes your present working arrangement.							
FCS Leadership	0%	0%	0%	100%	0%	0%	—
FCS Staff	16.7%	0%	16.7%	0%	50%	16.7%	—
Survival Band	Tribal Order	Exploitive Empire	Authority Structure	Strategic Enterprise	Social Network	Systemic Flow	Holistic Organism
Instinct Driven	Safety Driven	Power Driven	Order Driven	Success Driven	People Driven	Flexible-Flow Oriented	Synthesis Oriented
Beige A–N	Purple B–O	Red C–P	Blue D–Q	Orange E–R	Green F–S	Yellow G–T	Turquoise H–U
FCS Leadership	0%	0%	0%	0%	0%	100%	—
FCS Staff	0%	0%	16.7%	66.7%	0%	16.7%	—
DESIRED: Choose the one that best describes the way you would like to work.							

Figure 1: Future Captains Sports team results from the work-focused instrument.

We drew a general hypothesis from the overall survey results that for the group as a whole, there were clear indications of a Second Tier transition. Let us take a look at just some of the data we used to reach this conclusion. The results in Figure 1 are taken from the work-focused instrument, where we asked each individual to choose the organising code and principle (the images and associated words) that, "best describes your present working arrangement", and the one that, "best describes the way you would like to work." It is possible to draw conclusions about Kosmic Address from this information, when analysed 1) in the context of the predominant vMeme profile offered by the suite of three instruments, and 2) with the knowledge that every thought, action, and behavioural response is an expression of an individual's Kosmic Address. In effect, our core adaptive intelligences (vMemes) speak through us both directly and indirectly.

For this group, the predominant vMeme profile was Orange-Green-Yellow. Additionally, under duress, the instruments indicated that the leadership tended to regress towards Orange, and the staff tended to up-stretch towards Yellow, thus indicating an emergent capacity to lead, manage, and design from the other side of the line, subject to achieving greater cultural alignment and resilience. With awareness of the predominant vMemes, the results in Figure 1 indicate that two members of staff recognised a Tribal Order, Safety-Driven and Authority Structure, Order-Driven organisation, which suggested that Future Captains Sports might be weak in conducting administrative functions. This weakness in administration became a hypothesis for testing later on in the triangulation process.

The high score in Green (50%) indicated that the staff perceived they were operating as a Social Network, People-Driven organisation. They indicated the need to bring attention to the management of their enterprise through a focus on Authority Structure (Blue, 16.7%), Strategic Enterprise (Orange, 66.7%), and Systemic Flow (Yellow, 16.7%). This ability to designate an earlier system as the most appropriate (i.e. shift their collective thinking from Green 50% Present, to Orange 66.7% Desired) indicates an Integral perspective, where the focus is on functional solutions that address the question, "What is really needed here?"

As part of the triangulation process, we did thirty-minute telephone interviews with each respondent in order to validate the survey results. Following the telephone interviews, we concluded the team members were ready, willing and Integrally able to learn how to develop their own Integral curriculum. This awareness cleared the path for us to develop a series of recommendations that included explicit training in SDi and the real-time, whole-team involvement in the design and development of their own unique Integral child development curriculum. The results also confirmed that it was time for greater team involvement in the administrative development and operation of Future Captains Sports. We advised Scott and David:

- This group will be able to work explicitly with an Integral template. An Integral approach is highly likely to create a space for new freedom and flow across the whole group. Individuals will benefit greatly from a personal exploration and application of an Integral perspective.

We wished to ensure that the knowledge transfer and the sustained energy to support and consolidate the learning from an intervention would be owned by a self-referencing leadership dyad. We concluded that Scott and David were able to hold an intentional vMeme space at least a half-step ahead of the rest of the team to support the healthy development of Future Captains Sports. Based on these findings, we then prepared a recommended programme to be delivered onsite in Media, Pennsylvania one month later.

Triangulation Step 2: Assess the Life Conditions Past, Present And Emergent

We assessed Life Conditions in four different ways 1) web, desk and third-party research, 2) online assessments, 3) structured interviews of the team, 4) onsite scanning:

1) **Web, Desk and Third-Party Research.** In analysing the Life Conditions for Future Captains Sports, we examined the following elements: social trends and norms; soccer-based child development locally, nationally and internationally; Integral theory on child development; American sports culture and the relative prevalence of soccer; and role model child development programs such as Tacade's, *Skills for Adolescence*. For each element, we undertook a vMeme analysis. Our challenges were to find appropriate childhood development material that would

assist in the development of an Integral curriculum, and to assess how to position an Integral curriculum to be no more than a half step ahead of prevailing norms.

2) **Online Assessments.** Through the online assessments, we gleaned the team's perception of the present organisation of Future Captains Sports, and what they thought was required to secure a successful future.

3) **Structured Interviews.** Through structured interviews of individuals, we gathered additional information on both individual and team Life Conditions. For example: Were they married. What roles did they play? How long have they been in their role? What is their educational background? What inspired them to join Future Captains Sports? etc.

4) **Onsite Scanning.** Prior to departure, we pressed upon David and Scott the importance of us having an in-depth exposure to the Life Conditions surrounding Future Captains Sports. Within hours of arrival in Pennsylvania, Scott took us to visit the home where he grew up. Here we met his grandmother, aunts, and cousins, and visited the communal soccer pitch that was so influential during the formative teenage years of both Scott and David. For the whole period, we lived in the family home where David grew up, and had daily access to family stories about both David and Scott, from birth to present, from David's parents, and other friends and family. We also took road trips around Media, to observe and experience the locality of both their homes and their business.

Our scanning of the Life Conditions using the four methods outlined above provided us with confirmation of 1) the validity of the results from the survey, 2) weak business administration surrounding Future Captains Sports, 3) the readiness of staff to lead the creation of an Integral curriculum, 4) the capability of the founders/leaders of the organisation to sustain and lead from at least half a step ahead of the staff, 5) the proposed business model fit the future needs of the overall Life Conditions.

Triangulation Step 3: Discover The Embodied Nature Of Kosmic Address Through Face-To-Face Interaction

In Triangulation Step 3, we require direct observation of the whole team in the work-based environment. Where possible, all interactions with the team are required to be as close to day-to-day reality as possible. "Interaction" is when all information gathered is validated through live contact with individuals, the group, and stakeholders. In the interactions through the training and workshops one is assessing the Kosmic Address of each individual, and also the resilience and alignment of the social holon (the group's Kosmic Address) in a range of situations both classroom and business development-based. What we are looking for is the embodied nature of Kosmic Address.

The training and Integral design workshop were run on an indoor sports field owned by AMPRO, and managed by Future Captains Sports. Being on the sports field created the Life Conditions where the team was habitually in flow. Tapping into this flow ensured inspired learning, enhanced by whole body experiences through freedom of movement and thought. This environment allowed one of the staff members to bring her three young children each day. The presence and spontaneous responses of the children served as a constant reminder of the target audience. Towards the latter part of the programme, by being on the soccer field, we were able to test session plan prototypes with live classes of three and four year-olds, and five and six year-olds, and parents. We were also able to handle drop-in guests of parents, managers of the facility, and other stakeholders who wanted to be aware of the novel practices and new venture. The SDi training we gave the team enabled us to have close interaction with each team member, and to assess their competency to utilise each aspect of theory and application.

The team's design, development and documentation of their own Integral curriculum enabled us to observe their ability to apply theory in practice, to a point where we witnessed a successful knowledge transfer; success that was demonstrated not only by team feedback, but by the responses of children and parents alike. The application of the theory, process and procedures to the enhancement of business administration provided additional evidence of the relevant team member's ability to think, design and act from the other side of the line.

Principle 3 – Be Integral, And When Appropriate, Stimulate Your Client To Be The Same

Throughout this document, we have spoken about the need for Integral thinking, and practices that encourage its utilisation. To support practitioner and client we have developed spatial methods that literally place the individual(s) in a space of the elaboration intelligence of Yellow and beyond; a practice that we call "standing on the other side of the line." Essentially, standing on the other side of the line is a means of polishing and refining a Second Tier awareness by using the metaphor of the Spiral and the descriptions of the stages and the change transitions to stimulate latent Integral thinking. We begin by accepting that the change has already happened; we are just learning to grow into it. The "standing on the other side of the line" exercise opens up an "acting as-if Integral" frame, or a new psychological space that invites the individual to utilise his or her own Integral intelligence. Remember, stance matters.

One of the characteristics of the transition into Second Tier awareness is that the stages of development, or vMemes, are not available to the individual through self-inspection. It requires a third-person perspective, like looking up at the vapour trail of an aircraft, to see the patterns that the pilot is completely unaware of. What we have found is that through the utilisation of metaphors and models such as SDi, the individual becomes aware of how these stages speak and emerge through them. Once tasted, a self-calibrating awareness is realised, and the individual becomes increasingly aware of the phenomenology of his or her own Kosmic Address. The SDi template is simply a guiding metaphor.

Imagine looking back in from a balcony placed in the early stages of Second Tier thinking, enabling the observer to look back in at the theatre of the Spiral. From this perspective the attributes and characteristics of each earlier stage of development become apparent and differentiated within the observer. Imagine standing in that balcony, looking back at the development of a child, at three years of age, and being able to craft the Life Conditions (the curriculum) that supports the healthy, ongoing development of the bio-psycho-cultural-social systems that are active within and around the child. This is the essence of the practice, "standing on other side of the line." Here are excerpts from the mentoring session that illustrate Christopher holding an "as-if Integral" frame with David:

- You are your own best teacher. The word in italics, *"existence,"* is the dominant value and motivational system for Yellow. The joy of existence is exactly as you've described it. The process by which you get there is through acceptance. In this moment, we touch all life. This is the signature of this stage of development. It's not to experience life as "out there." It's to experience life through an explosion of our capacities to sense life in its entirety.

- Notice the difference between knowing the truth and experiencing the truth. This capacity to experience the truth in Yellow gives us a new compass heading: to choose to no longer exploit the planet; to recover the Life Conditions that enable us to truly thrive; the capacity that allows us to regenerate the vitality of life that we have lost over the last 300 years. All indicators suggest the human immune system is being compromised.

- Notice the means and ends values (in Turquoise). The means value is experiencing, learning to experience everything at once before acting. Don't expect quick responses from yourself, and accept that others won't always give you the time to develop an answer that is aligned with all life. The end value is the communion with life. The individual experiences the "I am that I am."

Applying Principle 3 To Client

The balcony is the place from which an Integral curriculum is designed. Through the utilisation of a growing theoretical and intuitive awareness of human emergence, we enabled Future Captains Sports' staff to guide themselves using a series of questions. This resulted in an overall curriculum, consisting of age-specific syllabi, coaching strategies, session plans, and activity plans, all designed to create the Life Conditions, as a flowing journey, to support the child into, through and beyond a particular stage of development. Here are the steps we took for working with the team, who, as you know, were already assessed as being ready, willing and able to utilise an explicit Integral theory.

1) Provide base level training of SDi, with an explicit Kosmological context to enhance relevance, meaning, and application.

2) Have participants lay out on the soccer field a spatial model of the whole Spiral, and working in pairs, coach each other through the

Spiral, in order to develop a working knowledge of what it means to think from the other side of the line.

3) With reference to appropriate child development theories, have participants stand on the other side of the line, to assess the Kosmic Address of the authors of the child development theories, to gain a collective understanding of the attributes of each child development age range, and to develop coaching strategies that release natural motivational flow by creating session-specific healthy bio-psycho-cultural-social Life Conditions, for a child, classified by age range. See Figure 2 for an example, the 3-5 year old category.

4) Provide a visual metaphor for an Integral curriculum, ensuring that terminology is defined and agreed.

5) Elicit the overarching purpose, vision, mission and ideals of Future Captains Sports as a means of bringing context and vitality to the content creation of an Integral curriculum.

6) Have participants stand on the other side of the line*, and as a large group, co-create a chain of existential states that provides the context for the development of the syllabi and session plans for child development from 18 months through to 20+ years of age.

7) Transfer the knowledge of how to create a chain of existential states to the participants.

8) Have participants stand on the other side of the line, and in teams develop a chain of existential states for each syllabus for each age range: 2-3 year olds, 4-5 year olds, 9-12 year olds. See Figure 3 for an example, the 4-5 year old syllabus.

9) Develop session plans for 2-3 year olds and 4-5 year olds. See Figure 4 for an example, Session Plan 5: Team Play for 4-5 year olds.

10) Test the session plans with live classes and review.

11) Make a plan, using chain of states method, for completing the Future Captains Sports curriculum, with clear roles and responsibilities, by the end of November 2013.

12) Work with the full team to explore the administrative functions that need to be in place at Future Captains Sports to support the successful delivery of a session plan.

13) Identify priority needs, and develop a chain of existential states implementation plan for website development.

14) Work with the founding pair to develop a realistic implementation plan, with supporting budget, for refinement of business administration to enable the successful utilisation of the curriculum.

Here are the questions we posed, in order to facilitate participants to, "stand on the other side of the line."

1) Life Conditions. What are the Life Conditions?

2) Coping Mechanisms. What are the dominant coping mechanisms being activated?

3) Motivational Flow. How do you create the Life Conditions in which motivational flow is released?

Age: 3–5 Years

Coaching Awareness

1. What's developing in the child at this age?
- Observational intelligence, awareness of what is a safe environment, imagination, motor skills, empathy, sense of humor, sense of right and wrong, comprehension of language

2. What's easy for the child?
- Running, walking, listening to stories, step-by-step directions, routine, recognizing primary colors, learning songs, free play, dancing

3. What's challenging for the child?
- Connecting numbers with objects, multiple step directions, movement with change of direction, attention span, tying shoelaces

4. What coping mechanisms appear to be underpinning this age/stage of development?
- Beige | Purple | Red

Coaching Awareness

1. What hot buttons do you want to stimulate?
- Rituals, give tokens, magic, safety, respect for elders, honor ancestors

2. What cold buttons do you want to avoid?
- Step on or desecrate sacred ground, introduce ambiguity, disrespect for elders, not trying to understand them, threaten family

3. What are the active learning styles?
- Step-by-step sequences of learning, repetition, mirroring, storytelling and acting out, chants, dance

4. What are tips for creating healthy Life Conditions at this stage of development?
- Bio: motor skills, counting, words, numbers with objects
- Psycho: stimulate imagination, give responsibility to care of object/person, free play, storytelling
- Cultural: rituals, empathy, humor, magic
- Social: don't threaten family, don't step on or desecrate sacred ground, provide a safe environment, give step-by-step directions

Figure 2

Participants used a book called, *Child Development: An Illustrated Handbook* by Jacqueline Harding, as the basis for developing "Coaching Awareness" and "Coaching Strategies" to release natural motivational flow by creating healthy Life Conditions. Here is their work for 3-5 years.

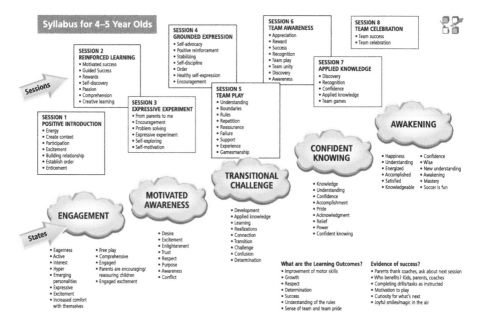

Figure 3

Based on the coaching strategies developed in Figure 1, participants developed an eight-week syllabus for 4-5 year olds.

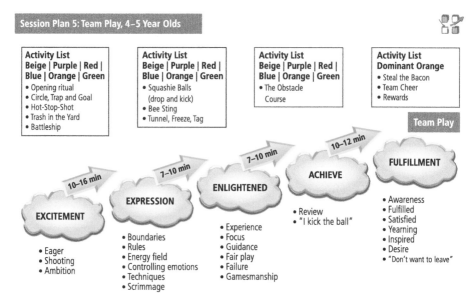

Figure 4

Based on the eight-week syllabus, participants developed a session plan for Session 5 Team Play, and then tested it with a live class.

Conclusion

In conclusion, a Solonic Practitioner is *acting as-if*, or *is* an Integral being. From this place of systemic awareness, on the other side of the line, the practitioner is well equipped to utilise the three principles of Solonic Practice to design and facilitate meaningful solutions in support of human emergence. A Solonic practitioner is in service of an emergent Kosmos.

It will take time for the full impact of our work at Future Captains Sports to be known. We are confident though that the context is set for success and what is needed is emerging. At the time of writing this chapter we had just received the following affirming message from our client.

> "Ohhhhhhhh yeahhhhhh!!!~!!!!!!!! Incroyable!!!!!! Thank you. Thank you. Thank you. Thank you. Beautiful..... I'm not even half way through it and I had to run upstairs and tell my parents how happy I am right now.... This document will be a huge part of the foundation for us to build upon. I couldn't have envisioned a better outcome from our ten days together. All of the knowledge gained, the unity achieved, and the documents you've sent will serve us for many years to come. We're so thankful for your generosity, skill, and professionalism. I'm grateful to you both deep down in my heart and soul. Christopher, I completed the exercise you gave me two nights ago and experienced my soul. I know what it is now....."

– David Brown

THE ARAB MEMOME PROJECT: DESIGNING FOR THE 21ST CENTURY ARAB RENAISSANCE

By Elza Maalouf

Chapter 7, from "Emerge! The Rise of Functional Democracy and the Future of the Middle East. 2014. Select Books, NY, NY.

> *I always ask: How can I help? What can I do for people? How can I improve people's lives? That's part of my value system. It's too late for me to change that system, but it isn't too early for me to say to the world that the Dubai narrative is all about changing people's lives for the better through smart capitalism, willpower and positive energy.*[1]
>
> —Sheikh Mohammed bin Rashid Al Maktoum
> Ruler of Dubai
> *Wall Street Journal*
> January 12, 2008

While oil wealth has brought Orange memes to the Middle East, it hasn't been able to attract the complex Orange entrenched in science, medicine, and technology. Because of this unique value-system interpretation of wealth, the culture has remained primarily centered in Purple kinship values. Business ownership and leadership succession plans in the Middle East look a lot like

---

1   Sheikh Mohammed bin Rashid Al Maktoum, "Our Ambitions for the Middle East," *The Wall Street Journal*, January 12, 2008, opinion pages.

business values that dominated the economic landscape of the United States from the late 1800s to the early 1900s. While corporate practices in the region can look Orange, corporations exist in PURPLE–Red Life Conditions.

These are businesses run by families with immense wealth. While historic Orange prides itself on scientific discoveries and continues to improve on human capacities as an expression of modernity, the Middle East has remained on the outskirts having the trappings of the Orange vMeme without the substance. The next frontier for the region is not how to get better management consultants to improve on the Orange memes already there, but how to get leaders to create the habitats that will naturally encourage the culture to emerge into more complex Orange expressions that can sustain their countries beyond the Age of Oil.

Genesis of the Arab Memome Project

Don Beck advocates for the pioneering view that human cultural memes mimic human biological genes. Beck continues his alignment with the most advanced scientific research regarding the function of human DNA. The Human Genome Project is one of the largest collaborative international scientific research efforts ever undertaken. Its primary goal is determining the sequence of chemical base pairs that make up the human DNA. The project intends to identify and map the genes of the human genome from both a physical and functional standpoint.[2]

While the Human Genome Project aims to decode human DNA in order to better understand the building blocks and evolution of our species, the Memome Project aims to decode human cultural DNA in order to better understand human sociocultural structures and the evolution of human groupings. Because of the double-helix nature of the value-systems framework that couples the "base pairs" of *Life Conditions* with *adaptive intelligence,* there is a physical and functional definition to memes. Beck will address these parallels in his upcoming book, *Humanity's Hidden Code.*

The idea for creating the Arab Memome Project came to us at the Center for Human Emergence Middle East while Dr. Beck and I were in the midst of our work on the Build Palestine Initiative. More precisely, it came to us after years of research and work diagnosing Life Conditions that exposed weak spots in the fabric of the development of the region.

---

2   The Human Genome Project (n.d.). In *Wikipedia.* http://en.wikipedia.org/wiki/Human_Genome_Project Retrieved August 1, 2013.

This is when we came to realize that far greater institutional complexity in the region needs to emerge in an indigenous way in order to accommodate the confluence of several factors that will profoundly impact the future of Middle-Eastern culture:

- The first factor was the deluge of global memes influencing cultural emergence and change through the World Wide Web. The Information Age knocked down the walls supporting traditional values, exposing the culture to numerous wildcards and scenarios. The density and rapidity of the information coming through in the last couple of decades has been so significant that it has the potential to accelerate the collapse of the existing socio-cultural constructs in the region.

- The second factor was the failure of development models, throughout the region to recognize the importance of building human capacities within the culture to deal with the rate and type of change.

- The third concern was, whether or not the Age of Oil ended in twenty years or forty years, there was no contingency plan to employ the culture of the Millennials who account for 60 percent of Arab society. This was and still is quite disturbing.

- The fourth concern was the marginalization of 50 percent of the culture—the women. To us, this represents the pivotal force for moving the culture to the next stage of emergence. Although there are subcultures of women in the middle and upper class who are leading businesses, the majority of women are excluded from the process.

- Our fifth and final main concern was, once we identified these threats to the future of the region, how do we move forward with funding the implementation of the Arab Memome Project?

No leadership outside the region or a single ally in the world could undertake this massive initiative regardless of their interests. This is an undertaking that has to come from within the culture and has to be a reflection of the indigenous will to emerge. This is the challenge that will define the shape of regional leadership for decades to come. The Center for Human Emergence Middle East (CHE-Mideast) can only act as a catalyst that informs business and political leadership on the trajectory of the stages of human and cultural development. We will design what we think is an effective and comprehensive cultural emergence plan that helps leaders navigating the road ahead. Most think tanks can only inform Middle Eastern leaders of the ominous challenges they face, but unless these leaders start to think from the future, emergence will continue to be arrested. The CHE-Mideast proposes to design region-wide MeshWORKS, with culture specific needs to initiate the transformational process. This is where we call on the Heroic archetypes in the region to rise to this challenge and create a new Arab Renaissance.

This is the New Frontier in Arab cultural emergence. What we aim to do is to memetically map out the entire Middle East. We have a global network of *Integral Design Architects* (IDAs) who are ready to support the CHE-Mideast and are proficient in the value-systems approach. Many hold advanced degrees in social and industrial psychology with decades of experience in organizational and cultural work based on the value-systems approach. All have had close work relationships with the founders of this innovative school of thought. They have developed proprietary technologies and can identify the functions that need to be performed. Unlike the linear plans that developed the physical infrastructure of the region, our memetically-honed strategies will be informed by local *Indigenous Intelligence Experts (IIEs)* that have the knowledge of the economic, political and religious construct of their unique culture. They will be trained in the value-systems approach relevant to their areas of specialty.

As we did in Palestine, we will conduct full assessments of Life Conditions within every country. Once this extensive data is collected, the same MeshWORKS approach that was used in South Africa, Iceland, the Netherlands, and Palestine will be used to design a resilient plan for overall Middle Eastern emergence. This is not a one-size-fits-all approach as we only design strategies after exhaustive assessment of the needs of an individual culture. We support the specialized experts in their field in shaping and implementing their strategies to support the sustainable movement of the culture to its next stage. This is where Seventh-Level Yellow leadership in the Middle East will be able to see the big picture with our help and be able to navigate it successfully and plan for a bright future accordingly.

We know from our experience in South Africa and Palestine that a systemic transition of a culture from the Purple Kinship and Red Heroic value systems to their next level of development involves the spreading of the memes of *prosper and let prosper*. While the Gulf Cooperation Council has experienced an entry level into the Enterprising value system through oil wealth, other parts of the region still struggle with the disparities between the haves and have-nots. The solutions for both parts of the region are to begin building institutions and laws to which all citizens subscribe, which also support the Millennials and women. These are the values on which a prosperous culture rests. A Seventh-Level Yellow leadership in the region will regard the design of institutions as a functional necessity for the emergence of their countries.

Goals of the Arab Memome Project

Based on our decade of experience with this theoretical framework in the region, and in preparation to launch the Arab Memome Project, our research has uncovered some areas of exploration worthy of Memetic analysis and closer examination. Below is a starting platform envisioned to ignite the conversation about the future of the region. It is intended to give birth to a new paradigm in developmental thinking about the future of the Arab world.

1. Developing A Robust Middle Class

There is no higher calling for the future of the Middle East than the building of an indigenously-informed capitalist system with a socially and economically-empowered middle class. This is the ultimate goal of the Arab Memome Project. Third level Heroic capitalism can lead to societal collapse if its efforts are not balanced by a system of checks and balances to assure that it serves the greater good of the people.

As cultural economist and Chief Operating Officer of the CHE-Mideast, Said E. Dawlabani, points out in his book *MEMEnomics,* this is precisely what happened in the United States as a result of predatory Red capitalism that led to the Great Depression. The only way forward for the United States was for its leaders to redefine its cultural and economic values through the power of institutions.

After going through more than a decade of severe hardship the culture emerged into a Blue order-driven stage of economic development. The building of government guaranteed programs regulated predatory businesses while encouraging institutions like banks, universities, and large corporations to be responsible to the country's citizens. This is an example of the types of institutions necessary to building a middle class. It was visionary leaders like Franklin D. Roosevelt who created many of the U.S. institutions that empowered the common family. This forever changed the economic dynamics of the most resilient capitalist society in the history of humanity. Much like Roosevelt's New Deal plans, the Middle East must embark on its own new deal that creates its own independent and resilient economy with fair opportunity for all who want to participate.

In light of where the global economy is today, visionary Middle Eastern leaders must look to empower innovation by funding research and development that adds value to the global economy. They must also look to empower a region-wide work ethic that builds capacities and skills within people. Empowering a robust manufacturing sector capable of processing all the petroleum byproducts today, will lead to many manufacturing innovations in the future. This sector played a major role in building the global middle class elsewhere, and it can do the same for the Middle East. More importantly, it can direct the Red energy of youth without formal education into productive pursuits and give them a new purpose away from destructive Red activities.

Leaders must also empower the educated Millennial Generation by providing it with the same institutional infrastructure that advanced countries have in place today. This will also involve the reformation of how business in the region gets done. The guidelines for business resilience outlined in my book *Emerge! The Rise of Functional Democracy and the Future of the Middle East* must be embraced region wide. There's no doubt that the knowledge economy is going to continue to grow. This is an economy empowered by Seventh-Level Yellow values. All stakeholders must participate in making sure the region embraces the knowledge economy, or be left behind. This is the new Arab Renaissance. The Arab Memome Project intends to address the building of an Arab middle class. It will require leadership, commitment, hard work and strategic planning capable of looking decades into the future.

Today, despite all the competition and threats the U.S. economy faces, its middle class remains the most powerful economic group in the world. This is due mostly to institutions that were put in place decades ago to guarantee economic security. Today, the wealth of this nation comes from human productive output that, unlike natural resources, is resilient, infinite and renewable.

Although many in the Middle East disagree with the United States' foreign policy, its domestic economic policies of the 1940s and 1950s are what is next for the Middle East. This is what made the United States an undisputed economic superpower for decades. While per capita wealth is much higher in smaller, richer countries in the Middle East like Qatar, Kuwait, and UAE, there is no other country in the world today that boasts a higher average income for a population as massive as that of the United States, the third most populous country behind China and India. The per capita GDP in China and India for 2012 was $6,072 and $1,492 respectively.[3] For the same year, per capita income for the United States was $49,922, more than eight times that of China and thirty-three times that of India.

No other system has distributed more wealth to its population than the capitalist system in the United States. This is due to a powerful middle class that was empowered socially and economically through institutions that were put in place by visionaries who built Blue Fourth-Level institutions. No culture in existence today has prospered long term without the prominent presence of a middle class and the purchasing power it creates in keeping local economies resilient and the population aligned with values of self-reliance.

It took decades for the United States to realign the values that embraced the spread of the middle class, and the Middle East will not be able to institutionalize change overnight. The region has received its share of criticism for having some of the worst economic data for a region so rich with natural resources. Based on the most recent available research, the value of economic output for all Arab countries in the Middle East and North Africa (MENA) region amounted to just 2.9 trillion USD for 2012, with oil and natural gas accounting for 73 percent of total exports and 78 percent of budget revenues.[4] Based on these figures and the population of the region, per capita income amounts to less than $650.

When compared to 2012 figures from the World Bank, this places the region in the 162nd place in per capita income, between Zimbabwe and Mozambique.[5] Importantly, should oil and natural gas revenues disappear without an economic emergence plan in place, based on income distribution today, the region will be tied in last place with Malawi and Congo for the world's poorest countries (based on 2012 income).

3   The International Monetary Fund, *World Economic Outlook Database April 2013, Report for Selected Countries*, http://www.imf.org/external/data.htm. Retrieved August 3, 2013.
4   Institute of International Finance, Economic research, the MENA countries, http://www.iif.com/emr/mena/. Retrieved August 3, 2013.
5   The International Monetary Fund, *World Economic Outlook Database April 2013, Report for Selected Countries*, http://www.imf.org/external/data.htm. Retrieved August 3, 2013.

These income disparities have been the primary cause of the Arab Spring. In rural areas of Egypt, for example where people live on less than $2 a day, the removal of food subsidies that caused the price of sugar and bread to rise 300 percent pushed the poorest people to the breaking point. This is the Middle East's version of the French Revolution happening much faster in the age of information and knowledge. Despite that, it will still take several decades for the region to emerge into an order-driven Blue stage of development. Just like the accelerated speed of the revolution, the emergence into a region-wide robust middle class will happen much faster if it is approached properly.

As we look to the future, the CHE-Mideast has formulated strategies that The Arab Memome Project can undertake to assure that the transition is an evolutionary process rather than a revolutionary one. Seventh-Level Yellow leaders have to begin today to facilitate the growth and distribution of per capita income to rival that of first world countries. By aiming for this lofty goal, the Middle East may be forever transformed.

2. Spreading The Memes Of Prosper And Let Prosper

The forward march of progress has become unstoppable. The Information Age has hollowed the manifesto of the Middle Eastern dictator. Social, cultural, political, and economic progress is all now informed by a global platform of transparency. The power is shifting to the people and the people want better lives than those brought about by war, repression, and enmity. Middle East development might parallel Dorothy's journey in *The Wizard of Oz*. Policies of repression could be compared to the arduous road towards the Emerald City. Along the road, many joined forces in seeking answers to what ailed them. They risked their lives on this difficult journey, only to realize that the great and powerful Oz, who was supposed to have all the answers, was nothing more than a little man behind the curtain. They found that the true road to redemption was self-reliance, which was always within their reach.

The little men behind the Middle Eastern curtain are dictators, former military rulers, and implementers of repressive policies that keep their cultures behind the times. What is next for the region is a painful transition from PURPLE–Red cultural center of gravity to BLUE–Orange values that are in touch with a changing global village, but with a pragmatic awareness of the disappearing oil reserves. The finite oil commodity has been the primary source of wealth for the region for a major part of the last century.

Historically, Europe lingered in the dark ages of closed Blue during the era of the Spanish Inquisition until the Industrial Revolution, the enterprising Fifth-Level system that acted as a superordinate pull out of the Dark Ages and through a socio-cultural transition to higher values. Beck's work in South Africa exemplified the powerful role that businesses can play in contributing to cultural transformation. Similarly, with our Build Palestine Initiative, we created an *optimistic, enterprising* superordinate goal for the Palestinians in order to give them hope about their future so they could go about building the needed institutions to support their vision. These are the values that informed the progressive Palestinian Prime Minister Fayyad to pursue the best future for his people.

The memes behind "prosper and let prosper" have acted as a primary catalyst for cultural progress for centuries. The pursuit of these values, if approached through the proper memetic channels, can render previous dynamics of conflict obsolete in time. Long-term prosperity has a way of moving many of the Zealots, Ideologues, and Flamethrowers toward moderate positions regardless of the issues in any culture. It is only through the Order-driven Blue and Enterprising Orange center positions on the Assimilation Contrast Effect graph of a society that a culture will have long-term prosperity and can shield itself from the destructive dynamics of closed Blue, complacent Purple, and feudal Red values.

3. Understanding The Memetic Implications Of The Miracle Of Dubai

In a region dominated by traditional values and oil wealth, Dubai represents what is possible for the future of the Middle East. This miracle in the desert has proven to the world that, given the right leadership, societal development can move through several stages of progress at what seems to be the speed of light. These are Arab values at their best: heroic Red leadership combined with a strategic Orange long-term vision for sustainable prosperity. Although much criticism has been leveled at the speed with which Dubai is being built, much of that progress speaks to the possibility of the region's diverse future. The values of commerce are deeply rooted in the region and in the history of Islam. As the Middle East emerges into Orange Fifth-Level values, many in the Muslim world want to adopt the enterprising virtues of the Prophet Mohammed. Historically oil and natural resources have only been the preferred mode of trade for the region for a short and temporary period of time. No one understands the implications of this better than the ruler of Dubai himself, who set out to build a diverse economy that sees beyond the limitations of oil:

> *Dubai's varied economic activities depend on a policy to decrease dependence on oil as the sole source of income. We promote the development of the trade sector, agricultural reform, national industry and national and international investment.*[6]
> – His Highness Sheikh Mohammed bin Rashid Al Maktoum, the UAE Prime Minister, Vice President, and Ruler of Dubai.

Understanding the importance of economic diversity for the whole region can act as a catalyst to propel the Middle East out of its current dysfunction and on the road to economic sustainability. The Middle East can learn from Dubai's heroic journey and adjust their visions and business practices to accommodate the most critical development stages for the future of the region. These are values that I often speak of at organizational and corporate leadership forums. They have given my clients a sustainable competitive edge. Now they are being echoed by the visionary leadership in the region. Economic diversity not only leads to minimization of future risk, it enables entire cultures to engage in more complex interactions and trade that will eventually become a source of self-sufficiency. It informs the designers of institutions on their need to be more in tune with the future instead of just honoring the past. It rearranges values at the macro-memetic level to anticipate what the future will bring and inspires its leaders, like Sheikh Al Maktoum, to serve that future promise.

In the past, without visionary leadership, cultures lingered in tribalistic Purple and feudal Red value systems for centuries. The right leader, or a benevolent monarch as in Dubai, creates Life Conditions that propel a culture toward higher levels of complexity. With the immense wealth that is present in the Gulf region, Sheikh Al Maktoum viewed money differently than many other leaders. He envisioned it as an important agent for the development of Dubai's infrastructure and institutions, and not strictly

---

6   Sheikh Mohammed bin Rashid Al Makhtoum, *Collection of Quotes*, http://sayingsearch.blogspot. com/2009/09/sheikh-mohammed-bin-rashid-al-maktoum_9184.html. Retrieved July 28, 2013.

as a facilitator of conspicuous consumption and personal wealth. This mature, long-term view of money and wealth will serve the region long after oil has disappeared. Economic diversity that is guided by leadership aimed at building human and institutional capacities has created a "pull" or a *superordinate goal* for Dubai that is redefining the current and future development of the Middle East. It is realigning the memetic stack of the tiny emirate and placing it in a position of regional leadership.

While this visionary development plan was designed to bring Dubai to a level of memetic complexity that rivals the West, Life Conditions in the region are integrating their own unique and indigenous expression, becoming the envy of the Middle East. This is the type of charismatic healthy leadership the rest of the region needs, leadership that sees common prosperity as the only way out of the current progressive stagnation and bloody stalemate.

What Dubai embarked on was a major systemic risk, but also one of the most ambitious development plans in modern human history. It is bringing individualistic values of personal success into a memetic mix rich with tribal generosity and tradition that is changing the Middle East and setting it up for advanced development. It is a unique and indigenous trail that is being blazed by risk, brave experimentation, and the ultimate desire to advance the culture. In the process, many of the memes that are unique to the Fifth-Level Orange system, including individual empowerment and scientific and strategic values, are taking root and will advance the future economies of the region.

As often is the case with initial stages of emergence into higher values, certain wild cards can derail a culture's efforts in its forward movement. Dubai was no exception. Between 2000 and 2008, without having free market Fifth-Level Orange complexity and with very little Blue commercial guidance in place, Dubai became an attraction to speculative investment and global predatory financial behavior. Buildings that touched the sky were being put up practically overnight. Global investors were buying properties off plans and selling them for many times the original price before they were even built. It was an unbridled RED–Orange feeding frenzy fed by an endless stream of global capital, and it was impossible to identify the real levels of demand and market prices.

Red capitalism combined with Orange greed unconstrained by Blue triggered the meme codes that provided the region with its first lesson on modern Fifth-Level Orange emergence. As the rush to build this city-state came to an end in 2008, many of its private sector participants learned the lessons of risk-taking, the understanding of free market forces, and the need to engage in strategic planning. These are three memes of a healthy, well-regulated capitalist system, which have emerged over the centuries to make capitalist cultures so unique today.

As a result of this massive speculation and the bursting of the first modern day real-estate bubble in the Middle East, something very unique emerged from Dubai. As an open system since the financial crisis, it turned its focus to building unique Fourth-Level, Blue order-system institutions that guarantee investor protection and provide Dubai with a future with long-term stability. This didn't happen willingly, as entry into the Fifth-Level Orange system falsely views the Fourth-Level Blue system as an inconvenience (at best). Unhealthy Orange will fight healthy Blue every step of the way because it gets in the way of free trade. Skipping a cultural development stage almost always results in vulnerabilities and wild cards that can set back emergence. Dubai's focus on building modern day Fourth-Level Blue institutions came just in time.

Blue was institutionalized by His Highness Sheikh Khalifa bin Zayed Al Nahyan, the ruler of Abu Dhabi, who agreed to bail out Dubai World, the state-owned holdings company that was left with hundreds of billions in debt at the end of 2008. Because Dubai World was born into a culture of speculation, without much Blue accountability, it lacked strategic long-term planning. As global cash dried up in 2008, it was left with many speculative and unfinished projects worth billions of dollars. Abu Dhabi's conditions on its bailout injected the necessary Blue that is now building a stronger institutional foundation throughout the UAE.

The brief history of Dubai, as an experiment of an open system within the context of a global economic village has given the region an example of how careful and visionary planning can move cultures quickly and place them on the path towards global competitiveness. Although Dubai might have stumbled in its ambition, its progress represents the most advanced emergence of both the Fourth and Fifth Levels (BLUE–Orange) of value systems in the region in tune with the future, while at the same time honoring a storied and proud past.

4. Creating A Regional Superordinate Goal

Just as His Highness Sheikh Mohammed bin Rashid Al Maktoum, the UAE Prime Minister, Vice President and Ruler of Dubai, created a catalyst for change by seeking a diversified economy and changing the regional dynamics, so must an economic superordinate goal set it on a trajectory towards long-term prosperity. Also, just as we did in Palestine by declaring a superordinate goal to create the "Mumbai of the Middle East" the rest of the region must create a pull that makes it abandon its current dysfunction and align its future with the memes of prosperity. It seems that the Middle East today falls into two dominant, and one peripheral, camps of thought:

- The first sees the solution for economic inequality as a return to traditional Islamic values. This is a healthy Ideologue Blue empowered by the enterprising traditions of Islam while being informed by the emerging global Blue values.

- The second wants to pursue prosperity but hasn't a strategy to implement economic policies that lead to long-term sustainability of their vision. This is a Pragmatic Orange that sees the culture in a modern light and chooses strategic compromises that result in a win-win-win situation for all.

- The third sees the need for differences to be respected and included. This is the Conciliator world-centric Green that deepens the understanding of the human bond and soothes the bumpy divide between sects, castes, and social classes.

Importantly, based on the foundational construct of a superordinate goal, the declaration of this goal must speak to these three competing camps equally. It must inspire them each in a way that challenges their leadership skills to the point where they are willing to override any threat to the achievement of this goal. If the goal speaks to all competing value systems along the values spectrum, it will seamlessly move culture away from its polarizing positions and elevate regional leadership to healthy positions on the values spectrum.

While the ultimate goal of the Arab Memome Project is to bring Orange complexity to the region, that superordinate goal has to be identified from a Natural Design perspective. Seventh-Level Yellow must see the need for current Enterprising Orange practices to evolve into more inclusive and sustainable forms that invite the scientific perspective and create the ecosystems that encourage research and development. A Seventh-Level Yellow superordinate goal begins to design structures that speak the specific language of each level of the culture. It begins to align those values in a way that everyone can relate to and aspire after. If it speaks to the emergent values of the region, prosperity will inspire all to participate. A carefully crafted superordinate goal for the Arab world would have language similar to the following declaration:

To bring long-term prosperity to the region through sustainable business practices that offer opportunity for all beyond the age of oil.

Today, although much of the region seems to be occupied with the Arab Spring, the calling towards a superordinate goal, although thinly veiled, is beginning to appear. While Life Conditions in Egypt pointed to the election of an Islamist president, this had the behind-the-scenes support of Zealots and Flamethrowers within the Muslim Brotherhood. This caused him to be overthrown. These are becoming the natural lessons for Islamists, perhaps teaching them to moderate their views. Zealots who support frozen ideologies are proving to be out of touch with the needs of the people once they are elected to lead. What people need most is a governing system that lifts their lives out of poverty, gives them an optimistic view of the future and enables them to make a decent living, send their children to good schools, and improve their quality of life. These are all elements that must be included in a superordinate goal empowered by the "prosper and let prosper" values of the future.

5. Aligning The Future Of Government To Meet The Superordinate Goal

The most pressing challenge, after creating a regional superordinate goal, is to design the form of governance that fits every country and be able to design a national system for governance that still aims to align institutions with the memes of prosperity. To design the form of governance that fits every country, a Seventh-Level Yellow leader would have to follow the MEMEtocracy principles that are outlined in the book *Emerge!*. For the region as a whole, its citizens should shift their thinking away from the belief that government knows best, although this might be true in the gulf region since governments there play a crucial role in developing the county's infrastructure.

Any regulatory structure of the Fourth-Level Blue system cannot be the guardian of innovation in a resilient society. It must design institutions that encourage the private sector to be free to explore every aspect of modern innovation in technology, medicine, alternative energy, manufacturing, and financial services. Moreover, it must fund the institutions that support all these endeavors. Governments designed from the Seventh-Level Yellow will align all their institutions to serve the superordinate goal.

As a part of the Middle East's emergence into Fifth-Level Orange values, leaders must evaluate the role of government and limit the extent of its involvement that is not aligned with the memes of prosperity. The function of government has to be liberated from its traditionally bureaucratic and domineering structure. It must also offer guarantees of private property rights and women's rights, the primary pillars behind the success of the capitalist system. As the region looks to establish goals toward a sustainable future, it must address the viability of a resilient private sector. It is the innovative nature of the memes of private enterprise that have historically brought culture into higher levels of expressions.

These are some of the many essential tenets of successful capitalism. In the case of Dubai, these realizations came to Sheikh Al Maktoum early on as he called for a very limited role of government. The result of those decisions opened up Dubai to global and regional investment like no other part of the Middle East had seen in its history.

In the Gulf Region, oil wealth has made welfare states out of many of the countries and monarchies. This is an entirely different level of "welfare" than the type that is seen in the West. The West's stage of development is

Order Driven-Enterprise (BLUE–Orange) values (in places like the United States, Australia, and the UK), plus Egalitarian/Humanitarian Green values in Europe and just developing in the United States and elsewhere. Their welfare programs are designed as temporary measures that aid the disadvantaged while they search for employment, for example. The focus of these governments is on how to make individuals productive members of society in the quickest way possible.

While Millennials in the Middle East who acquire high levels of education in countries with Enterprising and Egalitarian values (ORANGE–Green) prepare themselves to assume responsibility for taking their culture to its next stage of development, they come back to a place where generational inequality dominates the landscape. These are the things that our technologies will bring to the forefront when addressing the future of the region. Our goal will be to create a balance between the traditional belief systems, such as those which are guided by the motto of *always respect the elders because they know best* to values that appreciate meritocracy and the acquisition of new skills that are essential for survival in a globalized economy.

A government designed from the Seventh-Level Yellow system has to gradually wind down its welfare programs as it shifts its values from the *benevolent caretaker* state (Purple) to the *accommodator of prosperity* state (BLUE–Orange). This has to be done even if the region discovers more oil or natural resource reserves. Otherwise it will not emerge into the complex expression of the Enterprising Orange system with built-in sustainability. The great majority of revenues from oil, as in Norway, can go into a national wealth fund that augments the long-term prosperity of the culture, not one that defines it.

Through the Arab Memome Project, the CHE-Mideast will design each half-step at a time within a value system from the center of gravity of the culture. We move with the healthy pace of emergence, not with the false expression of a higher value system that collapses due to misalignment with the needs of the people. We remove blockages in lower systems to make them healthy. These are the crucial design elements in our philosophy as new systems begin to replace old systems.

The road to advancement would change the functions in which government operates. A globally competitive government must fill its key positions based on meritocracy. Key positions go to the most qualified in the function they are looking to regulate, as governance requires technocrats, not bureaucrats or members of the extended family, to run its affairs. There will be no room in the future Middle East for nepotism and favoritism. These are the old passive values that eventually lead to perpetual obsolescence of the culture. These are the things that keep societies behind, especially when the rest of the world is moving forward at a much faster pace.

Based on some of the concepts discussed in the book *Emerge!*, parts of the region that are going through rebellion now would have to be memetically evaluated. Sadly, they might need to go through much more bloodshed and even prolonged civil wars to come to a place where they say "never again." That place of crisis is where the foundation of an Order-Driven Blue culture is reached. In passing through the fire, it can begin to build anew. For those nations, the memes of prosperity will act as a pull that will hasten the realignment of culture to the regional superordinate goal. However, a predictable scenario for the next stage of MEMEtocracy for these states will be an autocratic form of democracy that runs the trains on time and builds order and discipline as a permanent infrastructure.

6. Aligning The Future Of Capitalism To Serve The Superordinate Goal

Looking to the future, the region faces many economic issues that need to be addressed in order to align them with a new superordinate goal. Many business practices that have become imbedded in the culture as a result of oil wealth in the Gulf Cooperation Council (GCC) have to be re-examined. Other practices in non-Gulf Cooperation Council countries that are a result of Red capitalist exploitation must also be addressed in order to depress the dynamics that caused exploitation in the first place. What would many GCC leaders do if they were informed by the same business models of global corporations like those of General Electric, which has a one hundred fifty-year strategic plan, or the Department of Natural Resources of Washington State, which has a two hundred fifty-year strategic plan?

What does economic prosperity look like beyond the age of oil? A newspaper article published in 2011 by the British daily *The Guardian* claims that Saudi Arabia will reach peak oil by 2030.[7] If these claims are true, are

7   John Vidal, "How much oil does Saudi Arabia actually have?" *The Guardian* [UK], August 8, 2011 http://www.theguardian.com/environment/blog/2011/feb/15/oil-saudi-arabia-reserves. Retrieved July 30, 2013.

there contingency plans being put in place to diversify the economy in such a short period of time? The premise that wealth from oil revenue can support the generous welfare programs that these states have is a fallacy that shouldn't even be entertained. Even the notion that revenues from sovereign wealth funds from oil will provide a substitute for economic diversity will be very short sighted. The fund managers at Dubai World should serve as a stark reminder that what seems to be safe and diversified one day could become a catastrophic financial liability the next. Should the future of the region be placed in the hands of global investment bankers, the entire Middle East will be set back for centuries at the first post-peak oil financial crisis.

The less affluent parts of the Middle East, due to past repressive leadership, are even further behind in the global race for advancement. Countries like Libya, Egypt, Syria, and the rest of the Levant have to be reformed and modernized. Institutions that are geared for basic human development need to be built for the first time. In short, metrics that align the culture with Enterprising Orange values have to inform every institution in every country in the region if it wants to be considered a global player on the global economic stage in the next century.

The most resilient quality of a capitalist society is its human capital. It is human resilience and investment in science, research, and development that will create diverse and sustainable economies. This is the shape of economic power of the future and the Middle East is already decades behind. At the core of a viable and diverse economic sector is a resilient educational system that must be geared to educate the masses in skills and knowledge.

7. Aligning The Educational Systems To Serve The Superordinate Goal

The most important source of economic resilience is the pursuit of well-developed human capacities. Educational policies designed to serve the superordinate goal of the region will naturally move the leaders away from developing oil fields and make them focus on developing capacities of their people. Our Arab Memome Project calls especially on the Millennial Generation and women to be an integral part of this process. This is the only way that the more complex forms of global economic values can become a permanent part of the future of the region.

Seventh-Level Yellow leadership in education must be present at the ministerial level in every country in order for the region to meet its superordinate goal. A committee of Seventh-Level Yellow thinkers must have full authority, full CAPI, for setting educational policy. They must make education as the number one national priority and that declaration must be heard in every home and on every street. This committee must be void of any nepotism and corruption and must have an independent funding mechanism.

Seventh-Level Yellow leadership in education must be able to set specific advancement and performance measures that meet the needs of a competitive global economy. They must be able to align the educational aspirations of Arab youth with the best educational practices in the world. A Seventh-Level Yellow education requires the pursuit of partnerships with educational institutions and businesses to offer both STEM (Science, Technology, Engineering, Math) and broad-based scholarships based on merit or need for students of all ages. Scholarships should also support the arts and the trades and continuing education for adults. This will act as an insurance policy against the generational ill effects of poverty. Leaders must be able to work effortlessly with regional economic centers of employment in order to determine future needs of the labor force, create a partnership with the private sector, and align with employers to provide internship opportunities and real-world work or research experiences.

An example is the newly created King Abdullah University for Science and Technology (KAUST) in the town of Thuwal along the shores of the Red Sea in Saudi Arabia. This is an institution like no other in the Middle East. In its short four years of existence, it is being dubbed as the MIT of the Arab World.[8] It is an oasis of research and development that attracts global scientific talent to its campus. This is indigenous, complex Orange in its earliest stages of existence in the region. It must be nurtured and made to grow. KAUST represents a self-sustaining ecosystem for scientific discoveries; a symbol of what is to come should the region move past the Age of Oil. An ecosystem made up of a multitude of KAUST-like institutions represents a resilient and organic emergence of a self-sustaining region grounded in the most advanced scientific practices. However, a university system alone cannot provide educational excellence for the entire culture.

---

8   King Abdullah University for Science and Technology, http://en.wikipedia.org/wiki/King_Abdullah_University_of_Science_and_Technology. Retrieved July 31, 2013.

Early childhood education must be aligned with the region's superordinate goal.

The minds of future generations have to be shaped from an early age when a child enters grade school. Since the Arab Memome project calls for an Integral Design approach, parents will play a critical role in embedding the memes of self-reliance and the virtues of resilience as early as possible in child's home life. The schools must place emphasis on the latest advancements in math and science as early as possible. While many of the elementary and secondary schools in the West tout the virtues of the Egalitarian-Humanitarian school systems, these models should not be copied in the Middle East. These schools will not be the proper memetic fit for the region. The educational system must go through several decades of teaching BLUE–Orange values that build the foundational stones of a culture while that culture attempts to compete on its own merits in a global economic marketplace.

Since this is a whole-systems approach, Seventh-Level Yellow leadership in education must address the qualifications of teachers and administrators and determine their alignment to the superordinate goal. Teaching, as a career that must be redefined as one of the most rewarding careers based on merit, and appropriately generous compensation should attract the most qualified teachers for the jobs. In addition to a focus on math and science, debate clubs must be fostered to encourage critical thinking and logical, rational and objective thought processes among students as early as possible.

Teachers recruited by a Seventh-Level Yellow educational system must be put through a prequalification process to insure their capacities and abilities to deliver on what's needed to meet the educational goals set to meet the superordinate goal. Administrators must also have awareness of the goals of the Seventh-Level Yellow leadership. They must always be searching for the newest teaching innovations that are adopted into the learning environment by the most successful schools around the globe.

These are just a few recommendations that the CHE-Mideast has identified as the economic, political, developmental, and educational issues that will inform the much larger Arab Memome Project. Final implementation plans would have to be adjusted as Life Conditions vary from one nation to the next as we're called upon to design for a specific country or part of the region. For now this will create a starting point for the debate on many of the reforms that await the Arab world. A more collective view on the future of the Arab child has to be debated in order for an organically designed system to emerge. Without addressing the kind of educational reforms the region needs to compete in a global economy, no economic reforms or superordinate goals of any kind would have a lasting effect.

A Region On A Hero's Journey

Building a modern-day Arab Renaissance starts with the goal of building a prosperous middle class that naturally turns the culture away from the ill effects of poverty and idle toil. This is an ambitious long-term project that requires the systemic involvement of all stakeholders in the region and in every nation, as that nation emerges at its own pace. The future survival of the wealthy and ruling class will depend greatly on their ability to be the visionaries of today. They have to believe that by adopting values of making wealth instead of taking wealth, they will increase the opportunities for all instead of continuing down the path of economics that create protectionist and destructive values. They have to be the ones who see with clear cognition that in absence of nationalistic programs for inclusion, the bloody Arab Spring will become the bloody Arab century.

The Arab Memome Project calls on these Seventh-Level Yellow leaders to take an active role in building the institutions that will transition the culture through one of its greatest historic challenges. Structural changes at all levels and sectors of society must begin today in order for the region to resume its glory from where it left off before the industrial revolution. As the title of my book implies, there is certain urgency for the region to *Emerge*. In order to do it right, the visionary leaders from within the culture have to rise and meet the challenges of joining an increasingly globalized world.

For me personally, although I live a comfortable life in the West, as a native of this land I feel the urgent calling of my ancestors to help. It is the historic duty that is embedded in the DNA of the Ghassanid Tribe and the entrepreneurial Phoenician spirit that runs in my veins. My ancestors were the nomadic people who originated from the Arab Peninsula and have never stopped caring about improving the lives of others for the better. They fought against the Persians and many other dynasties to preserve the Arab character of the region. Many have embraced the virtues of Islam while many remained Christians. Today, as Arab Nationals we have to redefine our values in terms of what the future looks like in the context of the global economic reality.

This is where a new journey for Arab heroism starts. The modern history of cultural emergence in the Middle East is filled with so many false starts. The region has suffered enough, from Nasserism and the fascist ideologies of the Baathists that were misaligned with the region's values, as well as from the military dictators who arrested the emergence of their people. Meanwhile, oil has done little to create economic values that add sustainable wealth and prosperity, and that must change.

My next-door neighbor in the West is a self-made Internet multi-millionaire, yet he takes joy in cleaning his own yard and trimming his own trees. These are the values that were created by the large middle class who emerged from the Industrial Age. It was the virtues of self-reliance that taught him and millions like him how to innovate and add value to a culture empowered by human capacities. By writing this book my hope is that my brother's children and their children in the future will live in a culture that champions the virtues of self-reliance and equal opportunity for all.

Today, the long-awaited journey for self-determination has begun. The Arab Spring is an organic movement that is led by a globalized Arab youth who can no longer accept the status quo. With unwavering bravery, they have answered the call without being aware of the bloody consequences.

There will be setbacks and many false starts. There will even be temporary downshifts and a possible return to dictatorships and military rule. There will also be a need for the Muslim Brotherhood throughout the region to reevaluate what the movement stands for. Should it disappear into the underground or join the democratic process? Would it choose to be further polarized into the fringe of radicalism, or come to the middle position of their spectrum of values, and push away their own radical elements? Their first chance at leadership in Egypt proved that their zealots and flamethrowers can hijack the future of the region. Would they go back to the drawing table and try to formulate a strategy on how to evolve the movement into a more pragmatic position and participate in fruitful governance, or would the radicals continue to define what the movement stands for?

If the goal of MEMEtocracy is to make democracy functional, a post-Arab Spring in the Middle East points to many more decades of functional autocracy and benevolent, but functional monarchies. Those are the right forms of governance that will guide the region out of its current dysfunction. They have to be informed by the *Indigenous Intelligence* that directs the culture at its own pace, while empowering all its stakeholders for a more prosperous future for their children and grandchildren.

This is how the bravest heroes set out on a journey, often filled with pain and trepidation, but most of all with hope. Similar journeys in other parts of the world were just as painful and trying. What the region has in its favor today is that time has been accelerated considerably. Social networks, the knowledge economy, and the region's wealth reserves can substantially shorten the cycle of emergence. Global memes will continue to provide transparency until the developmental gaps between the region and the rest of the world narrow. Leaders who embrace the virtues of transparency, and recognize the invaluable power of institutions and the importance of a resilient private sector, will be the ones who will lead the Arab world to its 21st Century Renaissance. Let the journey begin.

HUMAN NEEDS, DISABILITY AND COMMUNITY

By Dennis Harkins

The following article is written for a relatively sophisticated audience in the field of long term care, and more specifically for those who are involved personally or professionally in the system of services to people with intellectual, physical and sensory disabilities. It is an audience generally unfamiliar with Spiral Dynamics Integral (SDi). The intent of this article is to use but a few of the key concepts of SDi, with minimal jargon or explanation of SDi, to help create a framework for accelerating the pace of evolution of Long Term Care systems within the more developed nations.

> *The way we are, we are members*
> *of each other. All of us. Everything.*
> *The difference ain't in who is a member*
> *and who is not, but in who knows it and who don't.*
>
> — Burley Coulter[1]

Something happens. A dive into a shallow river results in a spinal cord injury; a car accident leaves the driver with a brain injury; Alzheimer's disease invades and addles a once keen intellect; a child is born and diagnosed with a label of Down Syndrome… The list goes on of those day to day occurrences which make disability a natural part of our lives. Most people with physical,

---

1   A character in Wendell Berry's novel, *The Wild Birds*. Thanks to John O'Brien and Connie Lyle O'Brien for this reference.

mental or sensory impairments live their lives without needing particular support from a long term care system. They do fine, often with a little help from their friends and families.

For people with impairments who need a little more help than they, their family or their friends can provide, the long term care system comes into play. Far too often people who encounter that system must trade needed support for systems-imposed limitations in how they are able to experience life, liberty and the pursuit of happiness. The most significant of those limitations is the unconscious belief, too often expressed through the behavior of those who fund, arrange and provide long term care services, that individuals with impairments who need assistance from the system do not have the same human needs as individuals who do not require such assistance. In other words, many of those who receive support from the Long Term Care system are not *the way we are,* are not *members of each other.*

Put this argument to a simple test. Walk into a place designed by the long term care system to provide food, shelter and support, such as a nursing home or a group home. Is that a place in which *you* would choose to live for a day? a month? the rest of your life? Would that place allow *you* to meet *your* needs for autonomy and freedom in how you live your life; for privacy; for companionship and intimacy; for self-expression and self-esteem; for respect by and connection with others?

Those are but a few of the needs we expect will be met as we select where to live, with whom to live, and how to live. They are so expected we take them for granted. Such needs are typically unmet and hardly considered when people are placed into living spaces that are not their own. This article suggests a framework for bringing those needs to conscious awareness, to enable those who work within and those who rely upon our long term care systems to *know we are members of each other,* and to act in ways that reflect that knowledge.

Evolution of Long Term Care

*If we are to properly understand events and influence the future,
it is essential to master four ways of looking at things: as they were;
as they are; as they might become; and as they ought to be.*

– Dee Hock[2]

Long Term Care systems as a response to disabilities are a recent human construct. In the United States they emerged in the 19th century. It is instructive to know that the oldest publicly funded institution in the United States for people with intellectual disabilities, the Massachusetts School for Idiot and Feeble-Minded Youth, was established in 1848 through the leadership of one of the most progressive social reformers of the 19th century, Dr. Samuel Gridley Howe. Dr. Howe noticed what we now view as the transition from an agrarian to an industrial age. He believed that creating a special school would offer young people with intellectual disabilities more powerfully effective learning, enabling them to return to their communities and be more successful within an increasingly complex economic system.

By 1866, Dr. Howe noticed that individuals were not returning home from such schools, and warned "We should be cautious about establishing such artificial communities...for any children and youth; but more especially should we avoid them for those who have natural infirmity...Such persons spring up sporadically in the community, and they should be kept diffused among sound and normal persons...Surround insane and excitable persons with sane people and ordinary influences; vicious children with virtuous people and virtuous influences; blind children with those who see; mute children with those who speak; and the like.[3] "Unfortunately, Dr. Howe's warning soon became a prophecy. A reform gone wrong was established within the first formal long term care system. It soon influenced how our communities viewed disability, the creation of new laws and public policies, and even how individuals and families viewed themselves.

Within a short period of time, social systems and cultural perspectives emerged that viewed and systematically treated individuals with intellectual, physical or sensory impairments as objects of pity, fear, ridicule or charity. Legislation passed in every state within the US creating dehumanizing

---

2 Hock, Dee. *Birth of the Chaordic Age,* Berrett-Koehler Publishers, Inc., San Francisco, 1999.
3 Howe, Samuel G. *In ceremonies on laying the corner-stone of the New York State institution for the blind,* at Batavia, Genessee County, New York, Batavia, N.Y.: Henry Todd, 1866.

institutions, requiring the sterilization of women, and denying public education to those with intellectual disabilities. A powerful eugenics movement sprang forth, led by university professors who published treatises blaming "feeble-mindedness" as a primary cause of poverty and crime.

This tragically flawed "science of eugenics" was used and reinforced by the US Supreme Court to support state compulsory sterilization laws[4], and in Hitler's Germany as the holocaust began with the extermination of as many as an estimated 200,000 people with intellectual and other disabilities. Generations in North America and Europe were raised within communities and cultures that had learned from our political, government, and educational systems to respond to an impairment within the brain or other aspects of the individual human organism in ways that devalued or even denied the humanity of those who experienced such impairments.

Over the past 75 years, disability advocacy movements have arisen and are today continuing the hard work of changing these perverse belief systems, the laws that reinforced them, and the internalization of those beliefs by so many individuals with disabilities and their families. Families took the lead in the 1940s in bringing attention to the hideous conditions within state institutions, eventually leading to their reform within all states, and their elimination in states that have best understood the harmful influence and impact of their very existence. Laws requiring sterilization were repealed, the last in 1979 in Virginia. State and federal legislation was passed requiring a free and appropriate public education of all children, and later requiring that education of children with disabilities be offered within regular classrooms rather than segregated schools or classes. Federal and state governments authorized extensive funding for services to children and adults with disabilities, with a gradual and growing bias towards using that funding within community rather than institutional services.

---

4   For example, the University of Virginia acted as a highly respected educational institution that pushed the thought and science of eugenics through research and education. In the words of Dr. H.E. Jordan, Dean of the Department of Medicine at the University of Virginia, "eugenics… will work the greatest social revolution the world has yet known… [for] it aims at the production and the exclusive prevelancy of the highest type of physical, intellectual and moral man within the limits of human protoplasm" (Claude Moore Health Sciences Library). Having a similar influence, the *Virginia Medical Monthly* published medical reports from superintendents of various Virginia institutions as a method to increase the loathing toward those deemed feeble-minded while also spreading eugenics theory and practice. These proponents continued to condemn the "unfit" to sterilization and with their continual insistence of the necessity of sterilization, public support grew. (Noll, Steven. 1995. *Feeble-Minded in Our Midst: Institutions for the Mentally Retarded in the South*, 1900-1940. Chapel Hill: University of North Carolina Press. p. 61).

Today, the leading edge within formal long-term care systems has evolved to promote the concepts of person-centeredness, of self-determination, of individualizing support and services to enable each person in need of support to have a home that is their own and the opportunity to live a fulfilling life as a citizen and community member. Despite common rhetoric that suggests these concepts are now the foundation of virtually all of our Long Term Care system, their actualization within those systems remains limited.

Today's Long Term Care systems remain dominated on the one hand by *how things were*, by the century and more of habits of viewing people who have impairments as primarily individuals in need of specialized services rather than as fellow citizens who have the same fundamental needs and aspirations as others. And, on the other hand, they are increasingly subjugated to *how things might become*, by the growing economic forces that identify people with disabilities as potential "covered lives," to use the current managed care language of state governments and corporate agencies. Both of these dominant perspectives view individuals with disabilities as *objects*. If we are to influence the future towards what *ought to be*, we must master strategies to support people to be seen as and to act as *subjects* in their own lives.

Human Needs and Aspirations Within the Long Term Care System

Human needs must be understood as a system; that is, all human needs are interrelated and interactive. With the sole exception of the need for subsistence, that is, to remain alive, no hierarchies exist within the system. On the contrary, simultaneities, complementarities and trade-offs are characteristics of the process of needs satisfaction.

— Manfred Max-Neef[5]

We are at a remarkable point in human history where it is possible to see clearly not only how we are living today as a human species, but how we have been living throughout our history. We can now see the common needs that cut across culture and history. Some domains of need relate to survival, as a species and as individuals. Others relate to our desire to not only survive, but to *enjoy* surviving, to be connected with others, to be healthy, to be free,

5   Max-Neef, M. (1991) *Human Scale Development*. Page 191.Apex Press, New York. May be downloaded at http://www.max-neef.cl/download/Max-neef_Human_Scale_development.pdf

to love and be loved. We seek not only subsistence, we seek fulfillment, and we have universally been on this search for tens of thousands of years.

There are many ways to identify and categorize universal human needs. The classification most commonly known today was developed by the psychologist Abraham Maslow. Maslow presents the following categories of needs and aspirations which impel human beings to think, act and respond as they do.[6] While subsequent research has brought into question the linear and hierarchical approach presented by Maslow, the categories continue to resonate across time and culture:

- Physiological Needs: for food, drink, air, sleep, sex; the basic bodily "tissue" requirements.
- Safety Needs: for security, stability, protection from harm or injury; need for structure, orderliness, law, predictability; freedom from fear and chaos.
- Belongingness and Love Needs: for abiding devotion and warm affection with spouse, children, parents, and close friends; need to feel a part of social groups; need for acceptance and approval.
- Esteem Needs: for self-esteem based on achievement, mastery, competence, confidence, freedom, independence; desire for esteem of others (reputation, prestige, recognition, status).
- Self-Actualization Needs: for self-fulfillment, actually to become what you potentially can be; desire to actualize your capabilities; being true to your essential nature; what you can be you must be.

The primary focus of Long Term Care systems quickly evolved, and to this day emphasizes meeting Physiological Needs and Safety Needs, although such basic needs as sex, and freedom from fear and chaos were not well-addressed during the period of rejection and dehumanization of those with disabilities, and for many individuals remain poorly addressed today. A look at today's bureaucratic rules, policies, and procedures that govern Long Term Care funding shows an overwhelming emphasis on security; stability; protection from harm or injury; structure; orderliness; and predictability. Services that adhere well to these rules and policies may receive the highest ratings from states and from private accreditation agencies while virtually ignoring the needs described by Maslow within the categories of Belongingness and Love; Esteem; and Self-Actualization.

---

6   Maslow, A. (1943) *A Theory of Human Motivation*. Psychological Review, 50 (4) 370-96.

Maslow's presentation of the universality of human needs enables us to see more clearly the essential human needs that are typically unmet within our Long Term Care systems. It is less useful in helping us understand why the system has evolved in that manner, and how we might help its transformation towards what we now know is both possible and what *ought to be*. The work of Manfred Max-Neef builds upon Maslow, and in combination with a perspective on how change occurs, provides a structure for accelerating the pace of that needed transformation.

Manfred Max-Neef is a Chilean economist who has worked on creating a model of human development which shines a light upon the different ways in which fundamental human needs are understood and satisfied, or not satisfied. In the book *Human Scale Development*[7] Max-Neef presents not only a complex and thoughtful approach to categorizing human needs, but also expresses the importance of distinguishing between needs and *satisfiers* of needs, a powerful distinction to make as we look at the evolution of our Long Term Care systems.

The network image below[8] shows 9 categories of human needs identified by Max-Neef. These categories of need are found in all cultures. What varies is how we *satisfy* the needs. The use of the network metaphor helps to show that these needs are seen as an interrelated system, not as a hierarchy (once the need for subsistence has been met).

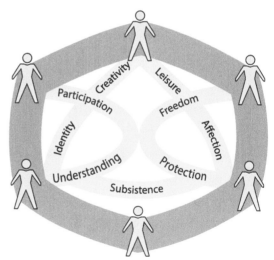

---

7   Max-Neef, M. (1991) *Human Scale Development*.

8   Image from www.holocene.net/sustainability/human_needs.htm, designed by Joanne Tippett

The following matrix[9] shows with complexity and insight a way of thinking about how those needs may be *satisfied*.

Fundamental Human Needs	Being (qualities)	Having (things)	Doing (actions)	Interacting (settings)
Subsistence	physical and mental health	food, shelter, work	feed, clothe, rest, work	living environment, social setting
Protection	care, adaptability, autonomy	social security, health systems, work	cooperate, plan, take care of, help	social environment, dwelling
Affection	respect, sense of humour, generosity, sensuality	friendships, family, relationships with nature	share, take care of, make love, express emotions	privacy, intimate spaces of togetherness
Understanding	critical capacity, curiosity, intuition	literature, teachers, policies, educational	analyse, study, meditate, investigate	schools, families, universities, communities
Participation Leisure	receptiveness, dedication, sense of humour, imagination, tranquility, spontaneity	responsibilities, duties, work, rights, games, parties, peace of mind	cooperate, dissent, express opinions, daydream, remember, relax, have fun	associations, parties, POW*, neighbourhoods, landscapes, intimate spaces, places to be alone
Creation	imagination, boldness, inventiveness, curiosity	abilities, skills, work, techniques	invent, build, design, work, compose, interpret	spaces of expression, workshops, audiences
Identity	sense of belonging, self-esteem, consistency	language, religions, work, customs, values, norms	get to know oneself, grow, commit oneself	places one belongs to, everyday settings
Freedom	autonomy, passion, self-esteem, open-mindedness	equal rights	dissent, choose, run risks, develop awareness	anywhere

*POW – Place of worship

Max-Neef's insights into the difference between *needs and satisfiers of those needs have important implications for the evolution of how we support people within our Long-Term Care systems.*

There Is A Fundamental Difference Between Needs And Satisfiers Of Those Needs

Shelter, for example is an essential Subsistence *need*. There are many ways to *satisfy* that need, such as:

- A cardboard box underneath a bridge;

- A semi-private room in a nursing home;

- A group home with 5 other people who happen to have impairments;

- An apartment that one leases, or a home that one owns.

---

9   Max-Neef, M. (1991) *Human Scale Development.* Pages 32-33

The manner in which the need for shelter is satisfied is not value neutral. How needs are satisfied makes a difference in how one is perceived and valued by others, as well as in one's own self-esteem.

The Manner In Which A Need Is Satisfied May Inhibit, Give A False Sense Of Satisfaction Or Even Destroy The Potential To Meet Other Needs

For example, using Max-Neef's matrix and applying it to legacy services provided to people with developmental disabilities:

Satisfier	Needs Intended to Satisfy	Needs, whose satisfaction is inhibited
Group Home	Subsistence, Protection, Affection	Affection, Participation, Leisure, Creation, Identity, Freedom, Protection
Sheltered Workshop, Day Services Facility	Subsistence, Creation	Understanding, Participation, Creation, Identity, Freedom

Inhibiting The Satisfaction Of Fundamental Needs May Lead To Individual And Systems Pathologies

We continue to be taught by people's "behaviors" when we create services and structures that prevent or inhibit their satisfying fundamental human needs. The "pathologies" exhibited by individuals within our Long Term Care systems have been increasingly understood over the past 30 years to most often be related directly to the manner in which basic needs for freedom, self-respect, love, growth and more are violated by the satisfiers our systems have created as services and outcomes.

Much of what our formal systems have created can be viewed as pathological, failing both people's inherent desire to satisfy their needs, and doing so in ways that have high costs. Those costs are monetary, in terms of excessive and poor use of public funding, and personal, by creating and maintaining negative attitudes towards individuals whose perceived pathologies are a natural response to the inhibition or destruction of opportunities to satisfy ordinary human needs.

Needs Are Not Deficiencies, But Are The Essential Requirements Of Living For Human Beings

Michael Kendrick[10], among others, amplifies this simple but often ignored declaration by Max-Neef. Within our long-term care systems we talk, write and teach about moving to strength-based rather than deficiency-based systems. Through an intensive learning course, *Optimal Individual Services Design*, Kendrick illustrates how our systems focus on satisfying impairment related needs at the expense of satisfying fundamental human needs. Participants in the course learn to reverse this process, with satisfying needs then seen as having the potential to engage and motivate potential within each person rather than simply responding to real or perceived limitations.

Needs May Be Met In A Synergistic Manner; In A Way That Simultaneously Stimulates And Contributes To The Fulfillment Of Other Needs

Max-Neef uses the example of a mother breast-feeding her baby as simultaneously satisfying the infant's needs for Subsistence, Protection, Affection, and Identity. At today's leading edge, we now see individuals with disabilities within our Long Term Care systems whose needs for Subsistence are met through thoughtful support to choose where, with whom and how to live, and in that process are simultaneously meeting needs for Affection, Participation, Leisure, Creation, Identity, Freedom, and Protection.

Needs Are Typically Not Satisfied Singularly, But Must Be Understood As A System, Interrelated and Interactive; Needs Are Universal; Satisfiers Are Most Often Culturally Determined

Fundamental human needs have evolved slowly and changed little over millennia. Satisfiers are more diverse across and within cultures, and are changeable through the interaction of individuals, of community values and beliefs, and of the systemic structures we create.

The manner in which our public systems *satisfied* the needs of individuals with intellectual impairments a century ago was almost exclusively through dehumanizing institutions. The manner in which needs for individuals with

---

10   Michael Kendrick's work may be viewed at *www.kendrickconsulting.org.*

those same impairments are satisfied at the leading edge today supports people in homes that belong to them versus supporting a government institution or a service provider; encourages education, careers and contribution rather than segregation in day centers and sheltered workshops; and focuses on community membership rather than the perceived safety of separation and exclusion. What accounts for these different responses to satisfy the same need?

The I, The We, And The It Of Long Term Care

I'm tired of well meaning noncripples with their stereotypes of what I can and cannot do directing my life and my future.
— Ed Roberts[11]

When there is an impairment that results in disability, an individual's needs will be satisfied both within and within the interaction among three primary contexts.[12] The table below points out that for some Individuals the impairment is such that they may respond with little or no help from others, essentially living one's life in the same manner as anyone else who does not have a disability. A person gradually experiences a decline in her ability to hear, but learns to compensate, to ask others to speak more loudly, to learn to read lips. The majority of people who experience a physical, mental or sensory impairment grow, adapt and live their lives with ordinary assistance from community or generic public resources. They satisfy their impairment related needs with little or no sacrifice in meeting other fundamental human needs.

---

11   Ed Roberts was perhaps the most significant of the many leaders of the Independent Living Movement. See *Ed Roberts: Godfather of Independent Living* at http://atotw.org/edroberts.html.

12   This perspective is modified, imperfectly, from Ken Wilber's Integral Theory (see, for example *A Brief History of Everything*. 1996). One modification is naming the lower right-hand quadrant *It* rather than *Its*, and leaving the upper right quadrant unnamed, described simply as the mind/body/ sensory system and thus also the place in which impairments to that system arise. While this is perhaps confusing, or worse, to those most familiar with Integral Theory, it is a simplification that has seemed to be helpful in sharing this perspective as a learning tool within long-term care.

Integrating Support & Services to People with Disabilities

INDIVIDUAL (I)	
Subjective Personal Can best be known by self, and for some people by those who best know and care about the person (Family often play that role)	

COMMUNITY & CULTURE (WE)	SERVICE SYSTEM (IT)
Place Businesses/Employers Faith Communities Community Associations Culture/Values/Beliefs	Government Funding and Support Provider and Health Care Agencies Schools Professionals/Paraprofessionals Political Systems

Like most people, individuals with disabilities get by with a little help from their friends. A little help from our friends may be thought of as the We in this table. Friends are only a part of the We. This is the home of our collective values; our cultures; our global, societal, tribal, and family belief systems; our communities and the associations we voluntarily join within them. For most people with disabilities the additional support they need to live the life they intend comes from here, with impairment related needs satisfied in typical and often valued ways. We call this care, and caring. We have been engaged in this practice since before we emerged from the caves.

For individuals who need more substantial support, the It of the lower right quadrant typically takes on more importance. The greater the need for support, or the less support available from the individual or family's own resources and the community, the more likely the involvement of the formal systems we have created to respond to particular human needs. Historically, and currently our formal systems have developed a habit of creating structures to satisfy impairment related needs that makes it difficult for individuals to have valued and fulfilling lives.

Bureaucratized and commodifed care are different than the care we provide to one another in our families and communities. When, as is typical today, that difference is not recognized, Long Term Care systems provide care, provide satisfiers of needs, in ways that promote stereotypes of what people can and cannot do, directing and limiting the lives and futures of those they serve.

Perspectives On Satisfying Needs Spring From Different Perspectives On Life

Satisfiers are culturally determined. Beneath this simple truth lies the deep complexity of how culture is expressed and evolves within any given time or place. One framework for understanding the nature of such evolution is provided through Spiral Dynamics Intergral (SDi), founded by Don Beck[13] based on the research of Clare Graves. SDi illustrates how different worldviews and perspectives develop through the interaction of external circumstances and the existential core needs of individuals and societies. It is a powerful lens by which to view both the challenges and opportunities in transforming our Long Term Care systems.

Change does not simply evolve in a linear fashion throughout history, but rather is highly dependent upon the interaction among differing and at times conflicting worldviews that are both historical and are present today. These worldviews are described within SDi as Existential Value Memes, or vMemes for short, and coded as colors to reinforce the importance of not viewing any one of these perspectives as better than another. Each of these perspectives represents a "center of gravity" from which we tend to approach the world, and at the same time we have within each of us elements of most or all of these and other perspectives. These exist within individuals, within communities, and within our organized social systems; within the I, the We, and the It.

The following matrix shows three of the most common perspectives in our world today in the left hand column, and displays aspects of the I, the We and the It in the right hand columns. The "Xs" represent a subjective weighing of the presence of each worldview within different life circumstances particularly relevant to long term care.

---

13   Don Beck has applied this understanding of human development and evolution to help create responses to some of the most globally intractable conflicts imaginable, including working with F. W. de Klerk and Nelson Mandela on the transition from apartheid in South Africa (*The Crucible: Forging South Africa's Future*, by Don Beck and Graham Linscott, 1991, New Paradigm Press). A web site that offers an excellent summary of SDi is found at *http://www.spiraldynamics.net/*.

Different Perspectives on Long Term Care

WORLDVIEW	Individuals who have an impairment (I)	Families (I)/(We)	Federal & State Bureaucracies (It)	Managed Care Organizations & Service Providers (It)	Community Members (We)
Blue vMeme Prime Importance of: Order Stability Security "Follow the rules"	X	XXX	XXXX	XX	XXXX
Orange vMeme Prime Importance of: The marketplace; Financial achievement; Entrepreneurship; Corporate Rights "Show me the money"	XX	XX	XX	XXXX	XXX
Green vMeme Prime Importance of: Community; Caring Connectedness; Value of all people; "Lets all join hands"	XXX	XX	X	X	XX

Individuals with disabilities who have become the most vocal leaders and advocates for change over the past forty years have tended to orient from the Green vMeme perspective of the importance of community and connectiveness, as well as from the Orange achievement focus. This has been particularly true of individuals with physical disabilities, and has been increasingly true of individuals with intellectual disabilities who have historically been placed into environments in which their voice was denied, with an emphasis on protection. This does not mean that individuals with disability do not value security and stability. It simply reflects a strong and growing tendency for a rejection of the forms of *imposed order and security that inhibit or destroy the potential for satisfying other needs.*

Like anyone else, parents of individuals with disabilities will orient from the different worldviews they acquired as they grew up within their families and communities. Some will be more likely to view the world through a lens of order, obedience and security, the Blue vMeme noted above. Those families will tend to favor their sons and daughters receiving services in settings such as institutions, nursing homes, group homes and sheltered workshops. Others will tend to see the world from a perspective that is achievement oriented, entrepreneurial and materialistic; focused on rationality and on achieving excellence. They are more likely to have higher expectations of their sons and daughters in terms of education and career. And still others will have an orientation with a heavy focus on community and connections, on workings towards enabling their children who happen to have a disability to be included in regular classrooms, and to have the same range of life experiences as their children without disabilities.

The same diversity of worldview is true of those who enter the work world of the bureaucracies that administer publicly-funded Long Term Care systems; of the large corporate and small business service providers who depend upon Long Term Care for their economic well-being; and of the elected officials and volunteer trustees of federal, state, and local organizations that fund or oversee the provision of Long Term Care. But, within that diversity, there is a strong tendency for bureaucrats to hang out at the level of rules and order, for managed care organizations and corporate service providers to orient from the perspective of monetary achievement, and for smaller service providers to work from the vantage point of valuing all people and deepening community connections. Our perspectives on the world are not etched in stone, and regardless of our world views we have a tendency to adapt to the circumstances that surround us.

Community members who have no personal connection to disability through family or friends will vary in their beliefs and perspectives. What they know about a Long Term Care system is typically what they have learned from the historical interactions among the I, the We and the It. How they view community membership for people with disabilities has been shaped by the history of excluding people with disabilities from their communities, and of the presence of special and segregated places for people to live, to be educated, and to spend their days. This history of exclusion has increased the likelihood that community members will view those who access long term support services as belonging to the It rather than to the We.

The relationship among these different worldviews and different circumstances is complex, highly interactive, and open to change. There *is a natural tension among different vMemes. There is a difference among how an individual with an impairment of mind or body, a parent, a state administrator, a managed care CEO, and a neighbor experience and view disability.*

All of these perspectives and differences are present, are real, and need to be validated and accounted for.

Moving Forward

An individual's impairments may challenge a person, their family, their community and the system of support regarding having or developing opportunities to satisfy needs in typical and fulfilling ways. Those challenges are best met by recognizing how most people get their needs satisfied, and supporting individuals who have impairments to satisfy their needs in typical, ordinary, and socially valued ways.

Deepening our understanding of *what is and what is possible* increases the potential to engage more in the learning and practice of *what ought to be.* We will best engage in that learning if we recognize and appreciate both the strengths and the limitations of different perspectives within our own lives, within our broader society, and within our Long Term Care systems. Order, stability and security are important, both to the individuals we serve and to the agencies that fund and serve them. Financial well being and achievement are important, both to the agencies that fund and serve and to the individuals they serve within a society that values such achievement. Caring, connectedness and community membership are important to all of us.

If it were simple to achieve this integration of differing perspectives, we would have done so long ago. The challenges faced within our Long Term Care systems mimic the great challenges within our human community. As human beings we value relationship and community, and we live in a world dominated by the presence and power of huge bureaucracies and powerful economic systems. It will take more than joining hands and singing Kumbayah to enable us to rebalance what individuals and communities can do for themselves, what the state can do for individuals and communities, and what the free market can do to enhance the opportunities of individuals and communities.

How we will best engage in that rebalancing is an emerging conversation. That conversation can be made more vibrant by developing and learning from economically strong and viable Long Term Care services that intentionally enable people to share the authority and responsibility of how to use scarce public resources to satisfy their impairment-related needs; invest in maintaining or strengthening the community connections so important to us all and learn to better individualize supports and services to enable people to have a home that is their own; relationships with those they love; work, careers and a good retirement; health, safety and security; and opportunities to uniquely express themselves as they have fun, create, contribute and worship as community members and citizens.

How we will best engage in that rebalancing is an emerging conversation. That conversation can be made more vibrant by including the following:

- developing and learning from economically strong and viable Long Term Care services that intentionally enable people to share the authority and responsibility of how to use scarce public resources to satisfy their impairment-related needs;

- investing in maintaining or strengthening the community connections so important to us all;

- learning to better individualize supports and services to enable people to have

- a home that is their own;
- relationships with those they love;
- work, careers and a good retirement;
- health, safety and security;
- opportunities to uniquely express themselves as they have fun, create, contribute and worship as community members and citizens.

CITIZEN DRIVEN COMMUNITY AND NATION BUILDING

By Bjarni Snaebjorn Jónsson

What is the truth?

The truth is not to be found in books, not even good books.
The truth is to be found in people with good hearts.

—Halldor Laxness

The above quote from the late Icelandic novelist and Nobel Laureate, Halldor Laxness, reflects well the basic philosophy behind this chapter. It is based on a research project that has, to a great extent, evolved from a search for a truth – not *the* truth, but a truth within a human system that finds itself in times of trouble. Another anonymous source has it that the truth is not only that of oneself, but must be sought in encounters with other people who have their own truth, and must bear in mind three basic principles: acceptance, respect, and understanding.

The question is, to what extent can a citizens' communicative engagement contribute to what could be referred to as "conscious social evolution"? The backbone of the research outlined below is a large-scale dialogue process initiated by a grass-roots group in Iceland called The Anthill. This 2008 process was followed by multiple similar events and one large-scale dialogue event organized by the Parliament of Iceland to initiate the rewriting of the Icelandic Constitution in November 2010. Since then, the same model has been applied in Scotland, raising a high degree of awareness and interest there as well.

The dialogue process, called "The Assembly Process" has now been used for a wide variety of issues ranging from specific organizational strategies to a visioning project for a whole nation. It is based on theories on Participative Action Inquiry, Dialogue, Grounded Theory, and public spheres. This carefully structured and facilitated process can create an environment of safety and creativity where every opinion counts.

This was an emergent process conducted in Life Conditions within the human social system and Nation State of Iceland. In the early part of this process Iceland's 2008 financial collapse occured, which was a powerful disruption to systems throughout Iceland. This event became an invaluable resource for researching a large-scale human system. We were presented with dynamics and responses to this sudden change that revealed profound impacts on the identity and overall wellbeing of the system. Further, the situation provided opportunities to study the overall challenges of the society, its Life Conditions and ways of thinking that, in many ways, led to the crisis. What emerged from the research was a model, called the "Conscious Social Evolution Model". This model outlines a study of causality and the forces that shape human systems for better or for worse.

The Conscious Social Evolution Model (CSE)

The basic idea behind the CSE model rests on the following assumptions, justified by literary sources and my own research activities:

1) Life Conditions matter. Individuals in a social system interact with their environment based on their worldview and culture, resulting in a co-creation of what can be defined as Life Conditions.

2) Actions are congruent with vMemes. Individuals will attempt to fulfill their basic human needs using means aligned with their vMemes.

3) Design to match capacity. Constructive development of a human social system should be tailored to its collective intellectual capacity.

4) Be wise in determining capacity: Properly evaluating the system's collective intelligence requires an authentic public space, sufficient and representative diversity of subjects, and proven methods of qualitative inquiry.

5) Change congruent with vMemes: New policies and suggestions for action are more likely to be accepted if grounded in the social system's core vMeme intelligence.

The underlying thesis is that these assumptions hold for every kind of human social system. They are components of the model for CSE shown in Figure 1 below and further discussed in this chapter.

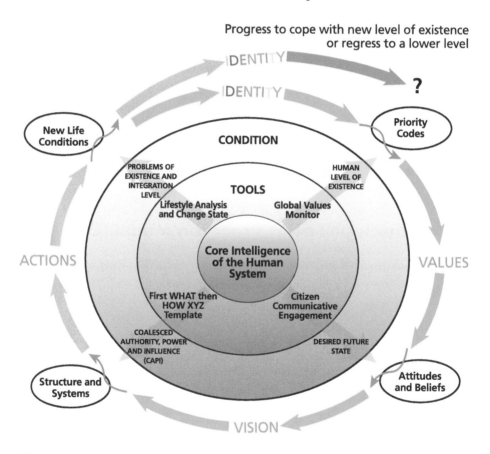

Figure 1. The Conscious Social Evolution model

Figure 1 is a management model based on the premise that a living system must either adapt to its environment or be unable to cope with the constant environmental change, eventually ceasing to exist in its present form. The adaptation is a highly complex dynamic, and due to the inherent autonomy of the system components, cannot be managed in the traditional sense. Although some may claim that it would be best to leave this complex system alone, I argue that such evolution of human social systems should not be left to chance or be willfully unconscious. Although there are many historical events that justify this argument, it is sufficient to refer to the financial crisis of 2008.

It would be highly arrogant to maintain that the CSE model has the capability of managing change within a human social system. A more modest objective is addressed by this model: What do we understand about the evolution of human social systems, and from that basis what effect can be achieved through communicative engagement centered on shared vision and superordinate goals? The argument is that detecting evolution of human social systems and strengthening awareness and social learning among the components (citizens) will create Life Conditions that support healthy vMeme expressions and, where appropriate, emergence of the next vMeme stages. At the core is the assumption that every human system has a collective intelligence steering it along its evolutionary path. The upper half of the model addresses the human system's situation analysis, its Life Conditions or problems of existence, and its capacity for dealing with these conditions. The analytical framework includes Adizes' Lifecycle Theory (1999) to examine the problems of existence and SDi to examine human system evolutionary process, as explained by its originator, the late Dr. Clare W. Graves (Beck & Cowan, 1996):

> Briefly, what I am proposing is that the psychology of the mature human being is an unfolding, emerging oscillating spiraling process marked by progressive subordination of older, lower-order behavior systems to newer, higher order systems as man's existential problems change. (p. 28)

The lower half explores ways to harness the collective intelligence to create effective action plans. This model ensures that we formulate an action pathway that is based on the premises of the human system itself. The Assembly Process previously mentioned was a significant setting for harnessing this collective guidance. It was noted in terms of the desired future and comments on how that future relates to respondents' beliefs and attitudes.

The model also involves ways and means that allow a vision to emerge from the Assembly based on the visionary highlights chosen by the participants. These highlights were chosen using an analysis model called "the Social Tectonic Plates" that emerged from the 2009 Iceland National Assembly data. The SEC model furthermore involves tools that enable a holistic approach to systemic intervention. Coalescing authority, power, and influence (CAPI) is an important element of the model. CAPI as it relates to the human systems change process is addressed in more detail below.

The Causality in the CSE model in Figure 1, the path as shown by the colored arrows, is described as follows, starting at the top with *Identity:*

- Assume a scenario in which the system is fully congruent with its environment ("perfect life"), resulting in favorable Life Conditions. The identity would be clear (I am who I am, doing what I want to and am best at, etc.), resulting in the system operating from a position of confidence.

- This would lead to a healthy and constructive expression of its vMemes, thereby serving the basic needs of the human system.

- This is followed by sensible, balanced beliefs and attitudes and a clear vision or superordinate goal.

- Combined with appropriate vMemes and beliefs, this would lead to optimal alignment of structure and systems, steering appropriate actions to successfully cope with the current level of complexity and further reinforcing success of the system.

- This would result in a new dimension or depth to the identity, which is now ready for a new level of existence.

If there is a change in Life Conditions manifesting itself in disintegration resulting in misalignment between the human social system and its environment, the situation becomes unhealthy. These changes can occur rather suddenly, such as in a war or natural disaster, but they could also be a gradual imbalance. Such changes inevitably threaten the identity of the system, resulting in fear, insecurity, and denial. Under threat, the system would tend to express its values in a limited or negative fashion, such as corruption, short-term thinking, blame, and so on. The beliefs and attitudes would then distort the common vision, which would lose its superordinate nature and become fragmented, leading to further disintegration within the structural elements of the system, and on it would go.

Case In Point

Given that a human system could only evolve on its own terms, taking into account its underlying mental and structural capacities to deal with different levels of complexity, any meaningful intervention would have to be with a deep understanding of the system itself. Take the Nation State of Iceland, a small, homogenous but developed and complex modern society. Since 2005, I have conducted quantitative research of the Icelandic nation's overall cultural traits. I also made extensive use of secondary sources, particularly a report on the financial crisis issued by the Parliamentary Special Investigation Commission.

The findings were put into the perspective of lifecycles to assess the system's overall level of adaptation to its Life Conditions. The conclusion was that prevailing Life Conditions seemed to have exceeded the collective cognitive capacity (Iceland was experiencing Orange Life Conditions with a collective vMeme profile strong in Red and weak in Blue). With privatized banking and a world awash in money, Iceland got ahead of itself in enjoying perceived success financed by foreign debt. The situation was a sort of fool's paradise: Perceived success, limited understanding of its causes, and totally lost overnight.

The key question here is then how the the human system's collective worldview elicits a response to perceived Life Conditions, leading to either healthy or unhealthy beliefs and behaviors. The quantitative surveys carried out in 2005, 2007, and 2009 regarding the prevailing vMeme systems revealed that a poisonous mixture of egocentric, power-based thinking (Red), together with strategic "means justifies the end" thinking (Orange), had become dominant in this era of material success. Other quantitative surveys on values in terms of beliefs and behaviour conducted in 2008 and 2010 using the methodology of Barrett's Valuecentre, showed a high degree of malignancy and entropy within the system, indicating a high degree of fear and limiting values.

When things started turning in the wrong direction, a strong confirmation bias took over (as explained in the Parliamentary Special Investigation Commission's report), leading to total denial and ultimately a financial crash of much larger proportions than anywhere else at that time.

The result was not only a massive blow to the nation's financial situation, but its very identity, that of a superior, overly optimistic, high-risk culture capable of turning everything it touched into gold.

It came as no surprise that the nation's response to the financial crisis was great fear, anger, and the search for someone to blame. Public protests and riots of unprecedented proportions occurred in the first months after the crash. The incumbent government was ousted and a massive criminal investigation initiated to prosecute those thought to be responsible. The situation was characterized by mistrust, blame, corruption, and more, as revealed by another quanititative study I carried out in cooperation with the Barrett Valuescentre.

Dialogue Process

It was in light of these developments that the dialogue process was organized. The goal was to turn negative energy into a constructive force by inviting a random sample of the nation's citizens to a carefully structured dialogue event using participative inquiry methodologies. By studying the data, a model for categorizing it into a comprehensive and holistic picture was conceived. While conducting this research, some important developments were revealed:

1) The process can harness the constructive energy of a human system, judging from participants' responses regarding their experience of the dialogue event (see Figure 35).

2) The process has been established as a universally applicable visioning tool for a wide range of issues and within various types of organizations and communities.

3) The process is not peculiar to the Icelandic nation, since it has been applied in other cultures with similar success.

4) It is difficult to establish with credibility that the Assembly Process is responsible for such direct visible effects as attaining certain measurable national objectives. However, it was concluded that the process is a viable alternative in participative democracy since it was applied to the rewriting of Iceland's Constitution. A pilot event

in Scotland has already led to serious discussion toward wider use of the tool by various societal bodies.

The grass-roots group "So Say Scotland" organized an event called *Thinking Together,* held in Scotland in February of 2013, based on the Assembly Process. Figure 2 is a "Word Cloud" comprised of words participants used most frequently to describe their experience:

Figure2. Words used to describe Thinking Process event in Scotland

The Social System And Its Citizens

As governance of social systems such as nation states become more complex over time, the distance between the citizenry and the social structures built for their benefit tends to grow. This results in a sense of victimization in citizens and a loss of accountability in leaders, as an increasingly centralized government fails to meet the expectations of the people it is intended to serve.

Mike Jay identified six factors in social change, each of which operates at a different speed:

- **Core** – The basic social operating system
- **Culture** – The solution set; that is, response systems and vMemes manifested in beliefs and behaviors
- **Code** – Algorithm developed through learning and evolving human consciousness
- **Conditions** – Iintensity of the situation or change
- **Context** – Perception of reality based on a frame of reference
- **Content** – The actual representation of reality as we perceive it (personal communication, May, 2010)

As scientific and technological advances enable us to create new systems and realities at an ever faster pace, the development of content is exponentially faster than development of the other dimensions, as illustrated in Figure 3:

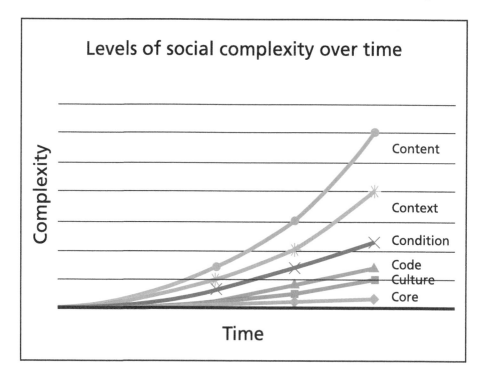

Figure 3. Levels of social complexity over time.

The discrepancy between content (an increasingly intricate social reality) and the society's tools for coping with these changes creates a dangerous incoherence (Beck & Cowan, 1996). The goal, of course, is not to hold the advancement of the society down to the level of its existing culture, but to grow the society's core, culture, and code at a pace that does not generate destructive conflict (Beck & Cowan, 1996; Adizes, 1996; Jay, 2010).

A number of societies at a similar level of growth as Iceland have moved toward technocracy, where all major input for public policymaking is in the hands of specialists and the public is not trusted to interfere in the process. The Iceland process argues that it should be the other way around: Specialists" should not be trusted to reign over the evolution of a society and citizens can be trusted to provide essential guidance. It is evident that there are great social imbalances and biases in most industrialized societies, and that changes are necessary in these human systems to promote resilience, health, and sustainability. It would seem wise to ensure citizen input in the visioning of needed changes.

Communicative Engagement And Visioning

David Bohm (1994) maintained that nations are established by thought and that all emergent human systems are planned and conceived by an individual or individuals governed by their thoughts and ideas; our thoughts command us as individuals with various, interrelated systemic and sub-systemic factors. Societies are also a composition of collective thoughts with similarly interrelated environmental, cultural, systemic, and sub-systemic factors. Thought is our being, or as Bohm (1994) put it:

> … thought is not merely the intellectual activity; rather it is one connected process which includes feeling and the body, and so on … we call that process a "system"—a whole system in which every part is dependent on every other part. (p. 42)

A related theory of human thought was explained by Lynda Gratton in her book, *Living Strategy* (2000):

> Human time is felt in two ways: First, by the ticking of the human clock, by the stages of human development, by the time it takes to build commitment and inspiration; second, by our deep immersion in time, in the memories

and commitments of the past, in the excitement of the present, and in the dreams and hopes of the future. We are not creatures of the moment. On the contrary, each of us has our own personal history and memory which influence the way we see our world and the expectations and hopes we have for it. (p. 13)

This is significant in that the key to anticipate the future and prepare the system to change is our foresight, which is affected by our experience of the past, a narrative knowledge. As Tsoukas explains: "Narratives not only allow for multiple connections among events across time, they also preserve multiple temporalities. As well as being linked to clock time, narrative time is primarily humanly relevant time" (Gratton, 2000, p. 255).

Gratton (2000) further noted the ways that our thinking processes operate in time:

- Past beliefs, hopes, and commitments influence our current behavior – the "memory of the past".
- Current behavior is influenced by beliefs about what will happen in the future – the "memory of the future".
- Skills and knowledge take many years to develop.
- Human development progresses through a shared sequence.
- Attitudes and values are resistant to rapid change (p. 16).

We have a tendency to judge the future by the past, evident in statements such as "We have tried this before," "Every cloud has a silver lining," "There is nothing to worry about; this is not the first time," and so on. If our thoughts delude us into perceiving a situation differently than it actually is, we may find a very serious trap awaiting us. The Assembly Process is a way to take participants out of their accustomed thought patterns and give them a fresh look at their situation. It helps them to not only envision a desired future, but shape their thoughts toward making that future a reality.

The New "New Deal" – Human Systems Change In The Internet Age

Most governance structures in today's societies were developed and implemented prior to the Internet Age. Evolving social media platforms are still in their infancy and fall far short in their current forms to play a constructive and systematic role in large scale-social change and governance processes. Rapid developments in technology for electronic collaboration (social media with a purpose) will open new dimensions for harnessing momentum, e.g. collaboration will be based on the needs of citizens themselves and with their own participation.

From the Wall Street Occupy Movement, to the Arab Spring which swept much of the Middle East, to the unrest overtaking many other developed economies, I believe that the tools and techniques discussed in this chapter together with a paradigm shift in communication technology hold promise for engaging the populace in the social and governmental changes now unfolding across the world. I believe that we can and should use these tools and techniques to engage those who are subject to socioeconomic forces to shape those very forces toward the greater social good.

Unity Out Of Diversity in Human Systems

The Assembly Process, developed with the aid of Participatory Action Research, Dialogue and Grounded Theory as discussed in the first section of this chapter, can establish a base for unity within a given social system. Maturana and Varela (1987) outlined the importance of interpersonal communication within a human system to its unity and growth. An authentic public sphere, in which participants can express their thoughts in a safe and uncritical environment, is necessary for social learning and to harness collective intelligence. This enables genuine joint meaning-making through sharing of experience and storytelling. The result is a representative view of the desired identity, values, and vision.

Theoretical Basis For The SEC Understanding Of Human Systems

The assumption that any human social system must grow and develop on its own terms is guided by SDi (1974), originated by the late Dr. Clare W. Graves, former professor emeritus of psychology at Union College, New York. The theory was further developed by Dr. Don E. Beck, who with Christopher Cowan described it in their book *Spiral Dynamics: Mastering Values, Leadership and Change* (Beck & Cowan, 1996). SDi assumes human emergence as an open-ended evolution, occurring in stages according to the complexity of prevailing Life Conditions.

Another significant theory supporting the above assumptions is the concept of lifecycles of living systems (Adizes, 1999). It holds that a human social system's evolutionary level may be gauged by studying its problems of existence (its level of unity or disintegration, and therefore the degree of adaptation to its environment) and framed in terms of its position in a lifecycle. Maturana and Varela (1987) stated that, when a destructive interaction between a living being and its environment occurs, the former disintegrates and loses its ability to adapt (p. 102). Adizes pointed out that lifecycle stages could be classified as either growth or aging. Many problems of existence experienced during the growth era are normal, while some could be abnormal or pathological. On the other hand, all problems of existence experienced in the aging part of the lifecycle are, by definition, abnormal or pathological; the system is disintegrating from the environment and ultimately within itself, losing its adaptation.

Another important factor in the adaptation of living organisms is *autopoiesis*. This concept was first developed by Maturana and Varela, who stated that living systems are characterized by three principal features: autonomy, circularity, and self-reference, which enable them to self-create or self-renew through closed systems of relations (Morgan, 2006, p. 242). The Assembly Process invited and evidenced this self-organizing principle of human systems.

SEC Application Areas

This chapter closes with a non-exclusive summary of human social systems where actual application of the model have taken place and been of significance:

- **Nation Building.** A citizens' communicative engagement organized by a government to capture the diversity and consider the way forward for the nation or to consider an issue of such national importance that it would require extensive public input. In this instance it is fair to assume that a vast array of remarks would appear from the crowd involving all aspects of the society. The government authorities would regard the respondents as a "sounding board" in controversial issues for further policymaking. In a geographically large setting, more than one event might be organized simultaneously. The complexity of the data would be such that categories would encompass larger subject areas. There are also other complexities relating to the placement of authority within different social institutions, be they formal or informal.

- **Community Building.** A communicative engagement involving a particular community, organized by local authorities and/or sponsors of some kind. These would typically be organized around a common goal such as employment opportunities, innovation/startups, community projects, and so on. Participants would present issues of a systemic nature in community building, as well as specific ideas for their own collaboration. The organizers would then be tasked with strategizing and monitoring results. Stakeholder groups in this smaller setting may be better aligned with overall goals, making it easier to establish the necessary combination of authority, power and influence. However, stakeholder analysis will still be required.

- **Organization Building.** Since 2008, many such events have been organized in Iceland using the Assembly Process. These typically involve most or all of the organization's employees, but in large organizations may involve multiple (not necessarily simultaneous) events tailored to the unit in question. Issues resulting from these sessions typically fall into the same categories as those of a National Assembly. In an organizational setting, authority, power, and influence are usually determined by corporate hierarchy.

My experience in Iceland and beyond, plus the theoretical frameworks that informed this experience indicate there is a way to engage the collective intelligence of a community, even as large as a nation. This collective intelligence can provide essential direction and a helpful influence on the healthy emergence of what is next for a community or nation. Transformation can be intentional.

Bibliography

Adizes, I. (1992). *Mastering change: The power of mutual trust and respect in personal life, family life, business, and society.* Santa Monica, CA: Adizes Institute.

Adizes, I. (1999). *Managing corporate lifecycles.* Paramus, NJ: Prentice Hall Press.

Althingi Parliamentary Investigation Commission. (2010a). Main conclusions from working group on ethics. In *Report of the Special Investigation Commission.* Retrieved from http://sic.althingi.is/pdf/ WorkingGroupOnEthics_Summary.pdf

Althingi Parliamentary Investigation Commission. (2010b). *Hrunið.* Reykjavik, Iceland: Althingi.

Barrett, R. (2006). *Building a values-driven organization: A whole system approach to cultural transformation.* Amsterdam; Boston: Butterworth-Heinemann.

Barrett, R. (2012). *Love, fear and the destiny of nations (Vol. 1). Bath, UK:* Fulfilling Books.

Beck, D. E. (n.d.). The many dimensions of change. Retrieved from http:// www.spiraldynamics.net/the-many-dimensions-of-change.html

Beck, D. E., & Cowan, C. (1996). *Spiral Dynamics: Mastering values, leadership, and change.* Cambridge, MA: Blackwell Business.

Beck, D., & Mackey, J. (2009). The upward flow of human development: Maps of the terrain. In M. Strong (Ed.), *Be the solution: How entrepreneurs and conscious capitalists can solve all the world's problems* (pp. 277-304). Hoboken, NJ: John Wiley & Sons.

Bohm, D. (1994). *Thought as a system.* London; New York: Routledge.

Bohm, D. & Nichol, L. (1996). *On dialogue.* London; New York: Routledge.

Burton, J. (1993). Conflict resolution as a political philosophy. In D. Sandole & H. van der Merwe (Eds.), *Conflict resolution: Theory and practice* (pp. 55-64). Manchester, UK: Manchester University Press.

Charmaz, K. (2005). Grounded theory in the 21st century: Applications for advancing social justice studies. In N. K. Denzin & Y. S. Lincoln (Eds.), *The Sage handbook of qualitative research* (pp. 507-508). Thousand Oaks, CA: Sage Publications.

de Blij, H. (2009). *The power of place: Geography, destiny, and globalization's rough landscape.* Oxford, NY: Oxford University Press.

Denzin, N. K., & Lincoln, Y. S. (2005). *The Sage handbook of qualitative research* (3rd ed.). Thousand Oaks, CA: Sage Publications.

Diamond, J. (2005). *Collapse: How societies choose to fail or succeed.* New York, NY: Penguin Group.

Gratton, L. (2000). *Living strategy: Putting people at the heart of corporate purpose.* London: Pearson Education Ltd.

Habermas, Jürgen (1961). Strukturwandel der Öffentlicheit, Herman Luchterhand Verlag, Darmstadt and Neuwied.

Jonsson, B. S. (2010). Notes from the field: Iceland National Assembly. *Integral Leadership Review, X.* Retrieved from http://www.archive-ilr.com/archives-2010/2010-01/2010-01-notes-jonsson.php

Kemmis, S., & McTaggart, R. (2005). Participatory action research, communicative action and the public sphere. In N. K. Denzim & Y. S. Lincoln (Eds.), *The Sage handbook of qualitative research* (pp. 560-578). Thousand Oaks, CA: Sage Publications.

Maturana, H. (2001). *Our genome does not determine us.* ASC 2001 conference, May 27-29. Retrieved from http://www.asc-cybernetics.org/2001/RH-Maturana.htm

Maturana, H., & Varela, F. (1987). *The tree of knowledge: The biological roots of human understanding.* Boston, MA: Shambala.

Pearce, W. Barnett. (2007). *Making social worlds: A communication perspective.* Malden, MA; Oxford: Blackwell Publishing.

Por, G. (2004). Notes on forms of collective intelligence (CI). *Blog of Collective Intelligence.* Retrieved from http://www.community-intelligence.com/blogs/public/2004/05/notes_on_forms_of_collective_i.html

Russell, D., & Ison, R. (2004). Maturana's intellectual contribution as a choreography of conversation and action. *Cybernetics and Human Knowing, 11* (2), 36-48.

Strong, M. (2009). *Be the solution.* Hoboken, NJ: John Wiley & Sons.

Surowiecki, J. (2004). *The wisdom of crowds.* New York, NY: Doubleday.

Thorisdottir, H. (2010). Manifestations of Life Conditions and trapped consciousness: The prelude and causes of the financial crisis in Iceland from the point of view of theories and research in social psychology. In The Althingi Parliamentary Investigation Commission (Eds.), *Report of the Special Investigation Commission (SIC)* (pp. 275-297). Reykjavik, Iceland: Althingi.

TECHNOLOGY AND INNOVATION – AN SDi ANALYSIS AND RECOMMENDATION

By Barbara Brown

Over the last century, Orange technological innovations have greatly improved the physical quality of life for those in the developed world. Unfortunately, the rapid pace of change and complexity of the science and engineering involved has reached the point where the average citizen is totally incapable of understanding complex Life Conditions of modern societies. Cultures cannot adapt as rapidly as technology changes. From climate change to banking failures, we see downward cultural spirals exacerbated by complex technologies which are not understood. Citizens lack the capacity to make political decisions regarding complex technology-driven issues and government solutions intensify the downward spiral.

As dysfunctional Blue corporate bureaucracies attempt to commoditize the process of innovation, technologists find themselves buried within massive organizations where novel invention is no longer possible. Toxic corporate cultures stifle their spirits and effectively channel daily activities into outdated and ineffective processes that maintain a technological status quo. During the past decade, technologists themselves have become increasingly aware of the problem and are seeking organizational and cultural solutions to remove these impediments.

Technologists vs. Humanists

At the cutting edge of innovation we see a split between the technologists, who envision a future driven by science and technology, and humanists who believe human minds and cultures must fundamentally evolve to cope with the demands of modern technology. Technology extremists tell us we do not need to fear climate change or resource shortages because the next set of innovative solutions will emerge as current problems become clear. Humanists reply that most people are not able to cope with current demands of the modern world, so innovation is needed in psycho-social and cultural arenas.

At the Orange (modernist) level, we have the history of technology-induced environmental degradation replaced by massive environmental clean-up programs which have largely mitigated the most severe effects in the developed world.[1] Although China could not skip this cycle, their efforts to implement large-scale renewable energy into their power grid, something which the West has yet to master, suggest Asia will run the course in decades instead of centuries. Five years ago, credible projections showed oil production had peaked and was no longer able to keep pace with increasing demand from the developing world. Enter the technologists with fracking and we now see projections(1) that the world may have enough fossil fuels from oil shale to industrialize the developing world. Environmentalists predict the resultant jump in fossil fuel usage will push the climate beyond the tipping point, with disastrous consequences. Technologists see time to perfect alternate energy sources.

There is a bifurcation in cutting edge ideas about how humans should be evolving. Orange technologists envision a world where digital controlling devices are everywhere from smart appliances, to the electric grid and driverless cars, to wearable technology, such as Google glasses or smart watches. Green communitarians respond that our social systems are failing and technology is not improving people's psychological lives. They recommend "enlightenment" as a solution to the malaise that has produced an American culture where, upon release of the American Psychiatric Association's newest DSM,[2] some psychiatrists now estimate

1   Sant, Roger, "This Time It's Different: 40 Years of Energy Policy", Total Energy USA, 2013, *http://www.examiner.com/article/total-energy-usa-2013-puts-it-all-together*
2   DSM-5, American Psychiatric Association, www.dsm5.org/Pages/Default.aspx, 2013

that over half the US population could have a diagnosable mental illness[3]. This bifurcation does not appear to be a simple conflict between Orange, individualistic thinking and Green communitarian feelings. Within the growing community expressing Second Tier capacity to work with post-modern complexity, we see the basic gap identified by Graves[4] between those most comfortable on the individualistic, self-expressive, left side of the Spiral and communitarians whose natural preferences lean toward the self-sacrifice, right side. Although Second Tier capacity comes with the ability to understand and appreciate the value of both the express self and the sacrifice self approaches, even individuals with great vertical capacity display a clear tendency to approach a problem starting from their preferred side. Not surprisingly, technologists tend to be individualist thinkers who are more comfortable with the self-expressive approaches.

A Yellow, left-side, analysis of Life Conditions comes from the large-systems and artificial intelligence fields. Led by Ray Kurzweil[5], a computer engineer who developed optical character recognition and current speech recognition programs, and physicist David Deutsch[6], this group looks at the evolution of the universe in terms of increasing complexity of information, including the massive information held within DNA and cortical neural nets. In his latest book, *How to Create a Mind: The Secret of Human Thought Revealed*, Kurzweil synthesizes the latest neurological research and fifty years of computer innovation to explain how the human mind carries out complex tasks, such as speech recognition. Since this understanding of how the brain works has led directly to functional speech recognition we now use in mobile devices, it's hard to think his insights can be too far off base. This line of thinking seems to be leading to the concept of replacing incompetent human decision-making with better artificial intelligence (AI) controls instead of developing human potential.

---

3   Lisa Collier Cool, DSM-5: *Will millions more Americans be diagnosed with mental illness?*, http://health.yahoo.net/experts/dayinhealth/dsm-5-will-millions-more-americans-be-diagnosed-mental-illness, 2013
3   Lane, Christopher, *The NIMH Withdraws Support for DSM-5*, http://www.psychologytoday.com/blog/side-effects/201305/the-nimh-withdraws-support-dsm-5, 2012
4   Beck, Don E and Cowan, C, *Spiral Dynamics Mastering Values, Leadership and Change*, Blackwell Publishing, 1996
5   Kurzweil, Ray, *How to Create a Mind: The Secret of Human Thought Revealed*, Viking Adult, 2012
6   Deutsch, David, *The Beginning of Infinity: Explanations That Transform the World*, Viking Adult, 2011

An alternate Yellow approach, from right-side, is well-defined by Barrett Brown[7], with his recommendation that "the 'consciousness' in Conscious Capitalism" be facilitated by active "Vertical learning" programs based on Bill Torbert's eight-stage model for business applications. Brown's approach emphasizes the Green communitarian aspects of development such as emotional intelligence, inspiration and deep connection. Not surprisingly, most of Barrett's examples come from Green non-profits, social entrepreneurs, etc. With the exception of a mapping of Warren Buffet's public career to his increasing developmental level, Brown has little discussion of practical applications or actual examples of vertical leadership in large Blue/ORANGE multi-nationals.

Leadership coach Mike Jay is now providing a synthesis of the two approaches in his book @F-L-O-W[8] and related coaching programs. Mike points out that we can look back on over 30 years of efforts at producing significant vertical growth using coaching and leadership programs. Lack of widespread success suggests that few people are actually capable of making significant vertical change in time frames that allow them to cope with their immediate problems. Jay recommends approaching the issue by identifying the individual's current capacities, including stage of vertical development. Instead of spending resources on developing new attitudes and behaviors that are not readily available to an individual, perhaps external support systems can scaffold people to produce the results they need to be happy without requiring "enlightenment". In addition to coaching and help from others, Kurzweil's AI systems could offer some of this scaffolding, providing users with everything from safety reminders to real time coaching in interpersonal skills.

Espoused Values at Odds with Theory in Action

It has been a tenant of Spiral Dynamics Integral (SDi) thought that our current culture wars are a result of conflict between a failing Orange capitalist system and a not yet healthy Green liberal society. There is general agreement that the Blue/Orange coalition that powered post-WWII was an example of a social contract that worked well for those Life Conditions. Green ought to be more sophisticated than either Blue or Orange, so why

---

7 Brown , Barrett C., *The Future of Leadership for Conscious Capitalism*, MetaIntegral Associates, 2013.

8 Jay, Mike, *@F-L-O-W: Find, Design, Use Talent to Emerge Happiness and Success in a Postmodern World*, Leadership University Press, 2012

do Green liberal programs appear to have caused more problems than they solved? One theory is that the rate of technology change has produced social fallout that is beyond the capacity of Green to master and therefore Yellow will be needed to develop working systems.

A more intriguing analysis starts with the observation that media sound bytes now inform much of public opinion. As more and more niche media become available, it is relatively easy for people to become mired in information that presents only one vMemetic viewpoint. Ideas which were originally generated at Green or Orange become slogans that are presented to Blue as "Truth" and to Red as "easy success" schemes, e.g. ORANGE/Green Libertarianism, which stresses personal freedom AND self-reliance, translates as "freedom" to do drugs and carry big guns at RED/Blue. Somehow, the responsibility part of self-reliance got lost in the downward translation. We hear parents brag of children who have reached Green by puberty, yet there is little evidence for their neurological maturity. A more probable interpretation is that the Blue "Truth" these children have learned to espouse simply has meme content which sounds Green. An obvious question arises, "What is the actual capacity of modern Western civilization?"

Jennifer Garvey-Berger[9] has looked at vertical development using Robert Kegan's Subject-Object Interview (SOI). Unlike the other self-report methods used for evaluation of development, SOI allows the researcher to inquire about the actual meaning making behind the media slogans. Using a typical corporate sample, Garvey-Berger's research shows a much lower center of gravity than more optimistic estimates from self-report instruments. Beck and Joiner may have measured a group that has self-selected to work in environments that encourage thinking at a more complex level. It is also probable that Jennifer's study participants would have selected more Orange and Green slogans on a self-report than they show in action during an SOI response. Garvey-Berger's distribution seems to more closely match what is encountered by those working with technology groups in large corporations. Having replaced innovation in the physical world with "virtual reality" and money as the only measure of business value, American multinationals are now trying to replace Orange innovation with Blue formula-driven change. American Capitalism's espoused myth of

9   Garvey-Berger, Jennifer, *Changing on the Job: Developing Leaders for a Complex World*, Stanford Business Books, 2011

Distribution of Population and Power by Value System (vMeme) - Form of Mind

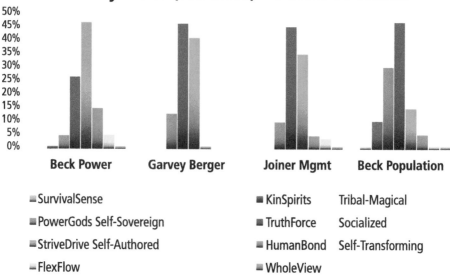

- SurvivalSense
- PowerGods Self-Sovereign
- StriveDrive Self-Authored
- FlexFlow

- KinSpirits   Tribal-Magical
- TruthForce   Socialized
- HumanBond   Self-Transforming
- WholeView

individual initiative has been replaced in action by bureaucratic policies and procedures stifling innovation at all levels in large corporate enterprises. While "display initiative" is on the job requirements, only pre-approved innovations are allowed. A large multi-national oil and gas conglomerate manages innovation with a process for identifying broken processes and another procedure for changing the bad process. No creativity required. The demonstrated inability to mount adequate, timely responses to severe technical problems such as the Deepwater Horizon explosion or the Fukushima nuclear disaster shows how inadequate Blue "safety" checklists are in coping with real 21st Century Life Conditions.

Nowhere is this disconnect more blatant than in the world of Dot-com startups and mobile aps. Between 1997 and 2001, trading in internet ventures with no profits, and often no revenues, caused the US NASDAQ to increase by a factor of five (5) before total collapse to the pre-1997 levels. The venture capital culture continues to push pro-forma (Blue) driven virtual business plans that stress quick payback, often by peddling a half-developed idea to a large competitor who will pay to shut down potential competition from an improved product. The November 2012 cover of MIT's *Technology*

Review[10] has the caption "You Promised Me Mars Colonies. Instead, I Got Facebook. – Buzz Aldrin." The US no longer has the capacity to carry humans into space. Long-term R&D projects on expensive technologies such as space exploration or alternate energy have been nearly impossible to fund, as investors continued to divert money to virtual "quick hits". As documented in Said Dawlabani's book, *MEMEnomics*[11], the Blue/Orange coalition that created useful physical technologies at affordable prices during the 1950's has disintegrated.

Mike Jay suggests that there is a payoff to encouraging unsophisticated consumers to concentrate on entertainment and virtual games, since the only current alternative is to sell the masses bling and toys that waste natural resources. Unfortunately, this diversion of funding into short-term entertainment and virtual ventures continues to make it difficult to fund work on real problems in the physical world. Although there is now a budding entrepreneurial private space industry[12], with entrepreneurs such as Golden Spike even planning a return to the moon, their strategies assume flights will continue to be funded by governments. Most alternate energy investments[13] are coming not from venture capital, but from large multi-nationals that can use government green energy subsidies to offset their costs. Because such subsidies are given only on old, not yet economic technologies, they divert funding away from unique solutions.

The Quest for Blue Solutions to Complex Technology Problems

In 1995, The Standish Group published its first CHAOS Report[14] attempting to document the results of the $250 billion spent annually in the US on Information Technology (IT) projects during the mid-90s. Their conclusion was only 16% of IT projects were on time and on budget with

10   Pontin, Jason, *Why Can't We Solve Big Problems,* MIT Technology Review, November/December 2012
11   Dawlabani, Said, *MEMEnonics: The Next Generation Economic System,* SelectBooks; 2013
12   *Golden Spike identifies steps needed to land a man on the moon,* http://www.examiner.com/list/golden-spike-identifies-steps-needed-to-land-a-person-on-the-moon 2013
13   *Total Energy USA participants say stop trying to mandate favored energy sources,* http://www.examiner.com/article/total-energy-usa-participants-say-stop-trying-to-mandate-favored-energy-sources, 2013
14   The Standish Group Report, *CHAOS,* https://www4.in.tum.de/lehre/vorlesungen/vse/WS2004/1995_Standish_Chaos.pdf, 1995

required functionality. Nearly a third (1/3) of the projects they reviewed were cancelled after significant cost. The remaining projects were deployed with a 198% cost overrun and an average time delay of 222%.

In response to this dismal record, the Project Management Institute (PMI) published its first Guide to the Project Management Body of Knowledge[15] (PMBOK) in 1996. PMI and its PMBOK efforts started as an attempt by successful Orange Project Management professionals to share best practices and innovation. Codifying the best practices began to put Blue administrative processes around tacit knowledge, allowing Blue organizations to use Orange know-how. In the world of physical construction projects, where the final products were generally clearly defined, such sharing was largely successful and professionally managed projects seldom had such failure statistics.

However, in Research and Development (R&D), innovation, and IT, a problem arose. The final results of a successful R&D or IT project were difficult to define in advance. During the 1-2 years required for project completion, business requirements and computer technologies were continually changing. In response to the increasing uncertainty, PMI published an expanded third edition of the PMBOK in 2004, adding additional Blue check-list processes to deal with each issue Orange identified. The ever-expanding PMBOK is now in its 5th edition.

One of the most difficult issues has been more accurate definition of the final product. Since cost and schedule overruns were a major problem, disgruntled business managers began to demand more detailed, locked down specifications prior to approving project start. In 2003, this trend to more detailed definition of IT products culminated in the founding of the International Institute of Business Analysis (IIBA®), which began to add to the ever more massive Blue checklists with its *Guide to the Business Analysis Body of Knowledge*[16]® (BABOK®). As a side effect of the growing overhead from massive Blue processes, costs for project planning and control increased and project timelines expanded, exacerbating the underlying issue of inability to respond to changing business and technology.

---

15   Project Management Institute, *PMBOK*, http://www.pmi.org/en/PMBOK-Guide-and-Standards/Standards-Library-of-PMI-Global-Standards.aspx, 1994, 2013
16   International Institute of Business Analysis, *A Guide to the Business Analysis Body of Knowledge®* *(BABOK®)*, http://www.iiba.org/babok-guide.aspx, 2005, 2011.

The Agile Manifesto

In 2001, in response to a continuing record of major failures in software projects despite expanding Blue controls, a group of 17 experienced software developers concluded that they were "uncovering better ways of developing software". Their ORANGE/Green *Manifesto for Agile Software Development*[17] recommended valuing:

- "Individuals and interactions over processes and tools.
- Working software over comprehensive documentation.
- Customer collaboration over contract negotiation.
- Responding to change over following a plan."

Many with an organizational development or team building background assume that the success of Agile methods is primarily due to the increased effort to apply Green principles, such as focus on teamwork and collaboration. In organizations that already have deep capacity for Orange, this may be the case. However, in massive bureaucracies where middle management is predominately Blue, it is more likely that the Orange systems thinking is responsible for the improvements. Agile principles[18] start with the proposition that "Working software is the primary measure of progress" and add an emphasis on "attention to technical excellence", producing a practical, Orange, results-oriented mindset.

Agile is systems thinking at its best. Since constant change is a demonstrable fact of current Life Conditions, Agile processes design in methods for continually changing requirements, replacing obsolete early designs with features the business now needs. Even when unnecessary features are removed before they are actually coded, most software projects have large amounts of rework. Agile emphasizes "Simplicity--the art of maximizing the amount of work not done."[(18)] This is often operationalized by breaking work into smaller deliverables with much shorter cycle times and by concerted efforts to reduce WIP (work in progress) so project flow is continuous and time is not wasted waiting on incomplete work or seeking feedback about project quality.

---

17   Beck, Kent, et. al., *Manifesto for Agile Software Development*, http://agilemanifesto.org/, 2001
18   *Principles behind the Agile Manifesto*, http://agilemanifesto.org/principles.html, 2001

Innovation From An Orange Middle

Over the past 10 years, the battle between ever-expanding Blue checklist approaches to managing projects and ORANGE/Green innovation has continued. Those individuals and organizations with deep Orange capacity have been able to effectively implement Agile methodologies, with visible improvements in project results. Executives, driven by these bottom line improvements experienced by their competitors, have asked their IT and R&D departments to implement these more cost-effective procedures.

PMI and IIBA have jumped on the bandwagon with attempts to provide Blue checklist processes for Agile projects, in addition to the conventional PMBOK/BABOK procedures. Blue IT organizations, with no capacity for Orange thinking, have attempted to use these systematic procedures with relatively little success. Going through the motions of working in a self-directed team doesn't produce innovation. People generally do their work exactly as they've always done it and simply add the overhead of following these new processes, as well as meeting all the old constraints.

Elliott Jaques[19], in his Requisite Organization designs, has proposed that hierarchies are a natural result of differing capacities among people. In an effective, functional hierarchy, those at the top have greater cognitive capacity than those they supervise. While Jaques measured increasing capacity as the ability to deal with longer time frames, he also emphasized the increasing ability to deal with a broader, more complex system. Jaques practitioners sometimes describe highly dysfunctional organizations as being upside down. Individuals with higher levels of cognitive ability appear to be trapped underneath ossified layers of inept bureaucracy in middle management, much as described in the "Peter Principle[20]".

Attempting to deploy Agile teams in a large Blue organization quickly runs into this capacity ceiling. Middle managers were selected for their ability to enforce Blue rules, not for their capacity for innovation or even for the capacity to get work accomplished. In spite of demands from board rooms for increasing productivity, project managers and CIOs are seldom leading major innovation efforts. Instead, Agile pilot initiatives are coming from talented, disruptive Orange individuals buried in the massive organization. These high-performance work teams are indeed fully self-organized and

---

19   Jaques, Elliott, *Requisite Organization*, http://www.requisite.org/, 1989, 1999
20   Peter, Laurence J., *The Peter Principle: Why Things Always Go Wrong*, HarperBusiness, reprinted 2011

find themselves constantly fighting for support from management as their efficient and effective processes are thwarted by requirements to follow approved processes, provide extensive documentation and deal with unresponsive quarterly or annual approval cycles.

Self-defined Agile teams often get a foot-hold in an organization when a visible project is in failure mode. Demand for results opens a crack for introduction of non-standard processes and requests to form an Agile clean-up team are often approved. If the team is successful, they are allowed to take on other difficult projects. As pilot Agile results get executive attention, an organization tries to form more Agile teams. As long as there is additional Orange capacity, a few Green collaborators to hold the teams together and an executive sponsor, the Agile initiative continues. The department quickly runs out of potential team members who already have the capacity to deal with their work in this way. The next step is to send staff to formal Agile training programs and to bring in Orange/GREEN Agile coaches to teach the teams collaboration and to facilitate new processes. Generally, this BLUE/Orange training approach has some initial success, as defined Agile processes replace some of the existing project management procedures.

Limits To A Self-directed Team Approach

Successful Agile projects were an objective validation of the value of the Green concept of self-directed work teams. Conventional Agile work groups are permanent, co-located teams of 7-9 members who work together on a single project and deliver completed project components on a short time schedule, defined as two weeks in the conventional Scrum[21] framework. In practice, iteration times range from days with continuous delivery frameworks such as those used to continually update our smart phone aps to monthly cycles on larger projects. Work items are broken into small, manageable chunks. Team members soon learn everyone's strengths, assigning each task to the most competent. The team meets for a short "stand-up" every day to visually verify that work is progressing as planned using tasks displayed on a wall board. As unexpected complications arise on a task, other team members quickly pick up the slack. A "retrospective" at the end of each cycle allows the group to fine-tune its processes to continually become

---

21   *What is Scrum?*, www.scrumalliance.org, 2013

more effective. Incomplete tasks on the backlog list are reprioritized every cycle, continually bringing the results more into alignment with current conditions.

In practice, this approach quickly reaches several limits. The first limit is ultra-specialization driven by the Blue checklist approach to technology. Most projects require work from technical specialists who are expensive and not needed full time by any single team. The department no longer has permanent team assignments, as specialists are shared by many teams and quickly become a limiting resource. Critical path project scheduling (Blue) tries for efficiency by taking all the slack out of the system, much as airlines try to optimize hub schedules. Just as a single late plane in a hub city can delay flights all over the country, so a single unavailable specialist will totally disrupt all Agile  projects. The obvious Orange solution, it's more effective and ultimately cheaper to have excess capacity, is in direct conflict with the Blue belief that statistical efficiency and 100% utilization should drive projects.

An Orange issue is that in the real world superstars do exist and they prefer to work together. The most competent often form a single high-performance team, leaving the rest of the organization with several "also-ran" teams that are not particularly effective. Blue middle management treats technical employees as a commodity resource and has little context for understanding and coping with these capacity-driven cognitive differences in team performance. Unless a Green coach can convince the most competent to work with average performers and teach them how to leverage their work, the organization cannot sustain Agile methods. The high performers are assigned as "team leads" and the organization moves back toward a command and control structure, dropping the capacity for team self-organization in favor of predictable, less stellar results.

Another common limitation is the conflict between the Blue need for long-range, detailed forecasting and totally predicable results and the short-term responses to changing Life Conditions which are at the core of the Agile methodologies. A typical project approval cycle fixes resources, schedule, budget and detailed deliverables on an annual and quarterly basis. Even minor changes must be approved by several layers of management, at best in a monthly review cycle. A critical change usually takes 6-8 weeks to make it through the approval process, in direct conflict with the 2-4 week Agile development cycle. The most effective Agile teams are supported by a project manager who can move changes through the system in a more timely fashion. Unfortunately, as the corporation tries to scale, such "exceptions" to the approved Blue planning cycle become too disruptive for the organization to support.

At an Orange, pragmatic level, the obvious answer is that it's not possible to effectively deliver large, long-term projects by locking in schedule, budget and scope 2-3 years in advance. In practice, resources (people and budget) and schedule (required delivery dates) are often fixed by corporate constraints and can't be altered by the amount of work requested. If it were possible to concentrate on the value of features delivered instead of obsessing on schedule and budget, self-directed teams could concentrate on rapid delivery of the most valuable features within the time constraints. Since a primary strength of Agile methods is continually triaging undelivered backlogs for current value, Agile is ideal for getting the most current value out of a highly constrained project system.

Between 2006 and mid-2009 IBM[22] used this philosophy, together with coaching and training, to deploy Agile methods to 7,000 team members. As the project continued, Agile processes began to bump up against both corporate procedures and entrenched leadership practices. As Agile procedures were added to the corporate playbook, the results were "more constraints and less flexibility." Orange solutions were not adequate to meet this challenge. Leadership needed a Green makeover. Surveys surfaced Trust in leadership as the limiting factor. Teams could figure out how to do their work, but command and control philosophies were producing churn. Deliberate efforts to shift to a Collaborative Leadership style delivered more value and increased productivity, while creating a more pleasant workplace. In a technical organization with deep Orange capacity, Green innovations can be quite effective. As capacity for collaboration and trust increases at all levels, better performance follows.

22   McKinney, Sue , "The Dancing Agile Elephant Meets Collaborative Leadership", *Agile Leadership Network Houston*, http://alnhouston.org/index.php/chapter-meetings/past-meetings/6-apln-houston-chapter-meeting-september-17-2009-600pm, 2009

Scaling Innovation In A Blue Environment

In practice, IBM's success story is rare. Most organizations managing large-scale IT projects lack the Orange capacity to effectively support Green collaborative work teams. Blue middle management needs to maintain their illusion of command and control, CHAOS reports[14] of continuing failure notwithstanding. Kurzweil's idea[5] that smart computer systems can provide capacities that humans currently lack is being put forward as a solution by cutting edge innovators. Classical Agile theory would consider the rapid delivery of working product as the appropriate measure for control. Entrenched Blue management procedures usually emphasize reporting of cost per item on a detailed level, with little consideration for the ultimate value of the result produced. Each individual's time should be fully allocated, even if much of that time is actually spent in needless rework or filling out time sheets. In some organizations the process of allocating people's time to individual product features becomes a significant proportion of the total cost. As standardized software tools become more robust and simple to implement, such reporting can often be provided with minimal effort on the part of the project team. This allows management to continue to have the security blanket of detailed cost accounting without burdening the project with huge administrative overhead. Non-productive activities, such as waiting for approval and fixing errors can be documented and the true impact of their reduction demonstrated.

Improving Enterprises[23] has taken Stagen[24] methodologies into software consulting. Allen Hurst reports they are using the latest version of a Microsoft tool called TFS to design Agile templates that can be quickly set up in an enterprise. The tool records activity and, with a couple of mouse clicks, links budget lines to detailed features and then records work on each feature automatically. This approach has been highly successful at a BLUE/Orange level, providing actual schedule and budget data on a timely basis. Unfortunately, efficient AI programs which gather data on how individuals spend their time can be used by toxic Blue as a nasty weapon. So far, Agile consultants using AI software systems have taken the Orange,

23   Hurst, Allen and Liles, Devlin, "TFS as a Springboard to Agile," *Agile Leadership Network Houston*, http://alnhouston.org/index.php/chapter-meetings/past-meetings/286-october-chapter-meeting-october-17-2013, 2013

24   Stagen Leadership Institute, Inc., *Next-Level Leadership*, http://www.stagen.com/perspectives/next-level/, 2006

pragmatic approach to what is fundamentally a Green issue of building trust in an organization. Consultants deliver their proprietary software templates with all access to individual time reporting totally disabled and then charge premium rates to implement the reports. Usually, cost-obsessed middle managers reject the additional charge.

Scaled Agile (SAFe™)[25] processes offered an explicit blended ORANGE/Blue approach to mitigate the problems of scaling project teams within massive enterprises. SAFe™ starts with the observation that in a large enterprise,

Implementing Scrum

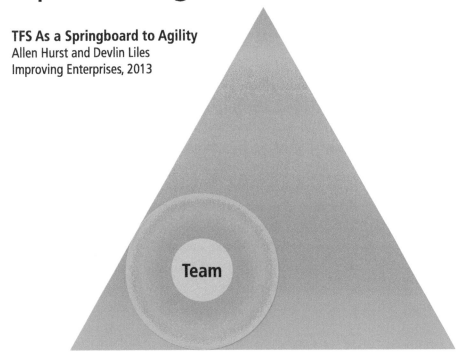

TFS As a Springboard to Agility
Allen Hurst and Devlin Liles
Improving Enterprises, 2013

software projects are constrained by available staff and budget. At a corporate, portfolio level executives determine what value streams they wish to pursue now. Approved work is then released down to a Program level, where items are scheduled based on technical sequences, e.g. you must buy your computer before you install the software, and overall resource availability. Once the Program Features are scheduled, small chunks of work are then released to

---

25   Scaled Agile Framework, http://scaledagileframework.com/, 2008,2013

Leffingwell, Dean, *Agile Software Requirements: Lean Requirements for Teams Programs and the Enterprise*, 2011

Leffingwell , Dean, *Scaling Software Agility: Best Practices for Large Enterprises*, 2007

many Agile teams in a standard cycle, usually two weeks. Every two (2) weeks, completed features are combined and the teams start on the next work items. Minimally usable feature sets are grouped and packaged for users on a planned basis. Again, software is available to help manage this process. In this case, managing the dependencies between sequential work items becomes more important than cost reporting.

A Future of Red/BLUE Human Drones Managed by Smart AI Systems?

The use of sophisticated software solutions moves toward the Yellow goal of increased transparency and Yellow-informed Blue controls proposed by Said Dawlabani in his book *MEMEnomics*[11]. Unlike the random information on the web, much of which is false or misleading, these tools are advancing the SOX[26] goal of allowing shareholders and the public to track what corporations are actually doing with their assets. When such tools are widely implemented, indicted executives cannot complain, as Enron's Ken Lay did, that the organization was so complex they could not see the fraud carried out by their direct reports. It is probable that such AI systems will become a critical component of workable Blue controls.

Unfortunately, when implemented by huge enterprises with minimal capacity to work beyond Orange, such AI tools also have the potential to greatly exacerbate social problems created by massive, impersonal enterprises. AI tools are already supporting the commoditization of technical talent. Many organizations have dropped Green development programs in favor of funding this technical patch. Use of AI to control organization behavior also appears to be widening the divide between the top and the work team. IBM's Green Collaborative Leadership[22] program, which reaches all the way down to individual work teams, is unique. More often, top-down leadership development programs, even if emphasizing vertical development for executives, die out when they reached the entrenched Blue middle where the capacity gap between the Orange and Green requirements of modern leadership and the limited current capacity of Blue managers is largest. Meanwhile, capacity within the work teams goes unrecognized and unrewarded, or in many cases punished because the continuing demand

---

26   Peavler, Rosemary, *The Sarbanes-Oxley Act and the Enron Scandal - Why are they Important?* http://bizfinance.about.com/od/smallbusinessfinancefaqs/a/sarbanes-oxley-act-and-enron-scandal. htm

from the highest performing teams for Orange innovation and Green collaboration proves too disruptive to command and control management.

At a smaller scale, Yellow solutions are slowly making an inroad in the technology sector. The Holacracy[27] business design model, invented by software developers, provides an explicit Green governance framework, using "social technology" as an alternative to the Orange AI-driven approach. While Microsoft is destroying collaboration and driving away high performers[28] by using such Agile AI performance tools to "stack rank" employees, Medium, a high tech competitor, has sought funding[(28)] to implement a Holacracy-based company.

In January, 2012 a group of 21 innovators met in Stoos Switzerland. At that meeting, they formed the Stoos Network[29], which is dedicated to facilitating a tipping point in transforming organizations. Several of the participants were familiar with SDi and presented the concepts to the entire group. In the last 24 months, the Stoos LinkedIn group has grown to over 2400 participants, with 19 local satellites on six continents. They have hosted five (5) follow-on meetings focused on looking for a "better way" where "the role of leaders should include the stewardship of the living rather than the management of the machine". The members are facilitating Yellow discussions within the Lean Agile community in the US and are beginning to explicitly advocate use of SDi to understand organizational transformation.

Change: From What to What?

Dr. Don Beck's Change Equation[(4)] reminds us that before we start trying to make change happen we must correctly identify the current Life Conditions and clearly define the proposed future state. Much of the proposed innovation in IT is driven by the view from executive coaches and Agile team development providers that organizations are nodal Orange and need a heavy Green infusion of collaborative leadership. If observations by Garvey-Berger and Hurst are correct, most large organizations are, in fact, nodal Blue, particularly in entrenched middle management. If we

27   Holacracy©, *How it Works*, http://holacracy.org/how-it-works , 2013

28   Hu, Elise, *Microsoft Vs. Medium: A Tale Of Two Office Cultures*, http://www.npr.org/blogs/ alltechconsidered/2013/08/28/216432137/microsoft-vs-medium-a-tale-of-two-office-cultures, 2013

29   *Stoos Network*, http://www.stoosnetwork.org/, 2012, 2014

mistakenly assess an organization as toxic Orange because Blue individuals have been conditioned to espouse Orange meme-bytes they don't understand operationally, we set up conditions for failure. There is not sufficient Orange capacity on which to build Green collaboration programs unless heavily scaffolded by Blue AI support systems and aided by executive identification of work team leaders with ORANGE/Green capacity to manage incremental innovation within a collaborative, high performance team.

In too many organizations, executive sponsored leadership development programs select and reward only Blue/ORANGE political maneuvering, without regard to any objective measures of the ability to get work done in a high-performance team. Yellow-designed AI systems, which manage Blue processes, should help better distinguish actual project results from self-serving political spin generated by non-productive but charismatic gamesmen. Executive sponsors can support a growing capacity for ORANGE/Green high performance teams by identifying actual capacity within professional teams. High capacity team-level leaders can learn how to get things done without confronting and disrupting the entrenched Blue structure in which the majority of employees are stuck. Seeding the project organization with such individuals and providing them executive protection from Blue retaliation for proposing changes will be a critical success factor.

Executive leadership will also need to be clear that mastery of Orange innovation is a pre-requisite for Green collaborative leadership. Blue managers have already mastered collaboration, or at least the collusion needed to maintain the ineffective status quo. Individuals working at Blue need to master personal, self-directed change before they are ready to collaborate at a higher level. Collaboration between technologists and humanists at a Yellow stage has the capacity to transform how our culture does technology. A critical key will be revitalization of Blue systems and structures which control and distort modern technology and stifle innovation. Yellow-designed AI systems which enable transparent Blue controls will be an important component of such transformations. As technology-based organizations fix their Blue systems, they will enable Orange innovation. Mastery of Orange provides a solid foundation on which to build Green, collaborative social technologies, which can lead to wiser use of physical innovations.

FOSTERING HUMAN EMERGENCE: TEACHING "INTEGRAL" AT UW-MADISON

By Alberto Vargas

"If you had a chance to teach something to the new generations, what would it be?" This was the question that was posed to me in early 2005 when I took a position of associate faculty at a Midwest Big Ten university, the University of Wisconsin, Madison.

My two main fields of interest were Latin American Studies, Environmental Studies and Sustainable Development. These are interdisciplinary fields which require integration of a variety of disciplines from science, to history, to law to political science, to sociology, to literature, to name a few. Although I had taught before and I had earned a doctorate degree, I did not pursue the typical academic track of research, publishing and teaching in which you become a specialist in a rather defined field that you focus on most of your career. In contrast, what I had done in my professional life was to engage in interdisciplinary applied work, consulting for international organizations, and working for a state agency. Trained as an agronomist in México, I completed an interdisciplinary Ph.D. in Environmental Studies at the University of Wisconsin, Madison which broadened my interests to other fields including the social sciences and humanities. In a way, I became a generalist, and one of my roles was to connect other generalists with specialists.

In order to teach something you must be passionate about it. I knew that I wanted to share with students my passion for what loosely has been called Integral Studies and complexity. And Spiral Dynamics Integral (SDi) is a central component of this approach.

I had discovered Integral Studies sometime in the mid-1990s when I stumbled on one of the books of Ken Wilber (Brief History of Everything, 1996). At that time I was writing my doctoral dissertation focusing on the evolution of institutions for community forest management in tropical Mexico. It all made sense to me, but I knew it would take me too long to fully incorporate what I had discovered into my thesis. So I put it in the back burner but continued with the reading. I defended my dissertation in November 1997 knowing that I had left something incomplete, and that I would be on a search for what that was until I found the answer. Things "Integral" turned out to be that answer.

My interest and passion for Integral Studies rose again with the dawn of the new Century. The twin towers attack in New York in 2001 launched many of us into a frenzy of confusion, perplexity and desire to understand and make sense of what the world was coming to be. I dove into readings on history, Islam, sociology and geo-politics but nothing seemed to be convincing. It all was rather fragmented accounts from one pole to another, with the occasional glimpses of universal human nature. I was particularly concerned because in 2001 my son was 9 years old and my daughter was 2. I felt sad and worried about what was coming for the young generations.

I discovered SDi at that time through reading another of Wilber's books: A Theory of Everything, 2001 The first chapter of the book is entitled "An Amazing Spiral", and it described beautifully the work of Clare Graves and Don Beck (among others). The description laid out a very articulate map of what we were all witnessing. Wilber used this approach to comment on the 9/11 events in the piece "The Deconstruction of the World Trade Center", which for the first time gave me a sense of peace and optimism. There was nothing to be worried about. It is what it is and it is evolving and all makes sense. Don Beck had made a similar claim earlier when he wrote "A Spiral View of Terrorism" (1996). It was as if Beck had foreseen what was happening. I was not aware of Beck's work before, and what was now in front of me made so much sense. Beck's perspective provided tools to interpret the world, and life in general, in a way that all the pieces seemed to fit beautifully.

Having tools to interpret reality helped but things were not getting better. The US descended into a fear-based, narrow, and regressive set of policies that led to the unnecessary and costly invasion of Iraq. And yet, there was room for optimism because the Spiral keeps on evolving.

Around 2003 I met my friend Tom Christensen through a Meet-Up group to study and learn more about Wilber and Beck's approach. At the beginning we were just the two of us, meeting at a café and trying to spread the word and engage in meaningful discussions. At one of our talks we decided that we would do what we could to invite Don Beck to come to our town and collect a group to interact with him in the intellectual and applied exploration of SDi. The question was: How?

We discovered other groups meeting independently in our area and started to weave a network of possibilities we felt could heal our world, society and ourselves. I mentioned these interests to another friend, also with a position at UW-Madison, Harry Webne-Behrman who I knew from my Jewish congregation. He in turn mentioned that we should talk with Darin Harris who had just taken a position at UW-Madison. Both Harry and Darin worked at the UW, but I was still working for a state agency that dealt with natural resource conservation issues. My room for maneuvering was limited and I had to do all this in my spare time between parenting and working. My curiosity was so strong though I did what was needed to deepen my learning.

I continued with the study and readings and dove into Wilber's magnum opus *Sex, Ecology and Spirituality* (1995). My passion was growing as I started to put into practice what I was learning at the personal and professional level. Personally, our family was able to navigate a difficult time when my wife went through spinal surgery, a result of an apparent minor traffic accident a few months before. Having the Integral framework available to us during this time, helped me respect and honor the Purple family bonds that moved to the foreground at this time and also to be patient with the health care system that was so Blue at times I had good reason to be frustrated. People are who they are, and accepting that, rather than lobbying for significant change, obviated a huge amount of stress and tension.

Professionally I kept on convening apparently disparate groups of folks working on the issue of coastal management and protection in our state. I had to work with legislators with ideologies across the spectrum, with scientists, engineers, lawyers, regulators, local officials, property owners. I convened a "work group" that had to go beyond the apparent disagreements into a workable, practical approach to advance the protection of resources without stifling economic interests. SDi revealed to me the differences in HOW these people were thinking, freeing me from the surface meanings of WHAT the people were saying. Those who had lost their homes to shoreline erosion, were wounded by the loss of their nest, their home, their Purple world. They no longer felt safe. They needed to find a safe place to live, to have their Purple satisfiers provided. Some were mad as hell, expecting either for others to "do something" or because they didn't want anybody, particularly the government, to tell them what to do with their land; and they were ready to take on something....but natural disasters don't lend themselves to behavioral change, and these people were frustrated. They needed some way to affirm their territory, their control over their lives. Regulators and service providers were very good at following the rules for disaster recovery, their Blue reality. But some people's situations were novel, and there were no Rules that fit. Thankfully there were people with a Green orientation, and they stepped in to make sure all involved were cared for. I was watching and participating in this all, with a rather new, but clear, SDi Lens. I directed when I was able, and did what I could to align resources and skills with where they were needed. This was a real threat. This was not a training, and I had all the pressure needed to force me into the Yellow perspective required to coordinate all of this.

At about the time I was attending to this village with already several homes collapsing on the shores of a tributary to Lake Superior, I started to teach Integral Studies and SDi to a variety of audiences, sometimes explicitly, sometimes implicitly. I was invited to give lectures to coastal engineers to put into context what they were learning and frame it into the world of policies. All of them listened carefully, although looking back on those early days of "Integral" there must have been more overwhelm than I wanted to see....teaching all of Integral and SDi in one hour? Only a newbie would have tried that. It was clear to me though that many appreciated the Integral "map", the Integral framework, that revealed to them just what actions were most likely to be effective, with whom, under what Life Conditions.

In 2004 I learned that the recently formed Integral Institute was convening a week-long seminar on Integral Ecology and Sustainability and I knew I wanted to participate. I applied and did get accepted to make the presentation, received a modest scholarship that helped convince my superiors this was a good thing to do, and confirmed my interest and competence in applying Integral Theory and SDi. In my proposal I chose to create a 15 minute video as the core of my presentation. I had no experience producing audiovisual materials, and "coincidently" a videographer and a script writer showed up and a very polished DVD was the result.

The DVD presented a distillation of several years of experience of the "coastal work group", essentially articulating the complex issue of the hazards of building too close to the edge of high bluffs in the Great Lakes region. There were scientific and engineering facts, policy issues, regulators, insurance and emergency management aspects to ponder, all at the same time. I used Integral Theory and SDi to organize all of this complexity, positioning appropriate elements in their appropriate quadrant, pointing out levels of movement up and down lines of development, and distinguishing the multiple vMeme interests present in those involved in the project. Here was a real world example of actual application of a great abstraction. I was affirmed once again, Integral is not just great abstract thinking; it reveals where strategic interventions can work.

But more importantly, participating in the Integral Ecology and Sustainability Seminar was a superb opportunity that led me to a "peak experience" or state of consciousness. I clearly remember being at the Denver airport on my way back home wanting to bow to anybody and everybody, feeling and understanding the awesomeness of human life in evolution. Integral theory and SDi was not an intellectual endeavor anymore, but a deeply felt and embodied reality. This realization gave me a lot of humility and also solidified my learning and application of Integral Theory and SDi. I met many colleagues at the Seminar, all sharing the desire to put Integral into practice in ecology and sustainability, which is what I do most of my time. One of the attendees to the Seminar, Marilyn Hamilton, is a collaborator with Don Beck and she was instrumental in getting in contact with him for subsequent activities.

Thus, by the beginning of 2005, what was apparently a disperse realm of possibilities suddenly became focused when I took my current position at UW-Madison. In conversations with Harry, Darin and Tom C. we designed a strategy to introduce SDi and Integral Theory into the UW-Madison.

Study Group and Madison Integrals

The first UW-Madison activity was a "study group" convened in the fall of 2005 and directed to academic and administrative staff at the university and the community at large. We would engage in the learning and discussion of SDi. The study group consisted of 6 weekly 2-hour sessions to host presentations and foster discussion about the concepts and application. The study group was designed to include a 3-day visit by Don Beck in the middle of the course. He would give a series of lectures, share question and answer sessions and raise awareness and interest about SDi the university. About 20 people signed up for the study group and remained highly engaged throughout the entire cycle. The Integral Institute donated five copies of "A Theory of Everything" to be raffled among the students.

The study group was a complete success. Don Beck's visit reached over 400 people who attended his lecture: "Change, Leadership and the Spiral". This lecture was embedded into the university-wide Managers and Supervisors Conference. From the study group a list serve with about 80 members was created to maintain contact among the life-long learners and continue the discussions. This group met bi-weekly for about three years afterwards. As I write there are still SDi related activities occurring in this group and in the individual efforts of members…this book being one of them.

Also from the study group two additional initiatives emerged: 1) a week-long session with Don Beck that took place in April 2006 to obtain the SDi Levels I and II certification training; and 2) the Journey of Facilitation and Collaboration, designed and implemented by Harry Webne-Behrman and Darin Harris; now in its 7th year with hundreds of graduates.

From the very beginning of our communication with Don Beck, his generosity and commitment to creating Life Conditions supporting fulfillment for humans all over the world was apparent. Don's enthusiasm and energy was contagious, genuine and inspired many of us to continue with our work.

Teaching SDi At A Big Ten University

With all this activity in the fall 2005 I was ready to engage in formal teaching to undergraduates and graduate students at the university. I knew I wanted to incorporate SDi and Integral Theory into my teaching. Thus the question I was posed in the opening to this chapter, "If you had a chance to teach something to the new generations, what would it be?" My answer had clarified. I wanted, and still do want, the next generation to know SDi and Integral Theory.

Implementing this commitment, I accepted a request to design and conduct two different seminars: One for undergraduates in liberal studies (mostly students in Latin American Studies and International Studies); and another one for graduate students (masters and Ph.D.s) in the Environmental Studies field. Both were conceived as highly interdisciplinary.

The undergraduate seminar in the spring was entitled "Current Issues in Latin America" and I have offered it 9 times since 2006. The graduate seminar in the fall was entitled "Sustainable Development: An Integral Perspective" and I have offered it 7 times since 2006. With about 25 students in each cohort for each seminar, over 400 students have been exposed to the material.

The topics of the undergraduate seminar ranged from US-Mexico Border, to Central American Civil Wars, to Film and Culture, to Feminism and Gender, to Land and Water and Agriculture. The graduate seminar, more rigorous, went more in depth into issues of land and water, climate change, energy, and biodiversity conservation and in general about the concept of sustainability. My aim was to present in the introductory sessions of both seminars a panorama of the complexity of the regions or topics and then try to use some the conventional, disciplinary lenses to make sense of this reality. Although useful, most of the conventional disciplinary approaches were too narrow or in too much detail and fragmented, thus leaving students in a state of perplexity as to what to do with so much information and angles to study it. I had foregrounded the problem.

Then early in the Semester I offered one full session to discuss the usefulness of SDi and Integral Theory. I presented them as tools (or "maps) to make sense of what students were learning, to reveal how all the pieces of such a complex problem could fit together. I also point out how the Integral perspective can address the heart-felt concerns hosted by so many of my students, for example:

How do you make sense of the senseless violence and destruction of the civil wars and repressive environments in the region?

What can we do?

Why do we keep on degrading the natural environment that sustains us?

Can we reconcile economic development with social justice and human fulfillment?

Even further, since SDi naturally invites students to turn the lens onto themselves also, they were often positively disturbed by what they found. Such disturbance often led to insights, self-recognition, and an appreciation for where they were, and what is likely ahead. That looks a lot like personal growth, and I was once again confirmed regarding the usefulness of things Integral. Further confirmation came from comments I received from students, noting a "refreshing", "illuminating", "clarifying" new way to viewing and interpreting the material. I received a Honored Instructor Award in 2009, sponsored by students, and a poster with some elements of my teaching experience received one of the Best Poster Presentation Awards at the Integral Theory Conference in 2010.

I didn't force or require students to adopt or use explicitly the concepts, but rather provided the information and left it there as seed to be discovered and used when appropriate. In each offering I introduced new ways of presenting the material and incorporated new angles to make it as clear as possible, leaving the opportunity for students to discover things on their own. There is no substitute for this and trying to download what I have learned into the students just doesn't work.

Integral Ecology

By 2007, it was clear to me that what I was trying to do at the UW-Madison was not an orthodox approach and that it was going to be a lonely enterprise. From the very beginning I reached out to other academic colleagues hoping to find a strong resonance and support, only to find a polite nod but a clear lack of interest. I checked to see if I was entirely off base. A colleague from the Educational Psychology field, who I knew on a personal basis, was reassuring and he told me that I should continue to pursue my interests, but I should take it lightly, as I would likely encounter a push back. His advice was to focus on the question: Is this useful? And he gave a confirming, "Yes".

However, I did start to encounter other professors who had similar ideas and curiosity to the approach I was pursuing. One of them was John Norman, a professor of Soils, a hard-core physical scientist, but with a keen interest and sensitivity to human related issues. He was giving a lecture on campus entitled "Science, Spirituality and Integrity" and I contacted him as soon as I found out about his interests. I invited him as a guest lecturer to my Seminars, which he kindly and generously accepted. His contributions raised questions that students appreciated. Through John, I met another professor in the biological sciences, Douglas Reinemann, who also shared an interest in SDi and Integral Theory as well as in Non-Violent Communication, a field that his wife Mary Kay Reinemann cultivated with care and enthusiasm. Also noteworthy is the interest and support of another colleague at UW at the time, Dr. Teri Balser, now a Professor at the University of Florida. Her commitment to education and the pursuit of integrally informed authenticity left a deep legacy at our campus, which is still a source of inspiration for many.

Doug and I talked several times and he decided to offer a seminar focusing specifically on the book "Integral Ecology" by Sean Esbjörn-Hargens and Michael Zimmerman(2009). I participated in several of the seminars which essentially were a forum for graduate students to read the book (one chapter per week) and have a discussion. The students who enrolled in this seminar, a self-selected group, were different from the ones enrolled in my seminars, because it was clear and explicit from the beginning that the main focus was to explore Integral Theory applied to ecology. They knew what they were getting into, thus discussions were very deep and fruitful. SDi was also used to further enrich the presentations and the discussions.

I also started to receive invitations from colleagues in other countries to participate in discussions about climate change, or urbanism or global environmental change and thus I have made presentations using Integral Theory and SDi at the National University in Colombia (Amazon-Leticia campus); the Autonomous University of the State of Mexico; the University of Guadalajara, in Mexico; and the University of Oslo in Norway. I see the integral seedlings spreading out and pushing our current teaching paradigm to a new level of complexity, all of which was foreseen by Graves, Beck and Wilber.

Conclusion

It has been a long journey from 2005 to where we are now and the experience has left me more motivated to continue than ever. For an academic to offer new research data and related conclusions is expected, natural, what fits the academic system. For an academic to offer a new paradigm, a new map of the same territory, does not fit so naturally into this culture. Why should it be any other way? The academic career trajectory has a very healthy Blue, Orange and Green structure to it; everyone knows how to advance; the purpose is clear; the steps are orderly and available to anyone; people know their place and what to do. But to shake things up, to try to add novelty at the level of meta-maps, new paradigms, something that is not on the road map, is, as it must be, disturbing to Blue, Orange and Green.

However, if a system is healthy, something will eventually disturb it. That is what opens the system up to growth that can include more. If I were the only voice of disturbance, then I most likely would have made no progress. I am not a Don Quixote. But if the system is ripe for a perturbation, is ready for a shift in its capacity to address complexity, then signs of this should be emerging in more than just me. My reading of Wilber, Beck, and my meetings with colleagues and friends in Madison and beyond, showed me that in fact there was an emergence of creative thinking that was shared by many. The system was trending towards change. This recognition allowed me to trust I was not tilting at windmills and allowed me to continue my efforts with confidence.

I do find it very intriguing that this change, this shift in the solidity of a Blue context, would be facilitated by Integral thinking. It appears to me that offering the Integral perspective supports a shift to Orange, creates a space for new thought, new vision, new possibilities for people's self-expression and achievement. But it also provides an intellectual context that has room to include everyone. That means Integral thinking while laying out the path to Orange, also provides a framework for those having the capacity to move to Green, to include everyone and everything. Even beyond this though, the very same Integral thinking creates the map, the intellectual framework that exposes what is essential for Yellow thinking to be effective. Integral thinking, which I use as an umbrella that includes SDi, is absolutely artful in providing the cognitive structure that fosters the necessary stability, and instability, necessary to occasion healthy growth at many vMeme levels. I do not want to imply, by any means, that there were no academic colleagues, who without an inkling of integral theory or SDi, were able to embody, intuit and practice a broad and consistent approach at Yellow. In fact I see this transformation happening in many people and places in academia. Students and other colleagues are hungry for an inclusive and comprehensive frame that helps to understand and decide on a course of action to respond to the challenges we are facing in this Century.

This has been the case for my students, and for myself. Many students have entered my classes with confusion, overwhelm, and too often a surrender to helplessness in the face of all the ineffective complexity they have become aware of. I watch with the greatest sense of reward as they wrestle with the Integral paradigm and often reconfigure in ways that includes much more complexity and provides insights into the leverage points where a difference can be made. They arrive confused. They often enough leave empowered.

In my case, I have been able to see the landscape of academia in a way that allows me to be strategic. I don't take a Red dominance stand and require that the University do what I say…of course. But I know where that kind of impetus comes from, and can dismiss it should the impulse to conquer emerge. I don't evangelize my Blue colleagues, in an effort to have them "see the light". As Graves said so wisely, "A person, godamnit, has a right to be who they are." I don't put up a big INTEGRAL THEORY sign on my office door, invent a new biz to achieve notice, position, or money, but do recognize any impetus to do so as the push of Orange. I do not have meetings with all the people I can find, hear their feelings about all things Integral, make sure they feel included, and meet again the next day to do the same…my Green inclusionary impulses.

On the best of days I do watch for HOW my students and colleagues are thinking, i.e. is it Red?, Blue? Orange? Green? What is the intelligence under the WHAT of their speaking? I then fashion my engagement with them based on what the existential need is under their communication. This does not change the world by Friday. But I have found that speaking to people where they are at, from which vMeme their thinking is originating, is the best way I have found to ensure needs are met and Life Conditions are set that are most likely to foster what is next for each person. This is how I am able to influence change, in the world I have access to: One moment, one person, one day at a time. That effort has led to countless people discovering what else is possible for each of them. That is my work in fostering sustainability on our planet. I am very pleased I can do what I can.

As a final thought I don't think I can say enough about how important it has been to me to have a cohort of similar thinkers available. If I can presume I am able to enact Yellow thinking, should I be entertaining this new breath of cognition all on my own, I would not have been able to identify the value of this new capacity, nor the breadth of benefits it offers. It seems pretty essential that highly complex thinkers, those moving beyond Green, have available a collection of similar people they find agreement with; a supportive cohort; partners in understanding and fostering human emergence. Nothing; nobody, is sustainable in isolation. If we are to thrive sustainably, we will honor our "we".

Bibliography

Beck, Don and Chris Cowan. 1997. "A Spiral View of Terrorism." http://www.spiraldynamics.net/wp-content/uploads/2011/07/spiral-view-of-terrorism.pdf

Esbjörn-Hargens, Sean and Michael Zimmerman. 2009. *Integral Ecology: Uniting Multiple Perspectives on the Natural World.* Integral Books. Boston and London.

Wilber, Ken. 1996. *A Brief History of Everything.* Shambhala Press. Boston and London.

Wilber, Ken. 2000. *Sex, Ecology and Spirituality. The Collected Works of Ken Wilber, Volume 6.* Shambhala Press. Boston and London.

Wilber, Ken. 2001. *A Theory of Everything: An Integral Vision for Business, Politics, Sceince and Spirituality.* Shambhala Press. Boston.

Wilber, Ken. 2001. "The deconstruction of the World Trade Center: A date that will live in a sliding chain of signifiers." http://www.kenwilber.com/writings/read_pdf/112

SDi MESHWORKS: HOW DIVERSE STAKEHOLDERS TRANSFORM COMPLEX CHALLENGES

By Fred Krawchuk

Introduction

Witnessing people suffer and even die as a result of divisive conflict inspired me to search for creative approaches to volatile and uncertain situations. My experiences as a military officer over the last 25 years, working across the domains of business, government, and civil society around the world, taught me that collaborative approaches to complex challenges can work. Harvard's Program on Negotiations, a trip to Northern Ireland to study the conflict there, and my support of a mediation process for an Israeli-Palestinian delegation were opportunities that provided me with pragmatic tools and rich practice in multi-party negotiations. Participating in Don Beck's workshops over the years provided me a comprehensive framework in which I could integrate and align my learning and experiences in order to successfully apply SDi theory to volatile and complex challenges. For example, designing a series of collaborative forums for groups of 300 diverse stakeholders from over 20 countries using SDi principles to explore alternatives to violence in Southeast Asia, I learned that no matter how difficult the challenge, you can always find people with the know-how to generate effective outcomes. In facilitating a variety of interagency and multinational initiatives in many hot spots around the globe (including Iraq and Afghanistan) using SDi Meshworks design, I learned the value of patiently cultivating relationships, developing collaborative processes, and discovering the possibilities of common ground for collective action in order to make a positive impact.

Purpose of the Article: In this chapter I share a Second Tier guiding framework to help others successfully create and facilitate productive collaborative endeavors based on my experience in applying SDi concepts. Research and input from a variety of scholar-practitioners also bolster this comprehensive approach to complex challenges by establishing superordinate goals and effective ways to achieve them. Finally, I share practical applications throughout the article taken from my work in Afghanistan to illustrate how to place these ideas into action.

Intended Audience: This chapter is intended for readers who want to learn how to apply SDi theory to make a positive impact on complex challenges that affect multiple stakeholders. I want to share my learning with civil society leaders who are searching for better ways to navigate turbulence in a sea of multiple actors. This chapter on Meshworks design will serve business managers who are seeking to enhance organizational performance and take their global ventures to the next level. Government officials who want processes with which to manage complexity will find a tried and tested framework in the following pages. Social entrepreneurs will learn new ways to broaden their networks and enhance efforts to make a positive impact. This article will also support leaders of non-governmental organizations that appreciate systemic approaches to dynamic challenges.

The "5P" Framework: The following outline illustrates my "5P" approach using SDi Meshworks principles, which addresses complex challenges and integrates the features that successful multi-stakeholder initiatives commonly share:

- **Purpose:** A specific issue, challenge, opportunity, or possibility that concerns all participants and provides the reason for convening.
- **People:** The participation of multiple state and non-state actors including representatives from government, business, non-governmental organizations, academia, and civil society.

- **Place:** A space where participants meet in person (and, as needed, virtually) for the sake of dialogue.
- **Process:** A process of shared inquiry, learning, problem solving, and (potentially) decision making in new ways that address stakeholder concerns[1].
- **Practice:** The efforts made on a regular basis by stakeholders to train and develop the "skills, mind-sets and heart-sets of collaboration"[2].

First, I explore ideas around why people join multi-stakeholder initiatives and the potential superordinate goals of such forums. Stakeholder vMemes play important roles in Meshworks. Then I examine the different kinds of people involved in an SDi enterprise. Stakeholders, the convening or management team, facilitators, and storytellers are the focus in this section. Having the best possible participants, in terms of diversity, will, and capacity, plays a vital role in the outcomes of an SDi Meshworks endeavor. The place where people come together to generate dialogue is the third critical component. Stakeholders need a safe container in which to open up, connect, and design new possibilities. A thoughtfully crafted process that galvanizes stakeholder commitment is the fourth key element. An expertly facilitated process creates the possibilities for discovering mutual interests, generating future scenarios, building new relationships, and fostering pilot projects. Ways to maintain momentum and share narratives about the endeavor are also critical aspects of the SDi Meshworks process. The fifth and final element is practice; collaboration, like any successful collective endeavor, requires training and development. This comprehensive approach shows how to take the design principles of SDi and apply them to a complex challenge faced by multiple stakeholders.

Definitions: I assume the reader has a basic understanding of commonly used SDi terminology, so I will not define those here. However, to facilitate the sharing of the 5P approach a few other terms should be explained. First, the term "stakeholder" refers to both the "participation of citizens as individuals and to the participation of organized groups" who are affected

---

1 Matthew Markopoulos, "Collaboration and Multi-stakeholder Dialogue: A Review of the Literature," International Union for Conservation of Nature and Natural Resources, Version 1.1 (March 2012): p.3. Markopoulos outlines the importance of people, place, process, and purpose in multi-stakeholder collaboration. I offer practice as a fifth component.

2 David Strauss, How to Make Collaboration Work: Powerful Ways to Build Consensus, Solve Problems, and Make Decisions (San Francisco: Berrett-Koehler Publishers, 2002): p. 128.

by a complex issue and care enough to do something about it.[3] Second, "complex," "messy," and "wicked" are used interchangeably throughout this chapter to refer to issues "for which there is no consensus on the problem or on the solution, and partisan interests (potentially) block collaboration."[4] Third, I define "governance" as the "systems that bring stakeholders and institutions affected by a specific issue together to share information, explore solutions, and make collective decisions," bearing in mind that not all institutions actively seek or engage stakeholder input.[5] Lastly, I define collaboration as one path of transformation for stakeholders who want to make a positive impact. It facilitates the growth of individuals and groups who are willing to come together to explore new paradigms. I believe that "collaboration is a practice of creating new observers and new possible actions together, in a mood of commitment to take care of the concerns of all parties as best possible."[6]

Purpose

The purpose of multi-stakeholder collaboration is to enable people to come together to think, feel, and act in new ways in the form of a shared inquiry with others.[7] Beck and Cowan emphasize the need to ask the right questions and clarify desired outcomes early in the design process to help formulate superordinate goals.[8] Organizers with input from participants may have a specific purpose in mind, for example. Or, they may prefer to allow the Meshworks dynamics to emerge organically as the process unfolds. Second, people come together to collaborate for many different reasons. Understanding what stakeholders care about and developing an overarching purpose can help focus the design of an SDi endeavor.

A helpful way to understand different stakeholder perspectives is by gaining an appreciation for their vMeme values. A worldview is comprised

3   Chris Ansell and Alison Gash, "Collaborative Governance in Theory and Practice," Journal of Public Administration Research and Theory, Volume 18 (2007): p. 546.
4   Peter Denning and Robert Dunham, *The Innovator's Way: Essential Practices for Successful Innovation* (Cambridge: MIT Press, 2010): p. 315.
5   *http://www.oneearthfuture.org* as of August 1, 2013.
6   Denning and Dunham, p. 339.
7   Don Beck and Christopher Cowan, *Spiral Dynamics: Mastering Values, Leadership and Change* (Wiley-Blackwell, 2005): p. 145.
8   Don Beck and Christopher Cowan, *Spiral Dynamics: Mastering Values, Leadership and Change* (Wiley-Blackwell, 2005): p. 145.

of a stakeholder's vMeme plus their overarching beliefs about how the world is and how it should be. Stakeholders will each have unique orientations that are influenced by their age, stage in life, living circumstances, and culture. These mindsets shape how they view collaboration, and can enrich the Meshworks process if managed effectively by designers.[9]

The following chart outlines key operating mindsets at work within individuals and groups.[10] This SDi framework can help everyone involved in the Meshworks enterprise work more effectively with the variety of perspectives among various stakeholders:

SDi vMeme	Orientation	Value/ Motivation	Worldview toward Collaboration	Meshworks Considerations	Meshworks Advantages
RED	Power-Oriented/ Rebellious	Power/Survival	Survival of the Fittest	Spontaneity, Risk, Impulsive Behavior	Brainstorm, Take Bold Steps
BLUE	Traditional/ Authoritarian	Order/Security	Positional Power	Stability, Tradition, Clear Rules	Set Ground Rules and Agendas
ORANGE	Competitive/ Achievement-Oriented	Success/ Independence	Meritocracy	Status, Goals, Results, Competition	Turn Ideas into Action, Generate Outcomes
GREEN	Egalitarian/ Pluralistic	Social Networks/ Affiliation	Organizations of Equals for Mutual Benefit	Tolerance, Consensus Building	Build and Sustain Relationships
YELLOW	Integrative	Process/ Systemic Flow	Interdependence of Complex Systems	Integration and Alignment of Systems	Manage Complexity and Create Synthesis

Bringing out the strengths of each of these orientations can bolster the Meshworks process. When a group is establishing the ground rules for the

---

9   Brett Thomas, "The Leadership Rosetta Stone" (presented by the Stagen Institute, Dallas, 2011): PowerPoint slides 8–15. During the late summer and early fall of 2013 I participated in a weekly "Integral Business Coalition" conference call led by Brett Thomas, co-founder of the Stagen Institute. This ongoing dialogue helped me to apply the concept of worldview to the context of multi-stakeholder collaboration.

10   This chart and discussion on perspectives and values is grounded in the work of Don Beck and his workshops based on his book co-written with Christopher Cowan entitled *Spiral Dynamics: Mastering Values, Leadership and Change* (Wiley-Blackwell, 2005): more information available at *http://www.spiraldynamics.net;* also, training I conducted on Integral Theory at Integral Institute (*http://www.integralinstitute.org*) that focuses on Ken Wilber's prolific work, such as a book he co-wrote with Terry Patten, Adam Leonard, and Marco Morelli entitled *Integral Life Practice* (Boston: Shambhala, 2008) also informs this chart and discussion.

endeavor, for example, stakeholders who care deeply about order (Blue) will be helpful contributors. The rebels in the room (Red) have much to offer when bold and audacious ideas are needed. When the group is looking at collective action plans later in the process, stakeholders who are results-oriented (Orange) naturally provide the needed push to get good ideas into action. Those who are inclined toward tolerance (Green) will work toward the inclusion of the diverse opinions present. Participants who have a knack for seeing complex systems (Yellow) can help others connect the dots and appreciate interdependence.

What is important to recognize is which mindsets are prominent among the stakeholders present. Upon this determination all can be integrated in the best way possible to support the organic unfolding of the collaborative process. Understanding the values of the participants and why they want to contribute to the endeavor is a critical aspect in the design of a successful collaborative enterprise.

Practical Application: Rugged terrain, a myriad of diverse tribes, nationwide poverty, a weak central government, widespread corruption, multiple distinct languages, 30 years of war, and a general distrust of foreigners combine to create an incredibly complex and uncertain environment in Afghanistan. At first glance, any possibility of collaborative action seems impossible. However, this case actually provided my colleagues and me a surprising opportunity to successfully apply an SDi approach in concert with multiple stakeholders. Assisting Afghans with rebuilding rural communities after decades of conflict required an intimate understanding of social networks, the socio-economic environment, and how to build partnerships to co-create sustainable systems to meet essential needs.

The wide variety of stakeholder groups offered an equally wide variety of motivations for their respective activities in Afghanistan. Some saw collaboration as a way to help their respective elements achieve optimal results. Others saw it as a way to improve their positional power. Certain organizations, feeling overwhelmed by day-to-day activities, saw the initiative as an unnecessary drain on their already-limited resources. A handful felt they could do things on their own and did not see the value in working as part of a larger enterprise. A number of groups wanted to find a better way to coordinate activities among themselves to avoid duplication of effort and inadvertently stepping on each other's toes. All of the groups, in spite of these differences, valued stability, and urgently wanted to alleviate violence in Afghanistan.

An appreciation for that diversity helped us assess the plethora of perspectives and concerns. Various international organizations aspired to build Afghan governance capacity. Regional stability, trade and commerce, and business development motivated select stakeholder groups (Orange). International security forces wanted safety and security (Blue). Several non-governmental organizations and Afghan civil leaders were striving for social justice, education, development, and human rights (Green). Certain groups wanted to increase their political power (Red) while others competed for financial growth (Orange). Many Afghan community leaders worked hard to meet the basic needs of their villages (Beige, Purple). In rural areas, Afghans wanted to farm, procure clean water, and raise their children in relative safety (Purple). Some stakeholders just wanted to survive (Red). We sought opportunities to coalesce around these diverse interests to create superordinate goals concerning rudimentary levels of stability, development, and governance (Yellow).

The diversity of worldviews held among the various stakeholders helped us to examine the challenge of violence in Afghanistan in a systemic fashion. This led to a shared understanding of the problem and closer alignment on collective actions. By coordinating our efforts, we avoided duplication of effort, filled gaps, and addressed the roots of violence in a more comprehensive fashion. Stakeholders learned to blend security, development, and governance programs more effectively, which helped reduce violence and increase stability.

People

The diversity of worldviews shapes not only the purpose of a Meshworks endeavor but also the people that make up the enterprise. Beck and Cowan stress the importance of carefully selecting the "Streams Team" that will help manage a collaborative SDi process.[11] In my experience, the Streams Team should include the convening group of sponsors who provide a vision, convening authority, and/or the resources that make it attractive for a diverse group to come together to engage in a dialogue. Stakeholders form an inclusive group representing diverse memes who are affected by the complex challenge. Facilitators support the Meshworks process with politeness, openness, and autocracy as needed so that stakeholders can listen

---

11   Cowan and Beck, pp. 152-4.

to, respect, and learn from each other, as well as they can, in a collective inquiry to address mutual concerns.[12] Storytellers capture the narrative of the SDi process, and assessors from the management team evaluate outcomes. The size, structure, and roles of these Stream Team elements vary to a great extent. They depend on the nature of the collaborative effort, the complexity of the Meshworks issue, the needs of stakeholder groups, and the available resources.

According to Adam Kahane, the success of a Meshworks project "will depend above all on the people... (as they) will have the greatest influence on the content and consequences of the process and will also be most influenced by it."[13] Inviting people with suitable skills, values, experiences, and the perspectives that best fit the SDi challenge will produce relevant benefits. This applies to the Streams Team that is managing the Meshworks initiative, the participants in the stakeholder group, the facilitators who guide the collaborative process, and the storytellers who capture the narrative. SDi designers want a diverse and inclusive range of participants who mirror the complex system in which they live.

Practical Application: The diversity of the stakeholders and the complexity of Afghan social networks led us to pay close attention to the people aspect of this complex challenge. We established an engagement team to build rapport with Afghan ministries and international embassies. This team also set up meetings between our leaders and their Afghan counterparts in order to share information, relieve points of friction, and develop new initiatives. Our units in the field took a similar approach. As a result, our organization and its component units engaged multiple stakeholders at the national, regional, and local levels. These relationship-building efforts also helped build healthy connections between top-down resources and bottom-up needs.

Another best practice that facilitated collaboration was the use of liaison personnel. With an appreciation for key stakeholder organizations, we placed the military version of Spiral Wizards in strategic locations throughout the country. They worked side by side with Afghan ministry representatives, diplomats, local government officials, development workers, and various military and police units. Video teleconferencing and face-to-face meetings

---

12   Ibid., pp. 118-22.
13   Adam Kahane, *Working Together to Change the Future: Transformative Scenario Planning* (San Francisco: Berrett-Koehler Publishers, 2012): p. 33.

with liaison personnel facilitated our decision-making process and raised the mutual awareness of needs and available resources. Together we formed a flat network of Spiral Wizards that quickly shared information and addressed stakeholder issues in an effective manner.

Place

In addition to having the right people, the place where a Meshworks endeavor occurs is also a critical component. People need to feel comfortable to open up, share perspectives, take risks, and connect with each other. As a result, SDi designers have an opportunity to integrate politeness, openness, and autocracy into the habitat of the enterprise. According to Beck and Cowan, consideration for politeness, openness, and autocracy in the SDi Meshwork's design "creates a far more pleasant place to be for all concerned."[14] The venue then must help generate a sense of belonging and promote a relaxed environment. If this is not the case, collaboration becomes even more challenging.

Creating a Safe Container: Social and interpersonal security are crucial aspects of designing a container for the Meshworks enterprise. If people feel at ease they will be better able to lower their guards in order to become more open and available to participate. Conveners can kick off a forum by declaring the meeting venue a safe space for learning, collaboration, and support. Organizers can also articulate what safeguards have been put in place to address social and physical security. Facilitators will find it helpful to acknowledge all of the diverse voices in the room and publicly articulate that everyone belongs there. Kathryn Schulz recommends a statement such as "We can foster the ability to listen to each other and the freedom to speak our minds," which also fosters politeness and openness.[15]

Logistical Planning Considerations: The physical space and logistical support for Meshworks activities also play important roles in creating a safe, welcoming environment that is conducive to collaboration. This is where autocracy in the form of providing structure and purpose to the overall physical setting supports collaboration. David Strauss stresses that "the physical environment…has a powerful impact on a meeting."[16] Good acoustics, suitable

---

14   Cowan and Beck, p. 122.
15   Kathryn Schulz, *Being Wrong: Adventures in the Margin of Error* (New York: HarperCollins, 2010): p. 311.
16   Strauss, p. 139.

technology for sharing presentations, comfortable seating, and esthetically pleasing views all help support optimal conditions for collaboration.

Arranging the space is another way to help make the Meshworks forum conducive to cooperation. According to Strauss, "one of the most powerful interventions you can make (in a Meshworks endeavor) is to arrange the seating before a meeting begins."[17] For example, U-shaped seating and semi-circles help focus attention on developing a shared understanding of problems and possible solutions. Successful facilitators use space accordingly, with an appreciation for the needs of the group and how to support constructive conversations.

Planning the space to facilitate networking and conversation during breaks also encourages collaboration. Insightful conversations take place and new connections are made "outside the immediate work of the group"[18] as well as within formal proceedings. Stakeholders can get acquainted over a meal or a cup of coffee. Longtime practitioners of collaboration realize that "you don't build trust until you actually get to know people a little bit."[19] Away from the formal meeting, participants may feel more relaxed and find it easier to speak with each other. Setting aside the time and space for these informal conversations is instrumental to the process.

Cultural considerations also influence the planning of the space. What works best in one region may be very different from what serves stakeholders in another part of the world. A key takeaway here is the need to understand the cultural context, the needs of the group, and the resources at hand. Meshworks issues and challenges are tough enough without adding unfavorable or uncomfortable meeting conditions. Planners find it to be in the best interests of all concerned to find and enhance the best possible meeting space for collaboration.

Practical Application: We conducted Meshworks events in different locations throughout Afghanistan and occasionally in the US, depending on the needs of particular stakeholders. Security played an important role; we did everything we possibly could to provide physically safe containers for meetings. Respect for Afghan cultural norms around community gatherings also influenced the way we arranged Meshworks events in the field. We often utilized NATO and Afghan transportation resources to help bring stakeholders together from geographically dispersed areas.

---

17   Ibid.
18   Yaffee and Wondolleck, p. 23.
19   Ibid.

To prepare military leaders for their deployments, we hosted collaborative events in the US. During these forums, we had video teleconferences between stakeholders in the field and their US counterparts. This provided real-time sharing of relevant experiences and best practices. To broaden this exchange, we brought in a variety of practitioners from other government agencies and non-governmental organizations with experience in Afghanistan.

Where we hosted Meshworks events played a critical role in our planning and coordination. The places where we prepared incoming leaders as well as where we conducted collaborative activities in the field had a direct impact of the successful outcome of these endeavors.

Process

Just as careful consideration in selecting the appropriate people and place are critical factors in a successful Meshworks effort, the process that stakeholders use also requires thoughtful planning. From an SDi perspective, this means creating alignment and integration in the Meshwork's design. In alignment, we gather pertinent stakeholders with diverse vMemes to identify the root causes of the challenge and paint a comprehensive picture of what is happening in the environment. This helps us to understand what we will do with whom. This thoughtful analysis sets us up for success during the integration phase where we put our strategic vision into action. We conduct pilot projects, learn and adapt, and scale accordingly all the while scanning the environment for patterns. In this phase, then, we focus on how we should support stakeholders to address their concerns.

A Meshworks process should enable stakeholders to listen to and respect each other and to suspend judgment in order for everyone to voice new possibilities to the best of their abilities.[20] This is not just an exercise in coming together to share information. The process evolves over time as stakeholders listen to each other and learn about each other's concerns. This in turn may produce a dialogue around desired shared outcomes and how to coordinate new ideas into actionable results.

This section will be divided into three parts: pre-Meshworks, Meshworks execution, and post-Meshworks. Although this approach may appear linear at first glance, I recommend that one actually view the multi-stakeholder collaboration process as a series of learning loops that evolve over time in

---

20   Isaacs, p. 36.

support of the needs of the group. In order to enable sustainable change, collaborative dialogue needs to be an iterative process, not a one-off meeting or singular event.

Pre-Meshworks Workshop Process (Planning and Preparation): Selection of participants and location are key activities for SDi designers to conduct prior to any collaborative forum. Part of this coordination can include surveys and interviews with stakeholders in order to sense desired outcomes, who is being affected by the current challenge, what is working well, what is not working well, and perceived obstacles to progress. Another critical element of the pre-Meshworks process is to assess the potential of, conditions for, and barriers to change?[21] The research and analysis will inform the organizers and fine-tune the process. This preparation will guide SDi designers to outline what they hope participants will know, feel, and do as a result of taking part in a Meshworks endeavor.[22]

Meshworks Workshop Process (Execution): Having the facilitators declare from the beginning that the Meshworks space is a safe container and that all participants belong and will be heard will help set the right tone for the forum. Facilitators should also engage stakeholders in establishing the ways in which the group wants to resolve internal conflict and ensure inclusivity. This means actively seeking ways to delineate the norms for conflict resolution and the collaborative process. A clear understanding of the "rules of the game" for these discussions will help generate a framework for conversations throughout the Meshworks.

Framing the Challenge: With ground rules in place and a collaborative tone set, facilitators should then work closely with stakeholders to frame the problem and/or opportunity. Helpful discussion questions include:

- What are the stakeholders' Life Conditions (time, place, problems, and circumstances)?[23]

- What are the root causes and the driving issues for these Life Conditions?

- What are the interests of the stakeholders and why are these interests important?

---

21   Ibid, pp 71-103.
22   Interview with Lida Citroen, an internationally-regarded branding expert and author who has made a career of helping people and companies create new or enhanced identities: July, 2013 (more information at *http://www.lida360.com*).
23   Beck and Cowan, pp. 52-56.

- What is currently working or functioning well? How can that be shared and/or scaled?

- What needs to improve?

- What are possible scenarios for the future?

- What are the shared interests, problems, and/or opportunities?

- What is needed in order to move from shared understanding of a problem or opportunity to shared action and commitment?

Mapping the Complex System: To support the framing of the conversation, participants should collectively describe the environment in which they face the complex challenge. To support this part of the SDi design process, Beck and Cowan recommend charting the "big picture patterns and flows in the milieu."[24] Participants can provide an inventory of ongoing activities and initiatives related to the complex challenge they face. They can also visually map connections among stakeholder networks, environmental factors, and ongoing actions. Additionally, a description of constraints and obstacles will help depict the current situation.

In addition to external environmental factors, understanding what is happening below the surface (i.e., in the inner landscape of the participants) also affects stakeholder dialogue. Concerns about the misuse of power, discrimination and other grievances may very well be an integral aspect of the Meshworks challenge. Facilitators should be prepared to include these concerns.

Painting a comprehensive picture helps participants develop a shared understanding of their environment, problems, and opportunities. The collective picture belongs to the group, not just one stakeholder organization, because it integrates the diversity of perspectives in the room. Throughout the process, moderators should strive for a collective picture of viewpoints, one that is inclusive of the voices represented by the stakeholders and their organizations.

Stages of Stakeholder Group Development: As in most group endeavors, the participants go through developmental phases during a Meshworks effort. One way to help groups move through this process is to help facilitate it in progressive steps. David Johnson and Frank Johnson

---

24   Ibid, p. 156.

have identified seven stages that groups navigate with the assistance of expert facilitation:

- Define and structure process

- Conform to process and get to know one another

- Recognize mutual interests and build trust (if not respect)

- Rebel and differentiate

- Commit to and take responsibility for the goals, process, and stakeholder concerns

- Function in a mature and productive manner

- Terminate[25]

Understanding that a process goes through many evolutions helps stakeholders understand that it is normal, and expected, to have ups and downs, tension, breakdowns, and breakthroughs during the course of a Meshworks venture. Facilitators enable participants to learn and adapt accordingly as the life cycle of the multi-stakeholder collaboration develops over time. SDi conveners also learn to be patient with this progression and support its natural unfolding.

Pilot Project Design: As the group develops a comprehensive picture of their complex challenges, facilitators can start exploring the possibility of discovering common ground and shared goals. Given that inequalities and grievances are often present, the group may need to build confidence and/ or co-create alternative future scenarios among themselves. By honoring differences and employing a dialogic approach, participants learn how others view the situation from their respective viewpoints. This fosters a possibility for collective action.

When common ground emerges during the Meshworks process, facilitators can work with stakeholders to design pilot projects and prototype possibilities. According to CEO and top designer Tim Brown, prototyping:

- Explores an idea, evaluates it, and produces useful feedback to improve upon it and drive the concept forward

---

25   David Johnson and Frank Johnson, *Joining Together: Group Theory and Group Skills* (Boston: Allyn and Bacon, 1996).

- Communicates an idea with sufficient clarity to gain acceptance across a variety of stakeholder groups, prove it, and show that it will work

- Avoids costly mistakes such as becoming too complex too early and sticking with a weak idea for too long, thus producing results faster[26]

Low-hanging fruit is a smart prototyping opportunity to pursue in order for the stakeholders to gain confidence and show others that progress is possible. Pilot projects help build momentum for the Meshworks endeavor.

Implementation: When a group aligns around a pilot project, facilitators should enable stakeholders to outline a way ahead. The group should provide a detailed implementation plan with desired output and outcomes. This should also include an inventory of resources and functional capacities that are currently available to use.[27] The SDi enterprise should also articulate the criteria for success and make commitments, including:

- What task or project?

- Who is responsible for the assigned task?

- Who is the customer and who is the executor for the task?

- When? (road map or timeline for execution)

- Why? (purpose/intent of the assigned task)

- What are the conditions for success? How will these be assessed?

- How will agreements or commitments be enforced?

- How will breakdowns be addressed?

Conversations that put ideas into accountable action also help us "place the right person into the right job (project) with the right tools and support."[28] Following up on these commitments requires people with the willingness, legitimacy, and ability to get things done. They need to have some level of power, influence, and/or authority in order to persuade those in their parent organizations or communities to take new steps. The ability of group

---

26   Tim Brown, Change by Design: *How Design Thinking Transforms Organizations and Inspires Innovation* (New York: HarperCollins, 2009): pp. 87–107.

27   Beck and Cowan, p. 157.

28   Ibid., p. 168.

representatives to negotiate with their own organizations is crucial to getting solutions truly framed, explored, crafted, agreed to, and implemented.[29]

Post-Meshworks Workshop Process (Follow-Through): Designers also help the SDi enterprise to adapt to shifts in the environment and changing needs of stakeholders.[30] One way to do this is to plan for the key activities that will take place after a Meshworks workshop occurs. Assessments, following up on commitments, sharing stories, and other ways of sustaining the momentum of the SDi enterprise are critical post-Meshworks event considerations.

Momentum and Continuity: SDi designers should consider having a process in place to help ensure that collaboration continues between events. Doing so helps stakeholders maintain momentum and generates a sense of continuity. Here are some ideas to consider that can help participants stay engaged in the Meshworks process and stay informed:

- Environmental scanning and the sharing of updates

- Newsletter

- Online collaboration platforms

- Interim workshops and seminars

- Video and telephonic conferencing

Scheduling progress reviews among decision makers with resources and project leaders who are implementing the action plans also helps promote collective action. Updates also serve to monitor trust levels and downplay status distinctions.[31] Collaboration works well when stakeholders are less concerned about who gets credit and more interested in healthier relationships and positive outcomes.

Another means for sustaining momentum is to always end a meeting by announcing the next event. This could be an online conference, a social event, an in-person workshop, or whatever activity best serves the needs of

---

29   Email correspondence with Jeff Weiss, August 15, 2013. Jeff Weiss is a partner at Vantage Partners where he leads the Sales Effectiveness consulting practice. Prior to founding Vantage, Jeff helped to build Conflict Management Group, a non-profit consulting firm that works with governments around the world on managing conflicts of public importance. Jeff was also a member of the Harvard Negotiation Project. His work on the topics of negotiation, strategic relationship management, cross-matrix collaboration, and partnering has been published extensively.
30   Beck and Cowan, pp. 169-70.
31   Ibid., p. 171.

the group. Connecting and building upon collaborative forums stimulates stakeholder interest and generates a sense of forward movement for the group.

Developing a Meshworks Narrative: We can think of a meaningful Meshworks initiative as an engaging story. Stakeholders come together to collectively face a challenge. These heroes face risk and uncertainty as they struggle with the given issue. They experience exciting highs and frustrating lows during their journeys of inquiry. Insights and "aha" moments might even generate transformational development as participants discover new ways of seeing themselves and others, and as they learn new ways to deal with the issues at hand. Resolution of a challenge builds stakeholder confidence while making a positive impact. As participants return to their organizations and communities, they bring back and share their stories of their Meshworks experience. This is also a healthy manifestation of the Red vMeme in which a mythology can grow amongst stakeholders who share this hero's journey.[32]

Creating a narrative about the Meshworks initiative also enables stakeholders to share their compelling journeys of challenge, struggle, and triumph. It is transmitted inside the group in order to learn from victories, setbacks, and best practices. Sharing stories outside of the stakeholder group can also be a powerful way to communicate the outcomes of the Meshworks, highlight the successes, and embolden others to participate.

Practical Application: The design and implementation of a systematic approach to helping community leaders provide alternatives to violence required a deep appreciation of Afghan culture. To learn about the complexities of life in Afghanistan, my civil-military interdisciplinary team designed a series of collaborative forums. On a regular basis we brought stakeholders together with experts in Afghan politics, culture, history, and economics to identify mutual problems and opportunities, search for common ground, and develop collective action plans.

We also expended considerable effort observing local customs in order to incorporate some of the effective ideas for security, governance, and economic development that already existed in villages. Witnessing these examples of positive deviance helped us co-design and implement a comprehensive strategy with our Afghan partners that incorporated relevant best practices and respected cultural norms. To scale this grassroots initiative, I prepared our senior leaders to engage senior Afghan officials in bringing

---

32   Ibid., p. 9.

parts of this effort into law, which bolstered legitimacy within the Afghan government. Senior leader engagements played a key role throughout this Meshworks endeavor to ensure that our efforts worked hand in hand with those of our Afghan and international counterparts.

Prototyping also helped us scale community mobilization efforts for rural areas. We frequently hosted video teleconferences so that our teams in the field, Afghan stakeholders, and interagency partners across the country could share best practices and address emerging needs. These collaborative forums facilitated rapid decision making and information exchanges. We constantly shared what experiments were (and were not) working well in water management, economic development, agriculture, security, and governance projects.

To assist in assessing and sharing the outcomes of these programs, I augmented my team with analysts from a think tank, including an Afghan-American. Together we synthesized reports from our field teams, surveys of rural Afghans, and analysis of economic and governance trends. We then distributed monthly assessment reports within our stakeholder network. This storytelling helped articulate impacts, allocate resources efficiently, and bolster Afghan confidence.

Additionally, I recruited an Emmy-award-winning photojournalist to help us capture stakeholder perspectives, lessons learned, and stories of rural Afghans rebuilding their communities. We made copies of the videos and shared them with incoming units and other partners who worked with us. We also distributed the videos to training centers in Afghanistan and the US and used them during planning workshops. These videos helped transfer knowledge to incoming teams and create continuity with interested stakeholders.

Practice

Practice is an integral aspect of the Meshworks endeavor because it helps us grow and develop along the Spiral. According to Innes and Booher, "collaborative dialogue…requires skills, training, and adherence to a set of practices that run counter to the norms of discussion to which many people are accustomed."[33] Just as an athlete trains off of the field in preparation for competition, the SDi practitioner practices the skills of collaboration

---

33   Innes and Booher, p. 37.

in preparation for successfully engaging in collaborative endeavors. These skills are not just conceptual understandings, but performance skills that are learned though practice. Through repetition and training, supervised by coaches, practitioners learn to embody collaborative behavior so that it can ultimately become second nature.

Practice is vital to Meshworks endeavors. *Theories* of SDi, conflict management, complex-systems thinking, project management, and facilitation provide intellectual building blocks for multi-stakeholder collaboration. Taking these concepts and putting them into *action* to see what works and does not work in a given situation is just as imperative to learning. New ideas are not enough. Stakeholders must experience coordination for themselves to genuinely appreciate its value and embody new behaviors.

I have found that practices that help people learn about themselves, how to relate to others, and how to respond to a complex environment support success in a Meshworks enterprise. Leonard Riskin offers, "For a person to appropriately implement the strategies associated with the new approaches to mediation and negotiation and lawyering (and multi-stakeholder collaboration), she must have a set of foundational capacities including awareness, emotional sophistication, and understanding."[34] Intrapersonal skills help practitioners learn to suspend judgment and be open to new possibilities. Through reflective practice, people can better appreciate their own perspectives, filters, strengths, and weaknesses. Building interpersonal capacity to listen to and connect with others serves stakeholders who engage with others on complex challenges. Having the ability to deal with unexpected changes in a chaotic environment helps practitioners adapt and overcome challenges in concert with other actors.

Conveners and managers of Meshworks endeavors ought to consider the component of practice in the overall design up front. Diverse stakeholders learn in diverse ways, therefore SDi designers ought to "create a learning environment that befits a variety of styles."[35] A variety of different practices that suit the needs of participants can be included in the process of a Meshworks event and taught in the planning and start-up of the activity. They can also be introduced as needed during the course of the Meshworks initiative. Sponsors might offer follow-up training and coaching to support

---

34   Leonard L. Riskin, "Mindfulness: Foundational Training for Dispute Resolution," *Journal of Legal Education*, Volume 54, Number 1 (March 2004): p. 83.
35   Beck and Cowan, pp. 149-50.

participants between formal meetings. Planners should consider what would be best for participants in terms of whether to provide collaborative practices before, during, and/or after a formal Meshworks event.

Practical Application: In Afghanistan, my interdisciplinary team worked in an ever-changing and chaotic environment. Consequently, I introduced some simple Aikido-based exercises into our routine.[36] We found that centering and blending practices helped us to be more effective in highly stressful situations. For centering, I invited my colleagues to each be aware of their body's center of gravity. With practice, they became increasingly aware of when they would "go into their heads" and become off balance. Sensing their feet on the ground, they would come back to center and re-engage the challenge at hand. In blending, my teammates and I would practice settling in our bodies, facing each other in an alert and relaxed manner, and then extending toward each other in a spirit of exploring what was possible without losing our own perspective. As we moved closer to one another, sensing each other's energy and mood, and our own physical sensations, we then blended our individual moves, thus creating a new collective movement. This practice helped us embody collaboration in concert with other people in a stressful environment. I knew I was on to something beneficial for the group when one of my colleagues stated that he would have appreciated starting this practice even sooner than we did (and practicing it more often).

Summary

In the early stages of an SDi enterprise we consider the issues, stakeholders and their intentions, and the complex environment in which they mesh. This helps us to broaden our apertures and create new understanding. As this exploration ripens we take our enhanced understanding and transform it into new possibilities. This can take the form of developing future scenarios and/or pilot projects. To maintain momentum and deepen learning, we share stories, practice new skills, and assess the outcomes of our initiatives. As we learn by doing, members of

---

36   I first started training in somatics with Richard Strozzi Heckler in 1991. He is the founder of Strozzi work and of the Strozzi Institute. A nationally known speaker, coach and consultant on leadership and mastery, he has spent four decades researching, developing, and teaching the practical application of somatics (the unity of language, action, emotions, and meaning) to leaders in business, non-profit organizations, and government, including the military. He is also a renowned martial arts teacher and has published extensively on the topics of leadership, coaching, Aikido, and somatics.

the Meshworks endeavor continuously refine, adapt, and align the five components to achieve superordinate goals.

Practical Application: An appreciation for Afghan culture played an integral role in our collaborative approach to successfully addressing socio-economic needs in impoverished villages. Close observation showed us positive deviance and culturally relevant solutions. Brainstorming helped us discover common ground. Collaborative forums facilitated collective action. Storytelling generated momentum. A collaborative approach, embraced by our senior and junior leaders, helped build a countrywide network of stakeholders. This network coalesced around mutual interests that focused on security, stability, development, and governance at the local, regional, and national levels. By building bridges between Kabul-based organizations and rural communities, we helped our partners connect resources with needs and thus make inroads in building sustainable support systems.

These collaborative efforts produced tangible results. Our assessments showed that security conditions improved where we instituted these collaborative programs, which also allowed Afghans to bring goods to market and generate income to provide for their basic needs. Afghan local police successfully withstood attacks and protected their communities. Rural Afghan citizens consequently began to respect and appreciate their local police. Logistical systems grew to connect Afghan central government resources with rural community needs and provide the beginnings of a pipeline of essential services. Rural Afghan leaders, seeing the success of these initiatives, requested similar programs in their villages. As a result, rural Afghans working with multiple stakeholders successfully mobilized over 40 districts and 100 rural villages in less than two years. Senior NATO, embassy, and Afghan officials applauded these collaborative efforts. Ultimately, this Meshworks effort continues to evolve, grow, and reach new villages every month, demonstrating its power and sustainability.

Conclusion

Applying SDi theory to multi-stakeholder collaboration is a challenging endeavor, but one that is sorely needed in our complex and uncertain world. Successful multi-stakeholder collaboration requires risk taking, persistence, patience, and a balanced and integrated blend of the 5Ps (Purpose. People. Place. Process. Practice.). A well-designed process and supportive container enable stakeholders to learn from each other as they collaborate and overcome the inherent challenges in tackling wicked problems. Appreciating one another's worldviews, participants develop overarching goals that transcend stove-piping and individual agendas. With sustained practice, stakeholders coalesce around a superordinate purpose to mobilize resources and align in collective action.

In Afghanistan, we applied Meshwork principles in a comprehensive fashion to help stakeholders address urgent and important needs. Senior leaders set a positive example in our organization and in the NATO headquarters in Kabul. They empowered their units to flatten communications and build partnerships with a wide variety of stakeholders. This also supported the strategic placement of liaison personnel throughout the country to form a dynamic network for information sharing, decision-making, and action. A dependable communications platform enabled the network to quickly bring stakeholders together to share information, solve problems, connect needs with resources, and build relationships. Our teams at the grassroots level built trust and confidence as stakeholders saw that the network responded to their concerns in a timely manner. As a result of this cumulative effort, we took isolated pockets of coordinated action and transformed them into a countrywide collaborative network.

A successful Meshworks enterprise requires competent facilitators, dedicated participants, an effective process, relevant pilot projects, and compelling storytelling. Members of an effective Spiral Streams Team seek a healthy balance between analysis, action, and reflection as they learn and develop a collaborative mindset over time. They also practice integrating the right mix of relationship building, task accomplishment, and process development as they address their common challenges. When done right, multi-stakeholder collaboration generates dynamic results that make a positive impact in society and create healthy social networks. A systematic approach that thoughtfully integrates the 5Ps helps create the synergy necessary to transform ourselves, our organizations, and the complex challenges we face into new possibilities for peace and prosperity throughout the Spiral of Life.[37]

---

37   For those readers who would like a more in-depth look at the 5P approach to multi-stakeholder collaboration, please go to the following web-site to download my report: *http://oneearthfuture.org/research/publications/multi-stakeholder-collaboration-how-government-business-and-non-governmental*

SDi AND SPIRITUALITY: A PERSPECTIVE FROM THE MINISTRY

By Rev. Dr. Jim Lockard

My early years in ministry, which began in 1995, were peppered with paradox as I tried to teach people to develop and expand an awareness of their inner divinity. My lived experience of spiritual community during this period saw misunderstanding, conflicts, people being wounded within the community, and my own degrees of frustration, exhaustion, and burnout. I wondered what the problem was. Were people just naturally resistant to one another and to the discovery of their own empowerment? Was I adequately prepared to be a spiritual leader and teacher? Was the philosophy that I had studied and worked to embody a false doctrine? Why was everything so hard?

I should point out that I am a minister in an organization called Centers for Spiritual Living, a metaphysical denomination. I am not in a traditional church, synagogue or mosque. The philosophy that my denomination teaches (more about it later) is very amenable to the concept of evolution and the discoveries of science. My perspective on the application of Spiral Dynamics Integral (SDi) is likely different than those of more tradition-based ministers.

After receiving certification in SDi 1 & 2 in 2003, I started to see what was actually going on. vMemes were clashing! I literally had no awareness that such a dynamic as evolutionary cultural development existed. Now, I thought, I could get somewhere. I began to create presentations of the model for fellow ministers in my organization, Centers for Spiritual Living1. As a member of the Board of Directors, I was sent to the SDi training to evaluate the model for use on an organization-wide basis. Over the next two years, most of our ministers were introduced to the model.

I became very interested in the model and began to use it on an everyday basis. For the first time, I was able to understand some of the differences in worldviews that I encountered in my own congregation and in other people in my life, i.e. family, friends, interfaith program acquaintances, etc. I quickly saw the value of the model in understanding that many worldviews were arising from vMeme differences. The resulting conflicts were, therefore, both predictable and resolvable to the extent that people could understand the model. That became my challenge. But first, a bit of an overview.

As Ken Wilber notes in his book, *Integral Spirituality* (Shambhala (2007), most religions operate at the Purple to Blue levels, providing some degree of structure for Purple and Red and the underpinnings for the Blue value system in a culture. The depictions of the deity are designed to be understood at these levels and are usually magical/mythical in nature. This system worked very well for hundreds of years in what was to become the developed West, because there was a balance of the vMemes or levels of existence and the Life Conditions present. The religions of the West, in particular, provided a sense of stability in the value systems, although, like their surroundings, they were operating at the vMemes of the day.

It was with the emergence of Orange/Modernism that the Western religions began to lose their traction within the culture. The scientific/rational worldview emerged during the Enlightenment, which was essentially a break from the dogmas of the Church which were inadequate to explain emerging scientific discoveries and the accompanying rise of rational thought. This new rational/scientific worldview was the hallmark of the emerging Orange vMeme and it spread into mainstream society which increasingly could no longer relate to the deities as represented by the major Western religions. This development, combined with the two great wars of the Twentieth Century set the stage for the secularization of Europe and, somewhat ironically, for the move toward fundamentalism in the United States. Although the US is becoming more secular, there is also a significant "fundamentalism factor" that has moved from

---

1   At that time, Centers for Spiritual Living was two separate organizations, Religious Science International and United Church of Religious Science. There was a merger in 2012 and the name was changed to Centers for Spiritual Living.

religion into politics. The evolutionary impulse being what it is, it is certain that the fundamentalism that currently exists will wane over time; however, it continues to have a significant effect on current American life.

There has been a rise in church attendance over the past 50 years in more conservative and fundamentalist denominations and among non-denominational Christian communities, while so-called mainstream Christian denominations have been shrinking. However, the fastest-growing category is among those who declare themselves "unchurched" or who live largely secular lives. Yet, many of these people, who are centered at the higher level Orange and Green vMemes, are highly spiritual.

A question for the United States, and, for that matter, all of the developed West, is: How to serve the more evolutionarily advanced spiritual needs of those in Orange through Second Tier? With the increased presence of those operating at the Green vMeme there is both a clear desire for spiritual connection, and a general rejection of the old paradigm, Purple to Blue based models of traditional organized religion.

The Moderns, or those in the Orange vMeme, seek ways to improve themselves. In our New Thought communities, where there is little or no dogma and the focus is on personal growth, these people want classes in prosperity and how to be successful in their lives. They want to network and they are very open to the church as a bazar, with things for sale, a book and gift shop for example. Orange wants to be recognized for their giving, often in a very public way (think of the big check for photo opportunities in the corporate/non-profit world). They want to be recognized as a "pillar of the church" and have their name published as a major giver in the bulletin. They also want the church to be run like a business.

Often called the Cultural Creatives[2] and said to consist of over 40 million people in North America alone, the growing population in the Green vMeme is just beginning to make their presence felt in the institutions of our culture. While those at Orange seek personal development in the realm of getting more and better (success, prosperity, relationships), those at Green seek connection and a deeper experience of the spiritual. This is often accompanied by a re-awakening of the Purple vMeme in the form of a strong desire for ritual, symbolism, and, in some cases, idols and talismans.

---

2 *The Cultural Creatives: How 50 Million People Are Changing the World*, by Paul H. Ray, Ph.D., and Sherry Ruth Anderson, Broadway Books (2001).

Cultural Creatives who attend church seek (and demand) authenticity, honesty, clarity, and deep connection. They do not want to participate in programs that convey status, e.g. naming buildings or "pillars of the church" as a way to raise more funds. This creates a challenge for raising funds when you have both Orange and Green present in significant numbers. They also want to know that their children are in youth programs that feature substance, good values and connection – and healthy snacks! If they are extraverts, the minsters will hear their ideas and suggestions loud and clear; if introverts, then the message will be delivered more subtly. But it will be delivered.

Cultural Creatives do not value loyalty as such (certainly not in the way that those operating at Blue do), so they will feel free to move around if something is not to their liking – after trying to influence the process to make the necessary changes. Being resistant to hierarchy, they will often feel that the organization of the spiritual community is cold or bureaucratic. They want personal connection and do not respond well to overall rules that (to them) inhibit doing what seems best for all.

A major challenge for spiritual communities, and, for that matter, for all organizations with multiple vMemes present, is how to serve the variety of value systems present. A much larger challenge is to do this without an awareness of SDi or other relevant cultural evolutionary models. I cannot address the latter, but as to the former, it is a matter of first recognizing that the differences exist and second, creating an environment of greater awareness of the dynamics involved.

Perhaps a word about Second Tier is appropriate here. I see a few people who are operating at Yellow or Turquoise in our larger organization, and, occasionally, in my own community. My experience with them is that if they find something with which they personally resonate strongly, they will tend to stay around. If that does not happen, they leave. What they resonate with is often our teaching (more about that later), but also, I find that they can find in our organization a vehicle for leadership that surrounds them with people who are in the higher levels of complexity. Centers for Spiritual Living is currently centered in Green, with a large contingent of Orange and a very few at Blue and a few Second Tier folks at the other end of the spectrum. This is a fairly rare situation in American religion today. It is, I would say, one of the few opportunities for a person at Second Tier to participate in spiritual community as part of a larger organization with international scope.

Centers For Spiritual Living

The Science of Mind™[3] is a philosophy developed by Ernest Holmes early in the 20th Century. The essence of the philosophy is that God, or Spirit is the Creative Intelligence of the Universe and is both infinite and personal. Spirit created the universe (and any others that may exist) out of Itself and the creation then became part of the Creator. The "Mind" in Science of Mind is Spirit and the intelligences of the creation (such as your mind and mine) are all aspects of the same Mind. Evolution is the means by which the universe becomes more complex in a self-organizing fashion. We humans are creative by means of our thought, and, as self-aware beings, we provide a conscious vehicle for the expression of Spirit.

The idea of evolution being an essential aspect of human and cultural development, as postulated in the SDi model, is consistent with the worldview of the Science of Mind. The Science of Mind is a spiritual and psychological philosophy that is based on evolution as an essential aspect of reality. The Science of Mind is the philosophy taught in spiritual communities that are affiliated with Centers for Spiritual Living.

From a historical perspective, the Science of Mind is considered a New Thought philosophy, part of a family of denominations which arose during the late 19th and early 20th Centuries. The historical roots go back through Mary Baker Eddy's Christian Science (although Christian Science is not considered New Thought today), the American Transcendentalists, and on back through the Western mystery schools, the Platonists and new-Platonists, the Gnostics, and beyond. A good description of this history is summed up in "The Perennial Philosophy", by Huxley[4]. The philosophy developed as part of the spiritual healing movement and has remained consistent with the modern research on brain/body/mind science and the influence of thoughts, emotions, and beliefs on one's life. The Science of Mind can be said to be a combination of mysticism, psychology, science, and theology to create a practical basis for successful living and the realization of spiritual connection.

---

3   For more information about The Science of Mind, you can read *The Science of Mind*, by Ernest Holmes (Putnam 1938) or visit *www.CSL.org*.

4   *The Perennial Philosophy: An Interpretation of the Great Mystics, East and West*, by Aldous Huxley (Harper-Collins1945)

The primary methodologies taught in the Science of Mind are affirmative prayer and meditation. Affirmative prayer, also called spiritual mind treatment, uses affirming statements and visualization to create new, healthier belief patterns in the subconscious mind. Meditation, taught in various forms, is for the purpose of learning to quiet the conscious mind to generate a more positive and empowered state of being. There is no specific dogma, or required beliefs in the Science of Mind philosophy, save the idea of an infinite God or Spirit that is best realized and related to from within each person.

The Centers for Spiritual Living is an organization of some 450 spiritual communities and other kinds of ministries around the world, but located primarily in North America. The most prevalent kind of ministry is a "center," which functions much like a church (the term church has generally been dropped, but is still in use in some places), with one or more ministers, practitioners (trained in affirmative prayer for others), and a membership that may run from a dozen or so to several thousand. Examples of how these centers are generally known are: *Center for Spiritual Living New York* or *Namaste Center for Spiritual Living*, although some do not use the Center for Spiritual Living descriptor in their name.

The prevalent vMemes present across the organization are Green and Orange, with a smattering of Blue and Second Tier at each end. It can also be said that there are strains of Purple that present themselves among some adherents as a love for ritual and symbolism. When ministers gather, the Green vMeme is most prevalent, and the business meetings take on this flavor – lots of processing is done, decision making is by consensus, collaboration is valued (every voice must be heard!), and hierarchy is always suspect. Those centered at Orange (who often have the largest membership in their centers) tend to prefer quicker decision making, more straightforward language, and more competitive election processes, but they are outnumbered as a general rule.

My Experience With SDi In Ministry

The center where I currently serve as Spiritual Leader is in Simi Valley, California, a bedroom community near Los Angeles. Simi Valley is fairly conservative in nature (home of the Ronald Reagan Presidential Library), and we are the only New Thought community in the city of 135,000 people. The membership of the Center for Spiritual Living Simi Valley is, in my observation, largely Blue and Orange, reflective of the general population. Those who regularly attend are, to be sure, more open versions of those vMemes. However, there are very few who are centered at Green, as would be the case in many other centers. Our board of trustees does not operate by consensus, and there are few of the Green-level concerns about every voice being heard, etc. As Spiritual Leader, I often have to remind people of those more complex values such as collaboration, so that we maintain a more spiritually mature tenor in our official business activities.

Simi Valley is the third center that I have served since learning about SDi. The first was in south Florida, in a more urban beach community with a large gay and lesbian population. The membership was heavily Orange with an emerging Green – little if any Blue. Due to the larger size of the community (it ranged from 300 to nearly 1,000 during my tenure), there were places and programs for those of different value systems, orientations, and preferences to go for activities. We all came together for Sunday services and for Science of Mind classes.

It was in Florida that I began to tailor written communications to the different vMemes present. The annual campaign letters contained sections for Blue (give out of loyalty and obligation), Orange (give to get recognized) and Green (give to be part of the community and for mutual support). I found that if you speak to someone's central vMeme they strongly respond to that and do not focus on the messages to other vMemes. We hired a planned giving consultant and, working with SDi, we were able to significantly increase the financial well-being of the community.

The next center where I served was in a wealthy community north of Los Angeles. Here, the primary vMeme present was Orange – people wanted success! There were fewer volunteers at this community. People were paid to make the coffee on Sunday, do sound for the services, etc. There was a dominant management class centered at Orange and they generally preferred to hire people rather than serve themselves. Into the mix were a few in transition from Orange to Green and I noticed that they became increasingly restive as they faced the realization that they no longer fit into the dominant group. Of course, this was often described as the group changing by those who did not have the degree of self-awareness necessary to notice that the changes were going on within them.

At this community, the messages that I gave and the written communication was largely at the Orange level with some emphasis on the mystical aspects of the Science of Mind philosophy for those willing to stretch in that direction. There was an emphasis on prosperity classes and classes to create better relationships and/or find one's soul mate. There were lots of social events, often high-end dinners and trips to the nearby wine country. That said, it was a fairly close knit community where many felt supported and there were long-term groups who met over periods of years in mastermind and other formats. I would come to see that these close connections were often defined by vMeme value systems and degrees of openness of the vMeme.

The Blue end of the spectrum presented shortly after my arrival in an interesting way. A staff minister (a lesbian) requested to start a gay and lesbian outreach program on one Thursday night each month. This center is located in a relatively wealthy, suburban area some distance from urban Los Angeles. The gay and lesbian population in that area is small as compared with a typical urban area, and we had very few LGBT members. The senior ministerial staff approved the outreach program and the minister placed a small ad in the local paper announcing the first meeting.

That weekend, my telephone began to ring. Angry members, some of them on the board of trustees, were calling. They were upset that we were undertaking such a "controversial" program as a gay and lesbian outreach without the approval of the board or a discussion with the membership. The issue was addressed the following Sunday during the services when the senior ministers spoke about being an open and inclusive community. A meeting was called during the next week and had a very angry tenor. A number of families left the membership, including some in leadership, as a result of the conflict.

Once this unfolded, I realized the dynamics at play. Since I had only been at the center for a few weeks, I had not fully identified the vMemes present and the degree of social conservatism present in a large segment of the membership. It was surprising to see such a response to a gay and lesbian outreach in our organization, as at least half of our ministers organization-wide are gay or lesbian. And, of course, I had personally just come from a center with a large LGBT population in the membership. It did show the difference in vMemes present between my previous urban/beach center and this high socio-economic suburban center.

Subsequently, I took the position as Spiritual Leader of the Center for Spiritual Living Simi Valley, California in 2008. While close geographically to my prior community, which I would describe as management class conservative, Simi Valley is distinctly more of a working-class conservative town. There are dozens of fundamentalist Christian churches of all sizes, several mainstream Christian churches, thirteen wards of the Church of Jesus Christ of Latter-Day Saints, two Catholic Churches, one synagogue, and two mosques, and us. Long a bedroom community of Los Angeles, Simi Valley is distant enough that the early settlers were ranchers and the suburbs grew largely out of the ability of police, firefighters, and tradespeople from the entertainment industry to live a distance from work in the 1960's and 1970's.

Our center draws from this community and beyond. Most of our members are progressives politically, but we have a sizeable contingent of conservatives as well. The defining characteristic of those who attend our center would be tolerance of differences – and don't talk about the differences. As I noted earlier, the predominant vMeme is Orange with a significant Blue presence and a smaller amount of Green. I find that those centered at Green who arrive, usually find their way to other spiritual communities closer to Los Angeles proper, where there is a much heavier Green presence.

Of course, vMemes, while significant, are not the only factor that draws people to spiritual communities. There are other aspects, such as social needs, the desire for spiritual education for children, intellectual level (the Science of Mind is a philosophy based on ideas and tends to attract people with strong intellects), and the temperament of the membership (things like enough introverts and extraverts, people with specific interests, etc.). We have a thriving men's group that meets for both social and spiritual reasons, a well-known youth minister who attracts young families on a regional basis, and my style of presentation and teaching tends to attract certain people and repel others.

That being said, the vMeme factor is significant. I find, for example, that some of the guest presenters who make a circuit of New Thought communities, and Centers for Spiritual Living in particular, are not well-received by my membership. Those presenters would tend to teach from a heavily Green perspective or from a Second Tier level without adequate translation to Blue and Orange. I seek out guest speakers and teachers with the capacity to speak to the more practical aspects of spirituality. Those I bring in include Buddhists monks (one who rides a Harley Davidson motorcycle), rabbis, other New Thought Ministers and a few secular presenters.

It is also important to recognize that none of us is completely in any particular vMeme and very few of us are heavily centered in just one. I believe that most of us at any given point are somewhere in transition from one level to another – in other words, we are in a place of uncertainty, even chaos. While this is the creative crucible from which the new emerges, it is also uncomfortable. As a minister, much of my counseling practice is for people in these transitional phases, in a Gamma Trap, as described in the model. My role is often to help them to recognize this and to give them tools to move into a smoother trajectory toward what is next for them.

This is one reason that I have conducted SDi introductory classes on a fairly regular basis at my center. I strongly suggest that those who are in leadership or who are interested in leadership in the future attend, but it is open to all. A result is a generally greater awareness of the existence of vMemes and their differences among the membership. SDi terms creep into the conversations, and often newcomers want to know what they mean, so their interest in the model is piqued. There is, I believe, great value in blending spiritual education with training in evolutionary development.

Tips For Using SDi In Ministry

First, we must have a solid foundation in the model. In a sense, learning SDi is like learning a new language. There are the major points, the vMemes and how they operate. However, the details and the subtleties are where it is easy to get tripped up. I often see people new to the model who go on a "labeling spree" of other people without realizing that people are complex and that all of the vMemes are present in each person to one degree or another. Sometimes the "center of gravity" vMeme is easy to identify, but that does not necessarily give an accurate picture of the person in general. I find that one common pattern is for someone to be predominantly at Blue in their home life and predominantly at Orange in their work life. As a minister or counselor, how I respond to them would depend on which area of their life a problem is located.

Many people I work with are in transition between vMemes. The SDi model identifies the Gamma Trap as that place between levels of existence where we find that what used to work no longer works. Here we tend to do the same thing with greater urgency and to little or no, or even to a deleterious, effect. Often, people stay in this in between state for long periods of time. I find many people in this place in my ministry, possibly because a major feature of our teaching is personal transformation.

When I counsel someone who is between vMemes or when I have them in class, I focus on helping them to realize that they do have the ability to direct their own experience to a greater degree, and provide psychological methods, such as visualization, to help them to get to the next level on a smoother trajectory. If appropriate to the situation, I may give them some instruction in the model and in the dynamic that they are confronting. This can give them an expanded perspective of both their situation and their capacities to direct their experience in a more empowered way.

But I must remember that the complexities of life cannot be fully explained by any model. "We do not grow absolutely, chronologically. We grow sometimes in one dimension, and not in another; unevenly. We grow partially. We are relative. We are mature in one realm, childish in another. The past, present, and future mingle and pull us backward, forward, or fix us in the present. We are made up of layers, cells, constellations." ~ Anais Nin

Bruce Sanguin, an evolutionary minister in the United Church of Canada and author of *The Emerging Church* (Copperhouse 2008), speaks of the role of clergy in terms of evolutionary development. "If we can create the kind of spaciousness to encompass the emergence of the new," Sanguin says, the spiritual community can fulfill its mission to create "the capacity and the willingness to pre-sense and presence the future that needs [the] congregation in order to emerge." The implications of such a Second Tier approach to ministry are significant. "Particular to an evolutionary worldview we open to and exemplify what Teilhard de Chardin called 'zest' for the adventure of becoming," says Sanguin. To understand this beautiful idea is to provide a sense of great joy; we would expect people to be "on fire with love".

The fact that so many of us are not "on fire with life" leads to another question from Sanguin, "What happened in your life and in your collective life (the lives of your ancestors) that traumatized you in such a way that you do not wake up every day with a sense of awe and wonder? What is the trauma that shut us down from being on fire with love?" This collective malaise, if not recognized and approached in a positive, therapeutic manner, can lead to the inability of the spiritual community to fulfill any mission involving the expression of an awakened love.

We are called, I believe, to a higher level of evolutionary expression. If any kind of organized religion or spirituality is to remain relevant in an evolving culture, there must be an awakening to the evolutionary impulse and how it manifests in human lives. The concepts of the deity and the understanding of the nature of reality must evolve as human understanding evolves. Fixed notions are no longer tenable. Everything is in flux except, perhaps, the Ultimate Reality that we call by various names, including God. But that Ultimate Reality is unknowable except through an evolving understanding of ourselves, of other humans, and of the universe in which we live. We may never arrive at the ultimate knowledge, but we will continue to expand and deepen our awareness.

I am encouraged by the interest among many in ministry in the SDi model. Seminaries and ministerial education programs of all stripes would do well to incorporate the model into their programs. At the same time, more research needs to be done involving the model and its applications. Cross-disciplinary conversations must occur to fully integrate the model into our culture in a way that will foster greater awareness and understanding of the evolutionary nature of human and cultural development.

As for my personal life, I do seek leading-edge concepts and models, but I do not always use them directly in my role as spiritual leader of the Simi Valley center. I have a variety of connections and groups that I participate in beyond my ministry. In addition to being certified in SDi, I am also certified in SD21[5], and share a ministerial coaching business with my wife. My ministry, as I approach it, is best served by meeting people and challenging them toward greater awareness where they are, and in such a way that they are best served in living the best lives of which they are capable. To do this, I need to have a rich life beyond my ministry. I find that my knowledge of SDi is essential in meeting the goals of ministry and in living my own life to the fullest.

---

5   SD21 is trademarked by Cindy Wigglesworth of Deep Change, Inc. and is a coaching and assessment process for spiritual intelligence, based in part on the work of Ken Wilber, Jody Frye, and SDi.

Bibliography

Anais Ninn, *Diary Of Anais Nin* Volume 4 1944-1947: Vol. 4, (Houghton Mifflin Harcourt, 1972)

Don Edward Beck and Christopher Cowan, *Spiral Dynamics: Mastering Values, Leadership and Change*, (Wiley-Blackwell, 1995)

Ernest S. Holmes, *The Science of Mind: A Philosophy, A Faith, A Way of Life*, (Tarcher-Penguin Publishers, 1938).

Aldous Huxley, *The Perennial Philosophy: An Interpretation of the Great Mystics, East and West*, (Harper and Row Publishers, Inc. 1944).

Paul H. Ray, Ph.D., and Sherry Ruth Anderson, *The Cultural Creatives: How 50 Million People Are Changing the World,* (Broadway Books 2001).

Bruce Sanguin, *The Emerging Church: A Model for Change and a Map for Renewal*, (Copperhouse, 2008).

Cindy Wigglesworth, *SQ 21: The Twenty-One Skills of Spiritual Intelligence*, Select Books, 2012).

Wilber, Ken, *Integral Spirituality: A Startling New Role for Religion in the Modern World,* (Shambhala Publications, 2011).

SDi AND MONEY

By Said Dawlabani

This is a slightly edited version of Chapter 3, MEMEnomics: The Next-Generation Economic System. 2013, Select Books, New York, NY.

> *The best way to destroy the capitalist system is to debauch the currency.*[1]

—VLADIMIR LENIN

The United States has been through three different MEMEnomics cycles. In Spiral Dynamics Integral (SDi) terms, these are value systems life cycles that relate to the economy as one of the vMeme attractors that form an entire value system. The first cycle began with the end of the Civil War and the beginning of Reconstruction, and the last is ending during this era. Special emphasis will be placed on the many factors that have aligned to create the perfect storm, which culminated in the financial crisis of 2008 and entered the United States into the entropy phase of the third cycle. Although the United States economy seems to be slowly recovering, the shocks from the structural faults that were decades in the making have permanently exposed the speculative and risky nature of the current expression of capitalism. In Chapter One of my book, I briefly chronicled the evolution of capitalism through the eyes of policy makers as it became identified primarily through financial innovation. Up until the time when the US dollar was taken off the gold standard in 1971, the finance function in an economy, whether it

---

[1] Michael V. White and Kurt Schuler, "Retrospective, Who Said 'Debauch the Currency': Keynes or Lenin?" *Journal of Economic Perspectives,* Volume 23, Number 2, (Spring 2009) 213-222.

was lending activities or raising capital, was a measure of current and future productive output of our economy.

In the last four decades, money has gone through a monumental shift that has violated that historic role; it has become a part of productive output itself. It is this dramatic shift in the role of finance, a classic case of the tail that wagged the dog in the functioning of an economy that must be understood from a vMeme perspective in order for capitalism to correct its course and emerge to higher levels of healthy expressions. To better understand the damage that continues to be caused by having a finance-based economy I will briefly chronicle the historic role money played in human emergence. Observation of the history of economic development through the vMeme prism differs from those observations of a traditional historian of economics. The goal is to show that the function of money was naturally and historically identified with the Blue system with a limited but highly regimented role in the Orange system. This meant that Orange financial innovation had to remain a function of Blue productive output in order for the system to remain healthy. The deviation from those historically proven standards and the false belief by policy makers at the top that financial innovation can move the functional role of money and place it squarely in the hands of the Orange vMeme, have been the primary causes of the financial collapse. MEMEnomics cycles have consistently proven that an economy enters the decline and entropy phases when money is removed from its historic Blue role. This is where we are today, overlooking the role money served for thousands of years and not having learned the lessons of history.

Money And The Tribal Order

Throughout human history money has played a crucial role in helping humanity emerge into more sophisticated forms of expression. Human beings have been involved in various modes of exchange of goods for many centuries. Before Adam Smith defined modern economics, simple bartering or gifting was a form of exchange that had been in use from the time humans banded together to form tribes in order to survive. From a vMeme perspective, the rewards received from an exchange of one item of consumption for another represented the earliest appearances of the Blue Truth Force vMeme. Although in its earliest appearances, Life Conditions were primarily tribal, and nations with rules and laws or modern religions that define the current Blue system were many centuries in the future, the tribes engaged in frequent exchange. This provided them with creature comforts they couldn't attain on their own. The two most prominent social contracts that represented the thin layer of the order system in tribal times were marriage and exchange or barter.

The earliest known manifestation of an ancient barter system was in Mesopotamia. The Shekel, which is the official currency of the state of Israel today, was named after a bushel of grain that was a standardized unit of exchange more than 8000 years ago.[2] Since grain did not suffer from the same spoilage factors as other foods for barter, it was stored in a common depository, and it became the first official form of exchange when accounts were kept on how much grain belonged to whom. As Life Conditions moved forward and tribes developed the capacity to save more of what they produced, modes of exchange started to multiply. Bartering evolved to a variety of goods, including items such as artifacts, jewelry, and precious metals, which eventually lead to the use of coins as a widely accepted form of exchange.

Ancient bartering was in essence the invisible force, along with tribal chiefs and holy men that provided for the early existence of tribal order. But unlike the other symbols of order within this early Purple system, bartering or gifting provided for peaceful coexistence with other tribes. For the first time, tribes traveled to other tribes not to pillage, steal, or kill, but to perform peaceful exchange. As tribes came to trust their trading partners, trade grew to more sophisticated levels and the number of trading partners increased. In the process, barriers that defined protected tribal living for centuries started to slowly disappear, and larger tribes began to form in bigger villages and ancient cities. During this course of tribal evolution, money in the form of commodity exchange formed the most widely agreed upon social contract and constituted what were the broadest acceptable symbols of hard work, prosperity, and social status.

The Emperor's Coin

As humanity continued to evolve and it entered the Red empire-driven system, money took on a more important role. Emperors needed to impose power over their subjects and at the same time allow for a system

---

2   Merrill C. Tenney, ed., *The Zondervan Pictorial Encyclopedia of the Bible*, vol. 5, "Weights and Measures," (Grand Rapids, MI: Zondervan), 1976.

of exchange that paid wages and permitted basic trade to function. This was made easier when rulers created their own money and passed laws that punished anyone who did not accept coin money as a legal form of tender. As this practice became more common, in the Red, feudal system it replaced previous forms of barter, but was still being identified as a vehicle that expressed a Blue order system simply based on the nature of its function. As the role of money evolved within this system, the *Babylonians* and their neighboring *city-states* took it to its next form of expression. They created the earliest system of *economics* as we think of it today, in terms of establishing rules on *debt,* legal contracts, and laws relating to business practices and private property.[3] Many other dynasties took their turns over the centuries to modify the type of commodity that would represent the impenetrable function that money provided in keeping workers paid, trade moving, and peace among the masses. From the early days of the Sumerian Dynasty to the Ottoman and British Empires, the more complex and widely spread the use of a monetary system became, the more laws were created that guided its uses and punished its misuse.

As this Red, feudal system continued to evolve so did the mode of exchange. By the time the Industrial Age and the era of nation-states began, precious metals like gold and silver became the preferred currency of the British Empire. In the late 1600s, with their colonies spanning the globe, the British single-handedly made gold the compulsory means of exchange the world over.[4] With its influence so widely spread, it became easier for the Colonial British to create a banking system backed by the economic strength of the empire from which evolved the notion of currency backed by the gold standard.

The Gold Of Nations

During the age of empires, commercial banks played the biggest role in advancing commerce and determining monetary systems and modes of exchange without much interference from anyone. As empires started to dissolve, and Life Conditions allowed for nation-states to emerge, the critical function of

---

3   Sheila C. Dow (2005), "Axioms and Babylonian thought: a reply," *Journal of Post Keynesian Economics* 27 (3), 385-391.
4   William A. Shaw, *Select Tracts and Documents Illustrative of English Monetary History 1626-1730* (London: Wilsons & Milne, 1896) [reprint: (New York: Augustus Kelley Publishers, 1967)], 166-171.

money in everyday life was further defined by the appearance of national banks. Through acts of national governments the use of paper money backed by gold became wide spread, and after many trials and errors and runs on banks, it gained the full trust and confidence of the public. From a vMeme perspective, this was a defining stage of the Blue system where finance played some of its most crucial roles in modern human emergence. The prosperity of a nation became deeply intertwined with how well developed its monetary system was. Development of infrastructure and institutions that would have not attracted the interest of the merchant class took place under a Blue governmental system that guaranteed their implementation by guarantying the currency.

As attention turned to nation building, the banking sector turned its attention to the development of a modern banking system that created much of the distributed wealth we see today. Once Life Conditions were identified with the safety and security of the rule of law in banking, debt financing for trade expansion and the creation of stock markets came into being to symbolize this new era of prosperity. Modern banking was being built on a more defined Blue structure that was initially identified and followed by ancient dynasties centuries before. The psychological motivation that compelled human beings to work hard, exchange wages for goods and services, save money, and borrow and repay when needed, became the foundation from which the West was propelled into the Age of Enlightenment and signaled the beginning of the Industrial Revolution.

Life Conditions in the West at the dawn of the Industrial Revolution were still in the nation-forming stage of the Blue system. Trade, however, was being redefined through the eyes of the Enlightenment Movement and was set to take a monumental leap forward into what would become the foundation of capitalism as we know it today.

Adam Smith, the Scottish moral philosopher, started laying down new grounds for the sentiment of exchange and trade by contributing to the new Blue code of the British Empire and examining the moral thinking of his time. Smith first introduced the *Theory of Sympathy*, which puts forth the notion that conscience arises from social relationships, and is the source of mankind's ability to form moral judgments. During the act of observing others, people become aware of themselves and the morality of their own behavior in spite of their natural inclinations towards self-interest.[5] A few

---

5   Adam Smith (2002) [1759]. Knud Haakonssen, ed., *The Theory of Moral Sentiments* (Cambridge University Press), xv.

years after this new Blue code of the Enlightenment Era that tied human nature to moral restraint, Smith authored his groundbreaking book *The Wealth of Nations* in which the argument for the spread of self-interest becomes the new meme that defined the systemic spread of wealth. Smith refers to an *invisible hand,* which performs this role in helping humanity emerge in this manner:

> "As every individual, therefore, endeavours as much as he can both to employ his capital in the support of domestick industry, and so to direct that industry that its produce may be of the greatest value; every individual necessarily labours to render the annual revenue of the society as great as he can. He generally, indeed, neither intends to promote the public interest, nor knows how much he is promoting it. By preferring the support of domestiek to that of foreign industry, he intends only his own security; and by directing that industry in such a manner as its produce may be of the greatest value, he intends only his own gain, and he is in this, as in many other eases, led by an invisible hand to promote an end which was no part of his intention. Nor is it always the worse for the society that it was no part of it. By pursuing his own interest he frequently promotes that of the society more effectually than when he really intends to promote it. I have never known much good done by those who affected to trade for the publick good."[6]

Life Conditions during Adam Smith's era were primed for a paradigm shift in human emergence. The empowerment of the individual came about in the most natural way, and a new definition of nation building was taking root. Except this time the effort wasn't being brought about by an act of government. Man, just by simply performing the craft he knew best, created an invisible hand that spread good deeds to building the wealth of a collective culture. These early stages of the Orange system established the self-empowerment of the Strategic Enterprise vMeme and forever placed Adam Smith into the history books as the father of economics and capitalism.

---

6   Adam Smith, *The Glasgow edition of the Works and Correspondence of Adam Smith*, vol. 3, 26-7, edited by W.P.D. Wightman and J.C. Bryce (Oxford: Claredon Press, 1980).

As this enlightened capitalist philosophy spread through Europe and the United States, further development of monetary controls within each country was needed to accommodate the spread of wealth and protect against the abuses of predatory and monopolistic practices. The Bank of England turned its attention from financing wars to the development of its industrial infrastructure. Modern day institutions that supported the evolution of capitalism, such as stock markets and central banks, started to appear all throughout the Western World. For most of the eighteenth and nineteenth century economic theories competed for the heart and minds of the industrial worker as the merchant class that had become identified as capitalists competed with socialist schools of thought, such as that of Karl Marx, over fair wages and worker abuses. Up until the end of World War I these institutions that helped spread capitalism through its early expressions of the Industrial Era, were backed by the gold standard. The role of money in human emergence was further recognized for the critical Blue function it played in developing humanity and advancing its cause through an endless quest for higher forms of expression.

Rise Of The Dollar

At the end of World War I an era began which saw the slow erosion of the Blue system in the role that money played in human emergence. The stable and consistent use of paper money and financial instruments created a natural departure from the gold standard. This precious commodity only came into demand at times of war and economic uncertainty when the survival of the predominant Blue system was being threatened. Trading nations had the long established understanding that although they subscribed to the gold standard, there would not be a demand for redemption of 100 percent of the money in gold. Paper money in the mid-nineteenth century started to stand on its own merit as a medium of exchange as long as its acceptance remained widespread and protected by the rule of law. During periods of stability and economic prosperity very few questioned the validity of paper money and whether it was backed by the gold standard or not. Paper had taken on the function of the exchange for value that for centuries had been backed by one form of commodity or another. By the beginning of World War I the complexity of finance could no longer be defined by an arbitrary system that relied on the availability of a certain precious metal and kept the boundless potential of economic activity and global trade limited to how much gold a nation had in storage. Just as it did in adopting the gold standard many centuries before, England took the lead in abandoning it, and soon many other nations followed.

The evolution of money up until the beginning of the twentieth century has consistently shown its functionality as a direct representative of productive output. Whether it was wages for work performed or financial rewards as a result of strategic planning and investment, the rewards were commensurate with quality and the quantity of human productive input. As Life Conditions in the West continued to move into the Orange, Strategic Enterprise vMeme, global powers looked to redefine the nature of the guarantee aspect of money. In essence nations looked to replace the tangible market value of gold and other commodities with the intangible market value of the power and credibility of the currency's issuing government. From a value-systems perspective this was a necessary step to move money away from its historical false Blue system attachment to gold to a new, yet undefined, Blue-Orange expression. If gold was a true expression of the wealth of a nation, then only those nations rich in gold deposits would have economic superiority. This was the presumption that made the world go round until the last century of the industrial era.

As scientific discoveries further shifted economic power to industrial countries gold became less and less important and the notion of paper money backed only by the faith of its issuing government gained more prominence. This is the phase known as fiat money; the word derived from the Latin "let it be done." This was a meritorious system of determining the true worth of an economy. Productive output of industry had a direct correlation to the presumptive value of the currency. From a value-systems perspective this new Blue expression of currency had boundless possibilities for expanding economic power and trade and was the truest representation of the Orange system, as long as a Blue structure remained in place that held the value of the currency to a direct relationship of total economic output and accounted for adjustments in balance of payments and trade. Unlike its previous and simple uses in previous centuries, the use of fiat money in a modern industrial era during the twentieth century represented a wholly different platform for economic expansion.

After the end of World War II the West entered into an economic alliance that would hasten the end of the gold standard and bring about the global acceptance of the US Dollar as the most stable world currency. The Bretton Woods system was set up to define the new role of money and through it the US dollar became the world's reserve currency. To the victor belonged the spoils, and to the United States belonged the unprecedented opportunity to set itself up as the undisputed champion of the Orange, Strategic Enterprise vMeme. As the United States rebuilt Europe, Japan trade agreements were enacted that further cemented the function of the US Dollar as the new Blue system to which this new world-order subscribed. The United States had set its currency as the world reserve currency, and although it guaranteed its redemption in gold for decades, no Western nations sought such redemption. The new role of this paper money served to make the United States an economic superpower and at the same time accommodated the distribution of wealth at a systemic level with its trade partners.

This experiment in the worldwide use of this new quasi-fiat Blue system was put to its first test in the 1970s. The challenges from the modern dynamics of an advanced industrial economy were intertwined with complex trade agreements that started to test the limits of the new powers of the US Dollar under the constraints of Bretton Woods. Deficit spending of the post WWII reconstruction effort, the overseas flight of the dollar, the cost of the Cold War and later the Vietnam War, presented insurmountable challenges to the long-term viability of the dollar as the world's reserve currency.[7] Since a member nation under Bretton Woods could not finance spending by printing more of its currency. The United States, after three short decades, abandoned the principles of this system and any remaining ties to the gold standard. Although the US dollar has been a fiat currency since 1971, the fact that the US economy remains the largest in the world has kept the dollar as the unofficial reserve currency of the global economy till this day.

Inflation: The First Historic Threat To Blue Monetary Order

The financial needs of the increasing complexities of Life Conditions in the 1970s and beyond could no longer come from a stringent and antiquated system with limited functionality. The shift away from the dollar as defined by the Bretton Woods framework symbolized an upward movement to an

---

7   Michael Hudson, *Super Imperialism: The Origin and Fundamentals of U.S. World Dominance*, 2nd ed. (London and Sterling, VA: Pluto Press, 2003), 63-68.

advanced expression of the Blue system that had rejected the gold standard. A government with a diligent eye on the money supply and its cost were the controls that were initially thought of as the new Blue system mechanism that will keep the function of money in check and as close as possible to the role it had under the gold standard but with a greater degree of flexibility. Backed solely by the perceived value of the corresponding economic activity, this new merit system symbolized the birth of the very first modern fiat currency with unprecedented global reach.

The fundamentals of this new system, along with the prevailing Life Conditions, are worthy of further examination, as they would eventually pave the way to the current expression of capitalism in the West. As is often the case with the emergence of a new system born out of the dysfunction of a prior system, the initial phase of a fiat dollar was quite tumultuous. With government spending out of control for decades, abandonment of the gold standard put market forces immediately into play. With levers and parameters that had not yet been tested the results sent shocks through every corner of the US economy. This act was paramount to a debtor unanimously declaring that he or she no longer wished to play under the same rules under which the extension of debt took place. This was the US government, the largest representative of the Blue system, declaring to its citizenry that it no longer wished to honor its debt obligations based on centuries old rules. Without the Blue role that gold represented, the US dollar was in a free-fall and inflation emerged as the biggest threat to the capitalist system.

In years past, upward pressure on prices was tempered by the notion that long-term inflation was determined by the growth rate of the supply of gold relative to total productive output.[8] Much of the power and control structure that was held to a definitive set of rules under the gold standard was now given to interpretation by free market economists, most of whom were top advisors to policy makers and presidents. From a value-systems perspective this was the shift that freed monetary policy from an *arrested* Blue system, one that was encumbered by tradition and limitation, to a new and *open* expression of what was still the Blue system, but was now being informed by market forces, which changed the dynamics of its expression.

---

8   M. Bordo, (2002) *Gold Standard, the Concise Encyclopedia of Economics* http://www.econlib.org/library/Enc/GoldStandard.html. Retrieved July 10, 2010.

As the United States faced competition from foreign manufacturers and experienced the effects of the oil crisis on the consumer, the blame for the failure to contain inflation was directed towards policy makers who were being accused of taking the economy off the gold standard irresponsibly and prematurely. The faith of the US Government in the backing of the fiat dollar continued to be put through strenuous tests and increasing challenges throughout the 1970s and early 1980s. Although this phase of monetary evolution caused much social upheaval, a return to the limited functionality under the gold standard would have made matters worse as Life Conditions were getting more complex and needed more advanced ways to deal with a rapidly diversifying economy. Money continued to evolve in search of a new and stable Blue role that would define the road ahead and the new expression of capitalism.

It had been a few decades since Keynesian economics gave the world the Bretton Woods framework and now it was time to replace it. FDR's New Deal policies that created much of America's middle class and improved the lives of so many had become outdated and burdensome to the very economic class they helped create. Policy makers' focus on the micro-economic dynamics surrounding price controls and Fed policies emanating from that view failed miserably in taming inflation and putting America back on the path to economic growth. These failures became directly associated with an ever increasing governmental role that was incompetent and out of touch with the citizenry. The heavy handed intervention of government was hampering individual freedom and burdening the tax payer much like the premise of Ayn Rand's *Atlas Shrugged*. Perception of the failure of government programs was spreading to new levels and their ineffectiveness became ingrained in the mind of the American voter. Along with the growing call to end the Vietnam War came the cry for government to get out of the pockets of Americans and American business. Calls for a long and sustained program for deregulation were growing louder by the day. Although many of the earlier attempts at deregulation came during the Nixon, Ford, and Carter years, Life Conditions had not reached the tipping point until a better picture emerged of what a new deregulated US economy looked like during the first Reagan Administration.

Inflation, as it relates to the role of money from a value-systems perspective, was the first shot fired across the bow to tell the consumer that paper money no longer held its end of the bargain in being an accurate representative of productive output. The faith in its Blue role was beginning to erode. The year that best demonstrates this was 1980 when the CPI was gauged at 14 percent and actual worker pay decreased by 0.3 percent for the year.[9] In less than a decade, one of the oldest social contracts in human emergence met the most complex Life Conditions under a modern economy, and that economy failed to deliver on its obligation to maintain the value of money as an accurate representation of hard work. By 1980 it was becoming very clear that the limited role policymakers, economists, and the Fed played in focusing on the micro-economic aspects of price controls was becoming obsolete. Within a few short years fiat money had shown policy makers that different thinking was needed to accommodate the ever-increasing complexity of an economy that no longer had the safe harbor of the gold standard. A wide ranging view with a central command over economic policy was needed as the Reagan Administration turned its attention to implementing its economic reforms which would come to define capitalism through a whole new role for monetary policy.

The New Fed, Debaucher Of Currency

Not much memetic analysis of the role of the Federal Reserve Bank has been given in this chapter until now. Since Congress passed the Federal Reserve Act of 1913 into law, which brought the central bank into its modern day existence, its primary role has been consistent with a Blue system. Since its creation and until the 1970s the US central bank was responsible for controlling the supply of money to insure the availability of capital for a growing economy. Its preamble called for a regulatory purpose more than any other and that was to establish effective supervision of banking in the United States.[10] This task became considerably more difficult with the dollar becoming a fiat currency and with the pressures from the prevailing Life Conditions of the 1970s. As one administration after the other failed to establish monetary stability and tame inflation, lawmakers started looking at different ways to empower the Fed to play a greater role in stabilizing the economy. In 1977 Congress passed the Federal Reserve Reform Act, which charged the central bank and its oversight committee with many new areas of responsibilities, such as insuring maximum productivity, promoting the

9   United States Department of Labor, Bureau of Labor Statistics, 1980, http://data.bls.gov/pdq/SurveyOutputServlet. Retrieved August 3, 2010.
10   Board of Governors of the Federal Reserve System, *The Federal Reserve System Purposes & Functions,* Washington: Federal Reserve Board Publications, 2005, 1.

goals of maximum employment, and insuring stable prices and moderate long-term interest rates.[11] This was a newly empowered institution that had brought the varying aspects of macro-economic debate under one roof and now had the power to direct economic policies with a mandate from the United States Congress.

Behind the scenes of the inflationary era of the 1970s and early 1980s, a new school of economic thought was emerging. The Chicago School, as it is commonly known, with economist Milton Freidman at the helm was preaching a new gospel for a whole new role for money. The destructive effects of inflation had given impetus for comprehensive deliberation on its causes and a new generation of economists were ready to tame this beast by methods far superior than price controls introduced in the past decade. This new macro-economic school of thought known as *monetarism had the view that productive economic output is influenced greatly by the money supply. Friedman's influential thinking advocated a* central bank policy aimed at keeping the supply and demand for money at equilibrium, as measured by growth in productivity and demand.[12]

This expanded definition of the role of money on the part of government was in keeping with the upward emergence of a complex capitalist society. The function of a central bank that supplies money in accordance with a targeted level of economic output was more in line with a culture's movement into an ever-increasing level of social emergence. Whoever had the power, authority, and influential thinking to alter the course of the next decade would become the hero who would be etched in the nation's psyche for many years to come. For Congress, what seemed to be a revolutionary idea at the time would become the standard way of thinking and was the beginning of altering the perceptions held for millennia of the role of money.

Life Conditions in the early to mid-1980s were such than any innovative ideas that advocated the limited role of government were fully embraced. The Reagan Administration blamed all that had gone wrong with the economy on a bloated government. It introduced sweeping reforms from which a new platform was launched to redefine not only the role of money, but also the new and evolving nature of capitalism. Reagan's economic policies, which became known as "Reaganomics," called for reductions across the board in

---

11   Ibid., 3.
12   Phillip Cagan, 1987, "Monetarism," *The New Palgrave: A Dictionary of Economics*, v. 3, Reprinted in John Eatwell et al. (1989), *Money: The New Palgrave*, pp. 195-205

government regulation, spending, taxation, and controls over the money supply in order to tame inflation.[13] The new powers granted to the Fed in 1977 would not prove to be of much consequence until the Reagan reforms had fully begun. In 1982 the Chairman of the Fed, Paul Volker, took the first monumental but unpopular steps to tighten the money supply, and inflation dropped from 13.5 percent in 1980 to just 3.2 percent in 1983.[14] The beast had finally been tamed. This was the victory the advocates of the Fed's new powers needed to create the new platform from which monetary policy would become central to the US economy. This institution had moved from mundane regulatory beginnings of providing supervision of banks to having a powerful presence at the biggest table of capitalism, and was now part and parcel of the entire economic debate of the largest economy in the world.

This shift in power cannot be underestimated. The traditional innovative leadership of a free market economy that lay in the hands of various corporations and industry leaders was now being helped along by an accommodative monetary policy that had the mandate to insure the economy was running as close as possible to full productive capacity. It became entirely within the powers of the Fed to provide liquidity as it saw fit as long as inflation was tamed. If laws governing capital markets were barriers to liquidity before, the new Fed had innovative ways to deal with them on the behalf of industry and the consumer. If the chairman of the Fed had certain views or ideologies on how money or liquidity should be used or what its role ought to be, then the entire economy would either benefit or become greatly burdened by the implementation of these views. This new concentration of power in the hands of so few had the potential to become elitist and misguided as it would exclude many valued views on the economy that have traditionally come from the different economic sectors. But, since this was money, the common denominator that fueled all economic sectors equally, the Fed never considered itself elitist especially after it had just tamed runaway inflation with its newly acquired powers.

From a value-systems perspective this was a turning point that moved the central bank from a regulatory Blue system role that was charged with enforcing specific policies to a quasi-Blue-Orange level system that had the potential for collusion with the unhealthy elements of the Orange system.

13   Niskanen, William A. *Reaganomics; The Concise Encyclopedia of Economics*. http://www.econlib. org/library/Enc/Reaganomics.html. Retrieved August 3, 2010.
14   United States Department of Labor, Bureau of Labor Statistics, 1980-1984 tables, http://data. bls.gov/pdq/SurveyOutputServlet. Retrieved August 3, 2010.

Money as a catalyst for emergence had just signaled humanity that it might not have to work as hard as it did before to reap the rewards of its labor. It could borrow without many restrictions and reap the rewards now. With Reaganomics in full swing, *Monetarism* and the new Fed had scored their largest victory and were now front and center in the economic debate. From that point forward money became an instrument of innovation from which unlimited types of products can be created and utilized just as if it were another segment of the economy that had its own productive output. The memetic dance that started with an act of a Blue system by a desperate Congress in 1977 was now putting in place an infrastructure of a new vMeme more closely characterized by the financial innovation of Wall Street than the supervision of banks on Main Street. Congress gave the Fed the powers to tame inflation.

As this succeeded, government agencies across the board, from the Treasury Department to the President's Board of Economic Advisors, threw out their antiquated belief in the Blue system to regulate commerce and fully embraced the expanded powers of the Fed. Most of these regulatory agencies were now staffed with similar value-systems decision makers anxious to deploy the promise of the new economy under its growing expression of financial innovation. These new powers would be used by the Fed to expand the US economy to heights that were never before attained and at the same time created a shift in the culture that became highly dependent on debt to finance its dreams and aspirations.

The role of money played in the Blue system up until this point in history had been determined by an unseen social contract that set forth the terms for rewards resulting directly from hard work and smart and strategic planning. Economic programs and policies throughout the twentieth century that helped create the American middle class introduced the meme of debt financing to the culture. Prior to the Fed becoming so central to our economy, consumer debt that financed partial purchases of goods and services still held borrowers to a position of accountability. Lenders demanded that borrowers have some of their own hard earned money into purchases of homes and consumer goods. Borrowers with too much debt or history of irresponsible spending were not extended the benefit of debt financing.

During these decades of wealth building, debt had evolved from its negative connotations of centuries past to becoming a partner meme that helped redefine money and its historic role. As long as this new mixture of debt and equity remained highly regulated, money would have continued its evolution into new and modern expressions of human emergence but would have remained firmly placed in its Blue role. But that role did not remain for long. As often is the case with the appearance of a new meme once its potential uses are fully quantified, the exploitive element of culture took its shot at corrupting it. A new infrastructure in consumer and corporate finance started immediately to build around the Fed's newly expanded powers, which along with the birth of the Internet and technological advancement created one of the fastest and most profound paradigm shifts in the history of modern economics.

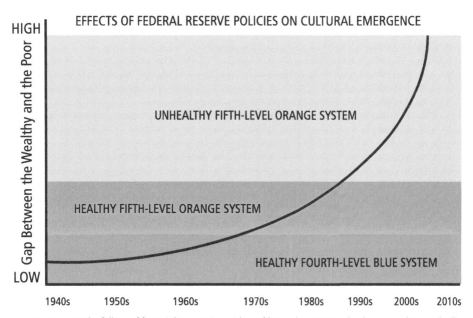

Fig. 12. Exposing the fallacy of financial innovation with a Fifth-Level vMEME Federal Reserve that gradually decoupled from alignment with Life Conditions.

FIGURE 12

The End Of Money As We Know It

As we have seen so far from the brief MEMEnomics history of money, it not only formed the highest common denominator for peaceful relations among tribes and countrymen. For thousands of years it has been the catalyst of change and human advancement. Even before the appearance of any of Abrahamic religions that offered humanity the notion of "Sacrifice Now for future gains" humans had to control their impulses for immediate gratification to "save" for future rewards and in doing so, evolved into a higher level of bio-psycho-social complexity. This sense of postponing gratification allowed for a trade system of bartering that gave birth to money and eventually to the complex global financial system we have today. According to Graves, humanity's greatest challenge is the transition from this egocentric stage of compulsivity to a higher level of existence under law and order. [15]

Over the centuries the need to accumulate goods and capital became the catalyst that moved culture away from its earlier savage nature. Money became the symbol that represented the Blue system and became a very important cornerstone for building the cultural codes that in part define who we are. The simple discipline required for the accumulation of savings became the means to separate compulsive acts for short-term gain from behavioral patterns directed toward long-term gains that lead to human progress. Simple things like payment of wages in return for hard work became the model that defined human interaction and the driving force behind better and more enlightened lives.

Through the prism of value systems, we see how money has historically had a dual role; first as a code of the Blue system and second as a catalyst that propels culture into higher value systems. As empires and nations fought destructive battles that further determined human emergence, in the end it was agreements among the feuding entities on resource allocation and monetary retribution that brought about peace. At the dawn of the Industrial Age that spread the Orange vMeme money played a crucial role in the development of nations and their infrastructure. With the development of monetary systems and capital markets, money continued its role as a representative of productive output to which humans in every corner of the world ascribed. It had brought humanity from its earlier tribal existence to its current level of sophistication and interdependence. This role more than any other has provided the motivation for humanity to pursue its quest for higher meaning in life, and until a more systemically accepted form of exchange spreads, money will continue to assume this role.

The role of money more relevant to the premise of MEMEnomics is its role as the most accepted form of an invisible regulator meme among the masses. The function of money in the Blue system is inherently intertwined

15   Clare W. Graves, *The Never Ending Quest*, eds. Christopher Cowan and Natasha Todorovic (Santa Barbara, CA: ECLET Publishing, 2005), 247.

with human nature and gives meaning to our current values and human existence. In a modern day capitalist system that is void of corruption, money plays a primary role in helping culture evolve to the next stage. But, what happens when that role is corrupted? What happens when a system that is thousands of years in the making is taken over by a segment of an exploitive vMeme that corrupts it to the core? What happens when consumer debt that has been a partner meme of money for decades decouples from that role and answers to a different master? What are the effects of a government that is supposed to be in charge of economic policy but chooses to ignore nagging structural problems and prints more money in an effort to postpone the inevitable? These are the questions that will define the modern day forces that corrupt money and hasten a MEMEnomics system to a premature end.

HISTORIC ROLE OF MONEY IN HUMAN EMERGENCE:

1. PROVIDE BLUE FOURTH LEVEL ORDER IN WHATEVER HISTORIC LIFE CONDITIONS EXISTED
2. ACT AS CATALYST (OPEN SYSTEM) TO DRIVE CULTURE INTO NEXT VMEME

PURPLE LIFE CONDITIONS: 6000–2000 BC:
- FORM: BARTER. Grain - Food - Gifting.
- BLUE FUNCTION: Peaceful coexistence among Tribes.
- Catalyst/Open System: Tribes became bigger tribes. Formed earlier cities.

RED LIFE CONDITIONS: 2000 BC–1700 AD:
- FORM: Emperor's Coin.
- BLUE FUNCTION: Wide accepted form of payment for slaves' labor, merchants' goods and war reparations.
- Catalyst/Open System: Ended wars between empires and established trade.

BLUE/ORANGE LIFE CONDITIONS: 1700–1970s:
- FORM: National currencies backed by gold.
- BLUE FUNCTION: Paid for basic societal functions, wages, trade.
- Catalyst/Open System: Allowed for globalization, single currencies, and abandonment of gold standard as an obsolete/false blue system.

ORANGE/GREEN LIFE CONDITIONS: 1970s–PRESENT:
- FORM: Fiat/paper money backed by the merit of country's economy.
- BLUE FUNCTION: Became subjected to exploitation by unhealthy orange. Still provide functions under blue Life Conditions.
- Catalyst/Open System: Unleashed debate about "Green-Yellow" money.

THE MEMETICS OF BUSINESS AND ORGANIZATIONS

By Jon Freeman

In his book *MEMEnomics* Said Dawlabani explores the development of capitalist ecologies, viewing economics from the perspective of social and cultural evolution. He applies the Spiral as the psychosocial DNA of capitalism. In my own book *The Science of Possibility* I set my exploration of what is known at the leading edge of science in a similar context. The ways that humanity views matter, spirit, truth and knowledge are also following a trajectory of emergence that can be viewed very clearly through the SDi lens. In the former we see the "only money matters" view of recent economic behaviour being replaced by awareness that people also matter, that the complexity of our Life Conditions can only be met by values shifts that recognize issues of sustainability and global order. In the latter we learn how the "only matter matters" view of science has devalued human understanding and placed a ceiling on the development of scientific knowledge. It becomes clear that scientific truth and effective epistemology similarly require that we evolve into sustainable, functional and holistic worldviews.

It will perhaps be obvious to those who know the Graves and Beck model of the world that these ways of thinking will apply in other fields. Politics awaits the fuller exploration of "memocracy", the stratified views of democracy that Don Beck has described. There is a place beyond what has so far been labelled in most Western countries as "democracy", and treated as the pinnacle of our collective governance despite the obvious evidence (need I mention the words "shutdown" or "Snowden"?) of dysfunction. In this paper however, I wish to explore the development of thinking in the area of business, organisations and management. New economics, science and representative governance would surely also demand new thinking in business and organisation. Indeed, we will see that the new elements are already showing up.

Since terms such as "business" and "organization" do not begin to apply until Blue systems are becoming embedded and developing genuine scale, we can justifiably ignore the Beige, Purple and Red stages. Although tribes have a political structure and it is possible for Red stages of thinking to encompass large populations, only with significant amounts of Blue does this transition towards structural stability. Plato and Aristotle respectively addressed the politics of incentives to socially acceptable behaviour and of communications. Machiavelli famously laid out the rules of political power as far back as 1515 and possibly could be said to define the management of Red-Blue behaviour. It is a further 260 years later, coinciding with the American Declaration of Independence in 1776 and 2 years before James Watt invented the Steam engine and kicked the industrial revolution into gear, that Adam Smith described the division of labor. Arguably only then can we view a genuine science of organisations as having begun.

Prior to that time the largest organisations were military and governmental. Military organisations had simple structures of hierarchical command and control. Government bureaucracies were not much different, overlaid by post-aristocratic class divisions and these hierarchical models, largely taken for granted, became the structural model for factories and businesses. Structurally this did not change for 200 years and there are still many businesses that continue with these forms even now, struggling to accommodate the effects of silo management and to integrate technical experts who may know more of the business than those who are responsible for managing them.

However, even while the Blue structures prevailed, management science began to look at other aspects of organisational behaviour. In the last decade of the 1800's German social scientist and philosopher Max Weber, who could be credited with founding the discipline of Sociology, began to introduce investigations of power, authority, and bureaucracy. His division of political leadership into the three categories of charismatic (familial and religious), traditional (patriarchal and feudal) and legal (modern law and state bureaucracy) can be mapped as similar to Purple, Red and Blue values systems. He also noted that the instability of charismatic authority inevitably forces it to "routinize" into a more structured form of authority. In *Economy and Society* (1922) he outlined his description of rationalization (including bureaucratisation) as a shift from traditional and charismatic organization and action to a goal-oriented organization and action (legal-rational authority). He is seen as the architect of classic, hierarchically organized civil service of the continental type.

Weber's approach can be viewed as Orange in character since he was seeking to analyse and improve the strategies within the Blue structural context. Orange values would not necessarily have an intention towards structural change. Its motivation and its goal-orientation focus more towards improvement in the efficiency and effectiveness with which those structures operate. In the same time-frame Frederick Taylor developed the study that became known as scientific management and was an early introducer of efficiency approaches such as work-flows and time-and-motion studies. Taylor's own early names for his approach included "shop management" and "process management". Many elements including analysis, empiricism, work ethic, efficiency and elimination of waste, standardization of best practices, transformation of craft into mass production and knowledge management (turning expertise into process) would be recognised today. His work paralleled the interest in economic efficiency. These Orange-oriented approaches have continued, via Peter Drucker's *Management by Objectives* (1952), Tom Peter's *In Search of Excellence* (1982) and Motorola's Six Sigma methodology (1986) to this day.

Meanwhile the early days of the 20th Century also saw the dawning of the Green values system. The births of Sociology and of Psychology are part of the emerging interest in people that characterises the Green stage. One development of the scientific management approach was an interest in getting more out of people and preventing the observable tendency for people to go at the slowest possible rate when performing mechanical and repetitive actions. Questions around human factors entered the picture. How could people be motivated? How could they be motivated and rewarded? While Taylor and others developed the concept of "piece-work" there was a developing interest in how human factors and psychology affected organizations. The Human Relations Movement focused on teams, motivation, and the actualization of the goals of individuals within organizations.

This movement shifted the perspective away from merely the organisational function. Chester Barnard provided a radical redefinition of efficiency, describing it as the degree to which organisations satisfy the motives of individuals and thereby contrasting strongly with economic efficiency. Frederick Herzberg introduced the corresponding concept of job enrichment, and developed the two-factor theory of influences on productive attitudes. He distinguished between Hygiene factors (such as security, physical conditions and pay) and Motivational factors such as job recognition, intrinsic job quality and potential for advancement. This can be seen as a broader conflation of Abraham Maslow's hierarchy of needs and indicating some sense of Maslow's view of the potential for self-actualisation as a human goal. Similarly, David McLelland developed Achievement Motivation Theory, sometimes known as Need theory. Interestingly, Douglas McGregor framed the contrast between Orange and Green in terms of two theories. Theory X presented how management traditionally perceives workers pessimistically and negatively. In its place he offered Theory Y, suggesting that managers could achieve more if they start perceiving their employees as self-energized, committed, responsible and creative beings and challenged the traditional theorists to adopt a developmental approach to their employees.

What we are seeing thus far is a development of thinking about organisations and behaviour that broadly fulfils what we would expect of a Spiral-based emergence. The transition from an accepted hierarchical structure simply performing however it may, into an efficient organisation as measured only in material and economic terms, and then into one in which there is a perception that human factors both influence material efficiency and are desirable in their own right fits easily within the Blue-Orange-Green profile of what we know of our wider social emergence.

Organizational science like other sciences seeks to explain, control and predict. All that I have described so far demonstrates that SDi can offer explanations. The remainder of this journey should show how its understandings take us further in our capacity to control or manage the way that organisations develop and what we might predict as the next required steps in organisational evolution.

As we know well from so many other areas, today's Life Conditions are those of rapid external change, global influences, major and continuous development of technology, high levels of interaction between multiple variables, issues of ecological damage, resource constraints, sustainability challenges and political turbulence. The sum of which led to the 2010 IBM finding that two-thirds of global Chief Executives named unpredictability as their biggest concern. Clare Graves' own prediction that we would face such conditions now resembles an SDi tablet of stone.

The last 25 years have witnessed the birth of viewpoints more compatible with these Life Conditions. Peter Senge's *The Fifth Discipline* introduced the concept of the Learning Organisation. As he says in his second paragraph, "The tools and ideas presented in this book are for destroying the illusion that the world is created of separate, unrelated forces." Giving up this illusion made possible "learning organisations" where "people continually expand their capacity to create the results they truly desire, where new and expansive patterns of thinking are nurtured, where collective aspiration is set free and where people are continually learning to learn together."

The Life Conditions into which he introduced this viewpoint included changes in the basic conditions of the Orange stage technological expression. The first industrial revolution brought mechanisation. The second is known to us through the introduction firstly of data processing and subsequently the vast changes which embedded intelligence and processes in electronic, faster-than-human systems, and then democratized and distributed the knowledge that we have been creating. This is well known to us all. Perhaps less familiar is the impact that such changes have had on corporate life and structures. Computers know more than managers. Those who write the systems know more about how a corporation functions than many Board directors. They wield a power which often has no relationship to their structural position and hierarchical authority. In companies led by technical knowledge of advanced engineering, chemical, pharmaceutical, automated production and other technological advances, the technicians and scientists similarly break the command and control structures of the past. The opening of systems and communication disseminates expertise to lower-echelon employees and many become experts in their own niches. This together with the democratisation of information and the commercial use of customer feedback by companies like Amazon has all added a Green people-oriented tone to the Orange mix.

It has also led to more complex organisation charts with "dotted" reporting lines and "matrix management". Added to employment rights legislation, the need to understand motivational issues and the high cost of replacing humans in whom much knowledge is invested and whose replacements often have high induction and training costs, the role of "Human Resources" functions has increased, which has also cut across traditional hierarchical authority.

Senge's learning organization is only one of many new aspects to our view of how business is to be done. Leadership development now calls for C-suite and managerial individuals to think in new ways. There are books on Inspirational, Resonant, Integral and Evolutionary Leadership; books invoking New Science, the Inner Path, New Paradigms and Values-driven approaches, and this is merely a small subset from my own bookshelves. Along with these varying approaches comes a coaching industry which variously seeks to raise traditional leaders from Blue hierarchical thinking, improve Orange excellence and strategy or to widen leadership capacity to manage others through increased Green sensibility.

Above all, Senge's approach as described in the quotes above is systemic. It represents a shift towards the integration of complexity. It is appropriate to remind ourselves of some of the things that Clare Graves said about the intelligence that we now label as "Yellow". "Those centralised in the cognitive existential state truly learn that life is interdependent. The world is seen kaleidoscopically with different views demanding attention. Knowledge in A'N' (Yellow) thinking exists in different settings; knowers think in different ways."[1] He goes on to describe the different ethics of the Yellow thinker based on the evidence of what will be beneficial to all, on the valuing of pluralism and on the readiness to change tomorrow as one set of problems solved lead to a new set in their place.

Clare Graves' view was evidenced both by his research on how individuals think and behave and on his data regarding how groups solve problems. He observed Blue, Orange and Green thinkers coming up with a number of solutions to a given problem. He witnessed Yellow thinkers in action and found what he describes as a "most peculiar phenomenon". "The A'N's (Yellow's) find unbelievably more solutions than all the others put together."

I am describing here a confluence of factors. The new problems demand new kinds of solutions. The emerging theories lead us towards systemic approaches that will support such solutions. The individuals who evidence these new vMemes and capacities are bringing varied, multiplex and continually changing solutions. There are paradoxical truths present here. One of Richard Barrett's four mantras is that "Organisations don't transform,

---

1   *The Never-Ending Quest* ed. Cowan and Todorovic, p. 370.

People do".[2] Yet we know that Values-driven change is an adaptation to Life Conditions. If the organisation does not change the conditions, new vMeme systems will be hard-pressed to thrive. Even Second Tier thinking will be obliged to adopt the First Tier solutions that fit.

The conclusion must be that to consistently apply Second Tier solutions calls for the organisation itself to transform. Those who know their SDi theory will recognise that this transformation is described at length in Section 2 of Beck and Cowan, which describes the toolkits for leadership, the Spiral Alignment procedure to put systems right and the Spiral Integration to make them work effectively. It teaches of streams and templates, all of it designed to produce organisations that are increasingly flexible, capable of articulation and flow, exhibiting the characteristics of natural design, organisations which have the adaptive plasticity of organisms.

We should expect to see, if our world is following this emergent trajectory, an increasing number of books, theories and toolkits that espouse Yellow ways of thinking or support the new needs of organisations and businesses. These are indeed visible. An early signal came from Tom Peters who in 1987 moved from excellence towards *Thriving on Chaos*. More recently in *MacroWikinomics* (2010) Tapscott and Williams describe the power of collaborative innovation and open systems and the need for organisations to "reboot". In *Conscious Capitalism* John Mackey and Raj Sisodia describe how this change can be delivered, and the need for Emotional, Spiritual and Systems intelligences that attach to its delivery. Richard Barrett's *The Values-Driven Organization* adds to the evidence which has been compiled by Raj Sisodia to show how corporations that adopt such approaches are among the fastest-growing. Dee Hock's *Chaordic Organization* implies in its name the blend of chaos and order that SDi flex-flow involves. Building their success on such ways of thinking, Google and Whole Foods Market among others are demonstrating in practice what kinds of growth can be achieved sustainably.

The toolkits to support such new ways of operation are also in evidence. Barry Johnson's *Polarity Management* offers a potent toolkit for breaking the "either-or" thinking that has attached to historical views of linear cause-and-effect. By encouraging a flexible and self-balancing creation of "both-and" thinking it leads naturally to a more responsive form of dynamic control and a leadership mindset that doesn't call for being right

---

2   *The Values-Driven Organization*, Preface, p. xxiii

once and forever, but meets the pluralistic and adaptively changeable mindset that Graves witnessed.

Another such tool is Brian Robertson's "holacracy", which blends hierarchy with distributed responsibility and provides communication mechanisms which are effective both top-down and bottom-up. In describing the growth of technical and niche expertise in many organisations, I indicated that leaders no longer know everything that there is to be known. To make good decisions in such conditions demands effective ways of ensuring that expertise can be supplied without undermining the responsibility that leaders have to lead or subverting their authority to do so. Holacracy is one example of an alternative structure which delivers this. It is also geared to "good for now" decision-making so that choices can be made which are responsive in real-time to changing demands but which are capable of subsequent change if conditions demand it.

In *MEMEnonics*, Said Dawlabani builds the conceptual framework for an economic system that integrates Value systems in functional flow. He echoes John Mackey in defining the sustainable corporation and he lays out the economic thinking that we need to support such a world. The task for organisations is to adapt to that world. It is not only businesses and commercial enterprises that must do so. The change in thinking that we are describing must affect national and local government too. We cannot deliver health systems, education, social care or not-for-profit activities in the old ways either. All are affected by shifting needs, resource availability, technological possibility and cultural demand. Apple Corporation's exhortation to "think different" is not just a linguistic trick. Doing things differently is not useful when it is geared to producing the same outcomes. We require the outcomes to change also.

I earlier described the need for our science of organisation to provide analysis, control and prediction. I have made the case for claiming that Clare Graves' theoretical approach has already shown itself to deliver useful analysis of our history and effective prediction of what we now see emerging. Our ability to manage and control is dependent on applying the tools that have been described here, plus the others that we determine as fitting to each situation. What the world needs is to take advantage of the toolkits and capacities that are on offer and apply them to the many urgent challenges of creating a sustainable management of the world, at all levels. What SDi deserves is an increasing number of opportunities for its practitioners to demonstrate such changes in practice. Cometh the time, cometh the Wizards.

Bibliography

Said E. Dawlabani: *Memenomics* (2013) ISBN 978-1590799963 Select Books

Allen, R.E. (2006). *Plato: The Republic*. New Haven: Yale University Press (First alphabetically of many translations)

Machiavelli, Niccolò (1961). *The Prince*, London: Penguin, ISBN 978-0-14-044915-0. Translated by George Bull

Frederick Winslow Taylor. (1911) *The Principles of Scientific Management*, available online through Project Gutenberg

Peter Drucker: *The Essential Drucker* (2008) ISBN 978-0061345012 Harper Collins

Tom Peters: *A Passion for Excellence* (1989) ISBN 978-0446386395 Grand Central

The Six Sigma Way: How GE, Motorola, and Other Top Companies are Honing Their Performance by Peter S. Pande et al, Robert P. Neuman and Roland R. Cavanagh ISBN 978-0071358064 McGraw-Hill

David McLelland: *Human Motivation* ISBN 978-0521369510 Cambridge University Press

David McGregor: "Theory X and Theory Y". Biographical article from "Thinkers" available digitally

Peter Senge: *The Fifth Discipline* (1990) ISBN-13: 978-0385517256 Random House

Don Tapscott and Anthony Williams : *MacroWikinomics* (2010) ISBN 978-1591843566 Portfolio Penguin

John Mackey and Raj Sisodia: *Conscious Capitalism* (2013) ISBN 978-1625271754 Harvard Business Review Press

Richard Barrett: *The Values Driven Organization* (2013) ISBN 978-0415815031 Routledge

Dee Hock – "Chaordic Organization" *http://www.myrgan.com/Inc/Literature_files/The Chaordic Organization.pdf*

Fuller story in *One from Many* (2005) ISBN 978-1576753323. Berrett-Koehler.

Weber, Max. *The Theory of Social and Economic Organization.* Translated by A.M. Henderson and Talcott Parsons. London: Collier Macmillan Publishers, 1947

SOCIAL AND CULTURAL INFLUENCES ON ORGANISATIONAL CHANGE: THE PRACTICAL ROLE OF MEMEPLEXES

By Dr John E. Cook

Keywords: Clare W Graves, Organisational Change, Memetics, Meme Complexes, Organisational Development

Abstract: Many change initiatives fail, primarily because of human responses to change. This article contends that it is possible to understand the complex dynamics of change by using memetics and proposes that, by applying a multidimensional assessment to identify a hidden culture, change states and natural ways of working, a picture will emerge as to how both individuals and organisations might cope with change. The article explores the background to memetics, culture and cultural theories and offers a method of categorising memes. It posits that memeplexes have relationships and that a meta-complex of nMemes (natural memes) are informed by vMemes (value memeplexes) and cMemes (catalyst change memeplexes), with an added influence by tMemes (technology memeplexes). Two small case studies are used to illustrate the usefulness of the memetics approach to change and the value of this approach for organisations which need to implement change effectively.

Introduction

The business environment now allows labour to cross local and international borders and technology offers a gateway to previously inaccessible markets. These factors often introduce widely differing values in both the labour force and customers, and twenty-first century organisations need to change to accommodate this diversity (Cook, 2008). This is reflected in the views of recruitment companies on the mobility of labour (South, 2012 pB19).

Without the ability to adapt to diverse demands, an organisation stands little chance of survival and it follows that those organisations which can effectively and speedily respond to the need to change are likely to be the most successful in their respective industries. Relative ability to implement change, however, depends heavily on the degree of receptiveness to change by individuals within an organisation; the unknown quality of change is primarily regarded in one of two ways, i.e. something to be feared or something exciting. Fearful individuals will, in all likelihood, feel forced into change; excited individuals will usually welcome new processes, and it is these responses which generally determine whether change is resisted or embraced, which, in turn, affects the organisation's change process.

Reactions to proposed changes depend on the individual's internal cultural profile, which is described in terms of memes. A meme is a unit of cultural replication (Dawkins, 1976, Blackmore, 1998, 1999, Distin, 2005) and individual memes have the ability to form clusters of hidden value systems which influence the individual's view of their environment and interactions with other people (Fog, 1999). Because genetic changes are plodding and slow, in 1976, biologist Dawkins proposed the use of memes as a way of exploring the speed of human change and development. The argument, however, that something other than natural genetic selection assisted human development goes back further: "….. even before Darwin's *The Origin of Species* (1886) in 1859, there were debates on the interplay between evolutionary biology and culture. In 1909, Dewey (Wilkins, 1998) was one of the first memeticists" (Cook, 2008 p67). Beck and Cowan (1996), also introduced the concept of memes, although as a subset of value memes which they called "semes" (small or little memes p31).

Meme clusters (meme complexes or, memeplexes), are regarded as the social equivalent of genes which reside as thoughts or ideas in the mind.

Simple examples of memeplexes are found in the cultures formed around popular music and fashion; in a business context, they would be identifiable in the latest management cultures, such as Corporate Social Responsibility (CSR) or an "ecological footprint".

One source of understanding culture is Professor Clare W. Graves' research from 1950 to the late 1970's, which preceded the emergence of memes and memetic concepts in 1976 (Dawkins, 1976). In terms of organisational change, however, Graves (1966) applied his work in quality management; Golin (2005) applied Beck and Cowan (1996) work in business consulting.

This article contends that a memetic framework can be used to measure an individual's internal culture in order to establish the degree of readiness for change. This would enable a prediction of the potential response to (and relative success of) change implementation. Knowledge of this state of change could also be used to design change programmes which match diverse individual needs with the needs of the organisation but, in order to achieve this match, an expansion of the current memetics view is required. It is therefore proposed that *catalysts of change* (cMemes, or cMemeplexes, which identify the change states of individuals or organisations) should be included in the measurement process.

What follows is an examination of the interaction between memeplexes and prevailing Life Conditions, an exploration of change catalysts and preferred ways of working, and a practical method of assessing memeplexes - all of which can be used to build memeplex profiles for effective change management.

Memeplexes

External (organisational) values are imposed through statements such as "we have a strong sales culture" and such a declaration would attract value memeplexes (Memes) of profit, bonuses and material rewards. By contrast, it is argued that the Gravesian vMemes are value memeplexes which develop *naturally*, under the influence of the environment in which we live. According to Graves (1966, 1977, 2005) and Beck and Cowan (1996), as societies developed over the last 100,000 years, vMemeplexes became an integral part of human existence, forming the hidden values of an individual. If it is accepted that memeplexes occur *naturally* in the interplay with the Life Conditions that create them, it then follows that they form part of a meta-memeplex, defined by the writer as "nMemes", or *naturally* occurring memeplexes.

It is proposed for this article that the social and cultural equivalent of biological DNA is known as the "Meme Complexes Architecture" (MCA), which comprises three components. These components suggest that, while memes might mimic genes in a virus-like replication and subsequently influence biochemistry, they are not *biological* entities, but instead social and cultural constructions:

- **nMemes** (natural memeplexes) – a useful term to define a series of interacting memeplexes which simultaneously embrace Graves' theory of social systems (1977, 2005), the Beck and Cowan (1996) vMemes and other naturally occurring traits. They indicate the degree of complexity of thinking needed to survive in given Life Conditions and are the meta-memeplexes which include vMemes and other traits and types, (such as analogue-digital thinking and personality types.)
- **cMemes** (catalyst/change memeplexes) – the predictors and enablers of change from less complex to more complex Life Conditions, or vice versa.
- **tMemes** (technological memeplexes) – enable coping with increasingly complex Life Conditions. Examples are simplifying information overload; sustainable business; the planet's survival. In this article, tMemes are included to complete the model and measurements require development for future versions of the model.

Figure 1 shows the relationships and interplay of the memeplexes which result in observable traits and personality types.

Figure 1.0 nMemes

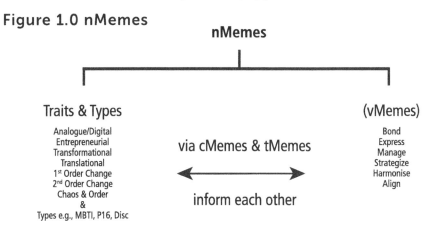

Figure 2.0 illustrates how each individual has a unique change (cMeme) fingerprint and there are approximately five commonly found patterns.

Figure 2.0 Change Patterns

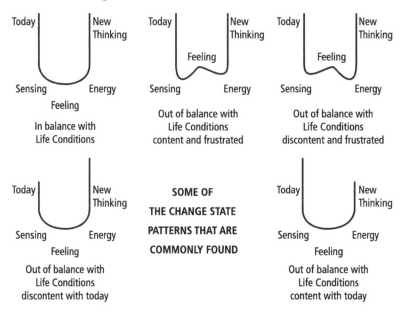

Because values are an individual's touchstone when responding to their environment, vMemes are the most important component of nMemes. vMemes are naturally preferred ways of thinking (Graves (1977, 2005); Beck and Cowan (1996), Lee (2002) and Wilber (2000) and are clusters of memes which form vMemeplexes which allow individuals and groups to survive and prosper in various contexts and in certain Life Conditions. They are influenced by our upbringing, family circumstances, education and physical environment and some vMemeplexes have a greater influence on the way we live than others. If change occurs in Life Conditions, proportionately more- or less-complex memeplexes are activated.

Graves' (1966, 1977) ground-breaking research into, and definition of, a social systems framework used paired letters to define vMemes, with the first letter denoting Life Conditions (external environment) and the second our capacity to cope with complexity (internal environment). In the summary below, the letters in brackets indicate the nomenclature relationship to Graves' (1977) original work.

In summary, these are:

- Intuitive (HU): still evolving – cosmos, planet, society;

- Align (GT): knowledge, competency supersedes rank, power, status;

- Harmonise (FS): reach decisions by reconciliation and consensus;

- Strategize (ER): optimistic, risk-taking, self-reliant, deserve success;

- Manage (DQ): impulsiveness controlled through guilt; each has a proper place;

- Express (CP): enjoys self to the fullest now, without guilt or remorse;

- Bond (BO): preserve sacred objects, places, events, and memories;

- Common (AN): food, water, warmth, sex and safety have priority.

Graves was thorough in confirming his research. He compared the E-C (Emergent Cyclical) concept to ten other similar points of view and covered leading conceptual thinkers of the time. (His review included, Ausubel (1952), Kohlberg and Turiel (1971), Sullivan, Grant and Grant (1954) Selman (1974), Broughton (1975), Issacs (1956), Issacs, Miller and Haggard (1956), Calhoun (1971), Loevinger (1976), Loevinger and Wessler (1970) and Erikson (1968, 1974).

Tests were conducted in Graves' laboratory (Graves, Huntly and LaBier, 1965), which included the use of overt and covert observations of groups, timed responses to words and pictures, essays, game play and psychological assessments (Lee, 2001; Beck, 2005). The work of Schein (1965) supported Graves' open emerging systems idea, by arguing that "his [Schein's] conception of Complex Man does say that Self-actualizing man of Maslow's is not the epitome of development," (Graves, 1977, Ch. VII, p. 44). The framework was also tested in action, to which Graves referred as a "test of application" (Beck and Linscott, 1991).

In addition to vMemes, the writer hypothesises that nMemes also contain other natural phenomena memeplexes: personality traits (e.g. a preference for digital or analogue thinking; Entrepreneurial, Transformational and Translational styles); personal priorities (e.g. a preference for Purpose, Principles, Profit, People or Trust); based on Beck 2002, a preference for 1st order change (incremental) or 2nd order change (revolutionary).

nMemes also include memeplexes of personality traits. For example, Myers Briggs Type Indicator (MBTI), is classified as nMemes because, over time, people remain reasonably consistent with their MBTI type (Quenk, 2000) and the memes are therefore regarded as "natural".

In an nMeme environment, there is a constant, iterative cycle which probes external Life Conditions and informs the individual on how best to survive and prosper at any given time. These cycles include the use of cMemes to predict and enable change, while the dominant vMemes determine the individual's response to change.

To indicate that nMemes are a meta-memeplex which contain components other than vMemes, a revised taxonomy has been devised: Bond; Express; Manage; Strategize; Harmonise; Align. This revision also offers more relevant definitions for organisational change today.

The Impact Of Technology

According to Blackmore (2009), tMemes is the third of three evolutionary influences - Genes, Memes and Technology. Technology is beginning to drive evolution and, for the first time in human history, we have the ability to alter all aspects of our planet for good or bad. Already software makes decisions and filters information for us. The next generations of cloud computing and intelligent appliances will become more self-evolving and make decisions on our behalf, thereby creating dynamic interchanges with nMemes. The tMeme is an expeditor or enhancer of the change process, and perhaps enables entry into the change zone. The next stage may well be the merging of tMemes with our biological systems (Blascovich, and Bailenson, 2011) and it is possible that this will influence Graves' (1977, 2005) social systems model.

Memes And Change

Graves defined change as the activation or de-activation of more, or less, complex thinking and described the neurological conditions under which change can occur. Beck and Cowan (1992), suggested a method of measuring the position of a person in relation to their environment and Cook developed an adaptation categorised as follows (Cook, 2008 p48-50).

1st Order Change: occurs when change arises within existing Life Conditions, or where basic assumptions remain unchanged. The change is based on past decisions and is an incremental approach, improving on what is already there.

2nd Order Change: Often caused by external influences and events and is the ability to make shifts to new assumptions and new memeplex systems. 2nd order change usually includes the unexpected and is driven by a vision of the future, needing a leap of faith from those required to implement the change. For some people, this is a natural way of thinking; for others, the thinking is forced by circumstance and they generally revert to 1st order as soon as possible.

Order: applicable to either 1st or 2nd order change, this is the need for change to occur in a controlled process.

Chaos: applicable to either 1st or 2nd order change, in which there is no need to control the process, person or organisation during change. It is accepted that there is no control over the change process and change emerges out of chaos.

It is contended that 1st and 2nd order change, order and chaos are naturally occurring memes and are therefore classified as nMemes, rather than cMemes.

cMemes: clusters or groups of memes which affect the process of coping with change. They are different from other memes in that they are *catalyst* memes, i.e. they assist and effect change, but do not change in themselves, and act only as an indicator as to whether or not change is possible. cMemes interact between Life Conditions and our capacity to handle complexity, measuring and indicating if we are in harmony with a given set of Life Conditions and measures.

Today; Sensing; Feeling; Energy; New Thinking: these areas approximate the Beck and Cowan (1996) change categories of Alpha; Beta; Gamma; Delta; New Alpha, but contain added flexibility for today's levels of integrated thinking and are particularly useful as a means of diagnosing the base change state in individuals:

Today (Alpha): the degree of contentment with the current way of living. In high alpha, the organisation or person is doing well in the environment; society is effectively meeting the needs of people; Life Conditions and environment are stable; organisations see no need to change. The basic assumptions, values and beliefs have created processes and systems which match the Life Conditions. This contentment with the status quo could lead to organisational stagnation and loss of market share to those organisations which see the need and adapt more readily to demands for change.

Sensing (Beta): in high sensing, there is a feeling that something indefinable is wrong. The previous way of surviving is no longer working; complacency and success may have introduced new problems to be solved. Symptoms may include individuals with personal problems; evidence of decline in organisations; stress, conflict and disagreement in communities. People do not understand what is happening in their world, but know something needs to be done and, in sensing, there are three potential approaches to change:

- Do more of the same in the belief that the problem lies in the implementation or enforcement of working systems.

- Attempt to fine-tune, or adjust, processes while keeping the main features, (a typical 1st order approach to change). There is a strong attraction to what was good in the past.

- Realise that processes are only processes and there are other available systems. This opens a new world view and allows change to occur, which typifies 2nd order change.

Again, if leaders are not alert to what these symptoms could mean, there is the potential of a severe negative impact on organisational performance.

Feeling (Gamma): a growing feeling of frustration, with a sense of being trapped, and can include an array of antisocial and self-destructive behaviours. The frustration often comes from knowing what is wrong, and why, and how to fix the problem, but change is prevented by strong internal barriers or uncontrollable external forces. In communities, a high gamma state may lead to violence, destructiveness, armed rebellion and revolt against the status quo. This is a 2nd order change strategy as individuals or groups literally or symbolically attack perceived barriers. In less extreme cases, physical, emotional or intellectual withdrawal from the situation is likely. In an organisational context, this state of frustration can affect morale and productivity and can also lead to high staff turnover.

Energy (Delta): the tipping point for change. The Delta surge of energy is often unrestrainedly enthusiastic. Previous Life Conditions give way to new solutions; the previously unthought-of emerges; new Life Conditions are formed. This passion produces creativity, resourcefulness and dedication to achieving goals.

This energy surge is also a strongly emotional time and can bring stress into relationships, sometimes triggering negative reactions in those left behind. If not properly channelled, the energy can lead to further frustration and reversion to old ways of thinking. A negative individual response to this surge will inevitably lead to staff turnover as those who cannot accept the new culture seek more comfortable working environments. Those who remain will be the champions of the new culture, leading to improved organisational performance.

New Thinking (New Alpha): a time of consolidation of the ideas and systems which emerged during the energy state. The individual and organisation stabilise; the organisation is aligned to its market place; communities are aligned with their environment. The cycle is completed and, in a sense, the New Thinking status becomes "Today". To remain competitive, it is important that organisational leadership remains aware that this is the start of a new cycle.

(The above categories are based on Beck and Cowan (1992, 1996 and Beck 2005) and their nomenclature - Alpha, Beta, Gamma, Delta and New Alpha - are included for clarity)

Measuring Memeplexes

There is some controversy surrounding the measurement of memeplexes: using the Beck and Cowan (1992) values test, Burns and Jackson (2011) raised this question in their paper "Success and Failure in Organisational Change: An Exploration of the Role of Values". Hulburt (1987) created the basis for accessing vMemes by testing the original Form A evaluation, which is the foundation of all current assessments, including that used by Burns and Jackson (2011). The currently available instrument, CultureSCAN, (validated with a small sample by Holwerda and Karsten (2006)) has both Likert and forced choice combinations, but is still considered ipsative in allowing individual and totalled group assessments. Brown, (2010) suggests converting to a binary system for analysis may ensure that ipsative assessments have a similar reliability to normative assessments.

The main issue with ipsative questionnaires is that the reasons for answers are unknown and Brown (2010) suggests that, by using Item Response Theory (IRT), causal latent traits can be revealed. Brown (2010) discusses the two types of commonly-used question types. Single-stimulus response format, (usually referred to as a 'Likert scale'), is multiple choice with five or more graduations between "strongly disagree" and "strongly agree". Forced choice questions have two options – "most like" or "least like". The CultureSCAN assessment used in this research contains both multiple and forced choices, and variations thereof. Brown (2010, p13) notes that "when giving a top rank (score) to one item, the respondent does so not because he/she agrees with the statement, but because he/she agrees with the statement more than other statements in the block." On forced choice, Brown (2010, p13) notes that "this scoring assumes that preferring one item to another is the same as agreeing with one and disagreeing with the other." Brown (2010 p13) using Meade (2004) "…. argues that the decision process that respondents use to select items 'is unknown and inherently alters the psychometric properties of the item level'". The debate on the correctness of applying statistical methods to ordinal data is long-standing and the writer regards Graves' work and assessments as a neutral way of initiating discussion on difficult subjects, which discussions offer clues to the causes of the latent traits.

More research is required to establish if the use of Item Response Theory (IRT) improves the validity of these types of ipsative questionnaires and, in this article, the shortcomings of ipsative data are recognised. In order to provide a form of triangulation, therefore, the nMeme structure is introduced to include other influences.

Case Studies

As an investigative starting point, two small case studies were conducted to test whether memetics offers a practical method to define culture and facilitate effective organisational change.

The specific aim was to determine how a memetic approach might be useful in the caring professions, where culture and change are important. Tutors from nursing and social services departments at a New Zealand Polytechnic were asked to voluntarily participate and two groups were subsequently formed, one of eight people and one of seven.

Measurements were based on the CultureSCAN (CS) instrument (developed by Beck and Cooke (2002)). To assist triangulation (Denscombe, 1988, Checkland and Holwell, 1998), four additional questions were included:

1) What is the biggest challenge you are currently facing?

2) How would you improve the environment in which you currently work?

3) What would be one thing you would appreciate from the (name of) Department to help you deliver better training outcomes for your students?

4) What is one thing that you can do or do differently that would make a positive difference to your group's success and opportunities?

The CS questionnaire contained questions with independent components of change, vMemes, digital-analogue thinking, personal priorities and present and desired states. Observations were made during feedback presentations to the two groups, and in two one-on-one sessions.

The CS questionnaire comprised eight sections.

Job and Cultural Fit: measurement of the gap between present and desired value systems, (or vMemes) is based on different sections and an overall score is calculated to a maximum of 64. Score ranges indicate:

18 to 14 – ideal, with good alignment to the culture

15 to 25 – some areas are causing dissonance and may need attention.

26 to 35 – there is misalignment and a higher degree of dissonance; some major issues need to be addressed.

35 and above – the sensing and frustration feelings are likely too high and major changes are required to align the person and organisation.

Without addressing the causes of dissonance and without alignment, problems occur for both individual and the organisation. Symptoms may include ill health, excessive time off and poor performance, (based on the CultureSCAN interpretation document - Cooke, 2008). The Job and Cultural Fit factor results facilitate individual discussions about the what and why of the CS scores.

Personal Priorities: the value systems (vMemes) important to the individual. Six vMemeplexes were measured: Bond, Express, Manage, Strategize, Harmonise and Align, where "Bond" is the least complex system and "Align" the most complex. This also addresses the complexity of thinking when an individual is under duress or stressed. The stressor can be work-related or external (illustrated in Group B's answers to the additional questions). Some people under stress have a natural tendency to think at a less complex level, while others have the capacity to rationalise and think through options to solve problems.

States of Change: cMemeplexes (Catalysts for Change), inform vMemes and nMemes. If there are high levels of sensing that something is wrong with today (Sensing) and strong feelings of frustration (Feeling), there is likely to be a shift in the complexity level of thinking (vMemes). This contributes to the range of the Job and Culture Fit factor. Change can be the biggest stressor and it is important for management to understand an individual's response when under stress, so that steps can be taken to reduce that stress and optimise performance in the change process.

Preferred Work Structures and Flows: the way individuals and the group perceive their organisation and how they would prefer their organisation to be.

Patterns of Thinking and Processing Information: patterns of thinking and information processing which individuals use. This indicates the range of capacities within a department, e.g. those who always "dot the I's and cross the T's" and those who prefer generalisations and patterns. How those capacities are used depends on personal priority vMemeplexes, (based on the work of Herman (1988) and Beck, Underwood and Cowan (1997)).

Forms of Executive Intelligence: preferred forms of working. The nMemes are naturally occurring traits, such as being extroverted or introverted. While the ability to be Entrepreneurial, Translational or Transformational all exist within each individual, people often show a preference for a particular form. "Entrepreneurial" managers create new with no continuity with the past. "Translational" refers to managing the present system as it is; "Transformational" describes a change or shift to totally new systems or environments. How they use their skills is informed by vMemes and cMemes (based on the work of Underwood (1987) and Beck, Underwood and Cowan (1997)).

My Work-Style Preference: the preferences a person has with regard to the type of organisation for which they would like to work. These preferences are very important to the individual and need to be recognised if an organisation is to benefit from staff diversity.

Four Additional Questions: used to gain supporting insights. The questions have already been listed and, for confidentiality reasons, actual responses are not reproduced here and only the analysis and a summary are documented. Due to the small number of responses, results can only indicate a suggested process.

The Case Study Process

All lecturers in the two departments received an email which detailed the process outline and confirmed that participation was voluntary. Questionnaires were completed online and an analysis of answers was produced for each individual. Participants were offered one-on-one sessions if clarification required. A feedback session on the aggregated results was held with each department.

The process included a type of triangulation, the eight sections of the questionnaire and their interplay, responses to the four extra questions, and observations from the one-on-one and group feedback sessions. The overall methodology was based on action research and accommodated the reflective cycle of the results analysis.

Findings

The CS assessment instrument is a multi-faceted questionnaire which builds a three-dimensional picture of the cultural and change landscape. The results are reported in the order of the methodology. For comparative purposes, the group's results are reflected against a global average of 9,149 people across a range of professions in mainly westernised countries. While recognising the limitations of ipsative questionnaires, the results were aggregated to arrive at group averages.

Group A

Group A comprised Nursing lecturers who teach to undergraduate degree level and who are required to comply with the rules of relevant nursing professional bodies.

Job and Cultural Fit: the group mean (25.8) indicated that there is dissonance caused by some major issues which need to be addressed. The current Job and Cultural Fit ranged from alignment with the current culture (14.0) to out-of-alignment (35.0)

As results emerge, other areas influence individual scores but it is suggested that the primary reason for the spread (range) arises out of three main areas:

1) Job Fit (part of the Job and Cultural Fit factor): 75% of the participants considered that they had a job fit; 25% found that the job either stretched or challenged them; 12.5% were either incompatible with their supervisor or felt they were in a short-term job;

2) Change States (cMemes): 50.0% of the group sensed that something was wrong; 37.5% felt frustration;

3) Present versus desired organisational vMemes: how participants perceived the organisation and how they would prefer it to be.

The above areas can comprise over a third of the Job and Cultural Fit factor score but other sections of the questionnaire also contribute to the score, as is later discussed.

In terms of personal priorities (vMemes), Group A results were: Manage 32.9; Align 32.5; Harmonise 29.4; Strategize 21.5; Express 21.0; Bond 20.3. The group has a vMemes centre of gravity which uses processes (Manage), looks at the whole (Align) and success (Strategize) as the three highest scores. This is compatible with a Nursing environment. The range of scores in the group reveals that there are people who are completely process- and rule-driven (Manage score 50) and those who wish to see the whole picture (Align score 54). This indicates diversity in the way each person works within the group. For example do individuals with a low Manage score bypass or massage processes to get results? Do those with a high Express score manipulate processes to their own ends? Or are the processes and procedures healthy enough to control these possibilities?

In terms of complexity of thinking, 75% use the most complex thinking by looking at the whole (Align) and thinking through all options to make informed decisions; 12.5% become defiant (Express).

Group A's results also showed that energy was present to make changes, but that they were not feeling trapped or frustrated.

The Group is cautious and prefers change in incremental stages as an evolutionary process. This fits the nursing profession, as processes containing checks and balances must be followed. There are also individuals who sense that something needs to change and who have high levels of frustration. Discussions are needed to establish the reasons, taking into account their respective vMemes under duress and personal priority vMemes.

In terms of preferred work structures, 37.5% see the organisation as either process or procedure driven (Manage) or success driven and self-reliant (Strategize); 12.5% see the organisation as exploitive and power driven (Express); 12.5% see the organisation as going with the flow, with lack of power and status and having the most appropriate person lead (Align).

The Group does not see the organisation as having the full range of vMemes and is skewed towards a more complex view of the organisation. 50.0% of the Group desires an organisation which is more people-centric (Harmonise); 50% believe that competence to do the job supersedes position (Align). This is logical for nurses, as different competencies exist and the one with the right competence leads. The Group needs to resolve the issue which does not allow it to see the Department as being people-centred (Harmonised).

The section on Patterns of Thinking (nMemes) shows that the Group has a range of thinking capacities and 62.5% are mixed system thinkers, which means they can switch between analogue and digital thinking. The range is important, i.e. if all are analogue thinkers, there may be too many ideas and dreams with little action to follow; if all are high digital, too much attention to detail may impede processes.

In measuring forms of Executive Intelligence (nMemes), there is a full range of skills but, as a group, there is a leaning towards Translational (41.7%) and Transformational (31.3%). With the group focus on the Manage vMemeplex and a tendency to use the incremental nMeme, change will be slow and follow a recognised process.

Group A's work style preference indicates a need for an organisation which "creates an atmosphere of mutual trust and respect among all" (62.5%). There is a second need for an organisation which "believes in purpose higher than that of being successful", a sense of calling and strong purpose (25.0%).

Finally, in the four additional questions, responses indicated a strong need to look at processes (Manage 7); a need for a sense of community and collectiveness (Harmonise 5); a need to be left alone to get on with it (Express 4). There was only one expression of need for improved technology and one of feeling frustration. The results supported the vMemeplex profile, except for an increased need to be seen as being able to get on to the job without interference (Express). Trust (1) and feeling of frustration (1) also supports the results from the other sections.

(To preserve the anonymity of participants, the detailed answers are not reported)

At the end of the academic year, four members of this Group resigned to pursue other options. On revisiting their respective questionnaires, their results reflected that they had not been aligned with the prevailing culture and that early signs of concern had been present. The reasons for their answers are unknown (Brown 2010) and follow-up discussions around the non-alignment could have prevented these resignations.

In this context, it is important to note that the range of results is significant, because the group averages hide the extremes. In fact, the average serves only as a reference point for the group.

Group B

Group B comprised Social Services tutors who teach to undergraduate degree level and who have a little more flexibility than Group A, but still have external compliance bodies.

The Job and Cultural Fit assessment: the group mean (23.0) showed that minor issues which are causing a small amount of dissonance need to be addressed. The current Job and Cultural Fit ranged from alignment with the current culture (11.0) to out-of-alignment (33.0).

As with Group A, other areas influence individual scores and, again, it is suggested that the primary reason for the spread (range) arises out of three main areas:

1) Job Fit (part of the Job and Cultural Fit factor): 85.7% of the participants considered that they had a job fit; 14.3% felt challenged; 28.6% felt incompatible with their supervisor. All saw a long-term career;

2) Change States (cMemes): 57.1% of the group sensed that something was wrong; 57.1% felt frustration;

3) Present versus desired organisational vMemes: how participants perceived the organisation and how they would prefer it to be.

In terms of personal priorities (vMemes), Group B's results were: Align 32.9; Manage 28.9; Strategize 28.0; harmonise 25.7; Express 23.4; Bond 15.4. The group's three highest scores reflect a vMemes centre of gravity which looks at the big picture (Align), uses processes and procedures (Manage) and "success", which is compatible with a Social Services environment. A better picture lies in the range of scores for the group, wherein there are some expressive individuals who are concerned with self-first (Express 37.0) and a range of others who want to follow processes (Manage 38), have people more involved (Harmonise 40.0) and who want to be successful (Strategize 41.0). These dynamics were also observed during the group feedback session.

Group B had a higher level of energy to change and break through to new ideas and new ways of doing things than did Group A. Results reflected that they, too, were cautious and preferred change to occur in incremental stages as an evolutionary process. The Group contains individuals who have high levels of frustration and sense that something needs to change.

As regards preferred work structures, 28.6% see the organisation as a place of safety and perhaps tribal (Bond); 14.3% see the organisation as being either exploitive or power driven (Express) or process or procedure driven (Manage); 28.6% see the organisation as success driven and self-reliant (Strategize). None see the organisation as going with the flow, having a lack of power and status and having the most appropriate person to lead (Align).

This Group does not see the organisation as having the full range of vMemes and is skewed towards a less complex view of the organisation. 14.3% desire a successful organisation (Strategize); 57.0% desire the organisation to be more people-centric (Harmonise); 28.6% desire an organisation where competence to do the job supersedes position (Align). In Social Services, people form the core focus, whereas a process-based organisation run by rules often does not have time for people and this Group needs to resolve the issues caused by the range of views between present and desired work structures.

Patterns of Thinking and processing information (nMemes) shows that the Group has a range of available thinking capacities, with 42.9% being mixed system thinkers, (moving between analogue and digital-style thinking).

Executive Intelligence (nMemes) results indicate that there is a range of skills on which to draw and the Group leans towards being Transformational (45.2%) and Translational (31.0%). There is less of a focus on the Manage vMemeplex than in Group A but there is a tendency to use the incremental nMeme, meaning that change will be slow and follow a recognised process.

Group B's work style preference indicates a need for a higher level of organisational trust (85.7%) and a lesser sense of calling, or purpose (14.3%).

Responses in the four additional questions indicated a stronger need to look at processes (Manage 16) and a need to Harmonise (9.5). They have a stronger sense of community than does Group A; some need to be left alone to do the job (Express 4). Today (3) indicates that the Group is content with the way things are and there is a small element of sensing that something is wrong and change is needed (Sensing 1). There is a need for a sense of community and collectiveness (Harmonise 5); a need to be left alone to get on with it (Express 4); a need for trust (1). There was only one expression of need for improved Technology. The analysis matched the vMemeplex profile, although there were no comments made on being successful (Strategize). The implication is that personal success is needed, but that it may not be politic to voice this in a consensus driven culture.

Summary of Findings

The analysis shows that the mean for each group followed the expected pattern for their respective professions. Both groups have a strong need to follow processes, "the correct way to do things", supplemented by being people centred. The strength of the analysis, however, is in the range of the individual's results. It is possible to play to the strengths within each team. For example, in one group there is an individual with greater skills than the others in looking at the whole picture, analysing a lot of data and arriving at solutions to current problems. There are people in both teams who can dot I's and cross T's and who prefer working with the detail. Others can take what is there and incrementally make improvements. Still others are Entrepreneurial and can create something completely new. From the analysis, it is possible to identify those who need work to be a place of safety; those who need to be allowed to be successful; those who centre on rewards for self.

(Note: After completion of the research, four participants resigned. Of these, three had very high job and cultural fits factors (29 to 35), which indicated that they were not aligned with departmental culture. Two found the job a challenge and one felt that the job stretched them. In addition, two of these people had very high levels of frustration and two had high levels of sensing that something was not quite right. It is not possible to formulate a final conclusion about the resignations without exit interviews but, if the results of the questionnaires had been earlier explored, these resignations may have been prevented. The remaining participants had a job and culture fit factor of between 14 and 29, with an average of 19.)

While complex, the data can only go so far, but it is a good place to start conversations about change and how different people within the groups respond and react to change. Some will need change to follow a slow process. Others will embrace change that makes them or the department successful. A few will require change to benefit them personally and others will need change to occur in a safe environment.

Conclusion

Irrespective of the size of an organisation, a Memetics approach can be used as a model for understanding behaviour and relative individual and group ability to handle planned change, and perhaps to overcome immunity to change (Kegan and Lahey, 2009). Memetics offers value because, by uncovering frustration levels, the application can serve as early warning that personal change is needed. As indicated in the follow up of those who participated in the Case Studies, Memetics has the added advantage of identifying potential staff turnover, which facilitates corrective action before valuable knowledge and experience is lost to an organisation.

Unlike previous measurement interpretations (in which meme components were regarded as being separate), the integration of Graves' original social system theory with nMemes and cMemes offers a richly enhanced profile of individual and organisational readiness and ability to change. The result of research into nMemeplexes now also creates a home for some aspects of other research which previously lacked a model.

The nMemes, cMemes, vMemes and tMemes framework is still at the theory stage. Still the limited case studies suggest the practical application of memetics in the context of change. The assessment results uncover much richer data for use in leadership, management and training than was previously the case.

Organisational change is a complex and dynamic process (Senge, Kleiner, Roberts, Ross, Roth and Smith, 2007, Johnson, Scholes and Whittington, 2006). The degree to which change is accepted or rejected by individuals in the organisation depends on the memetic MCA fingerprint of those required to implement change. While organisations can adopt an attitude of "they are paid to do what is required", prior consideration of individual needs in relation to those of the organisation allows management to lead a successful change process with flexibility, efficiency and effectiveness. Additional research into the practical application of the memetic model for understanding change, culture and values is needed but, in addressing Martin's question "Can Organizational Culture be Managed?" (Martin, 1992), at least MCA is mapping the change terrain (Martin, 2002).

Authors Notes

1) This paper is an edited version for this publication. A full version is available from the author including tables of results.

2) To illustrate the practical use of Graves' framework in an actual business, an example called ABC Inc. using a new instrument CultureView CS3 which includes introvert and extrovert characteristic is also available from the author.

References

Ausubel, D. (1952). *Ego Development and the Personality Disorders.* Grune and Stratton, New York. USA.

Beck, D. E. (2005). discussions during level 1 and level 2 training Aug 4th to 9th Auckland New Zealand and a talk Forum North, Whangarei, New Zealand – 5 Deep Ltd PO Box 1488 Whangarei New Zealand. (a full audio recording of the six days of training was taken).

Beck, D. E. and Cowan, C. C. (1992). *The Values Test Overview Basic Guide for Administration and Interpretation,* National Values Centre Texas USA.

Beck, D. E. and Cowan, C. C. (1996). *Spiral Dynamics - mastering values, leadership and change.* Blackwell Publishers Ltd Oxford UK.

Beck, D. E. and Cooke, C.G. (2002) first dated CultureSCAN assessment instrument. Available from http://www.5deepvitalsigns.com/contact

Beck, D. E. and G. Linscott (1991). *The Crucible: Forging South Africa's Future,* New Paradigm Press, P.O. Box 787 Denton Texas. USA.

Beck, D. E. Underwood, S.B. and Cowan, C.C. (1997) *Mapping the Mind, Thinking Patterns and Systems, and Multiple Intelligences.* Third Edition. National Values Center, Inc. P.O. Box 797 Denton, Texas. USA.

Blackmore, S. (1998). "Imitation and the definition of a meme", *Journal of Memetics - Evolutionary Models of Information Transmission,* p. 1-13 http://wwwcpm.mmu.ac.uk/jom-emit/

Blackmore, S. (1999). *The Meme Machine,* Oxford University Press, London.

Blackmore, S. (2009). "Evolution's third replicator: Genes. Memes and now what?" New Scientist, Issue 2719 31st July. Downloaded 20/12/09 from http://www.newscientsit.com/article/mg20327191.500-evolution-theories

Blascovich, J and Bailenson, J. (2011) *Infinite Reality.* William Morrow AN Imprint of Harper Collins Publishers. New York. USA.

Broughton, J. (1975). *The Development of Natural Epistemology in Adolescence and Early Adulthood.* Unpublished doctoral dissertation, Harvard, USA.

Brown, A (2010) PhD Thesis *How Item Response Theory can solve problems of ipsative data.* Universidad de Barcelona, Spain.

Burns and Jackson (2011) "Success and Failure in Organisational Change: An Exploration of the Role of Values". *Journal of Change Management,* 11:2, p133-162.

Calhoun (1971) "Re Evolution, Tribal, and the Cheshire Cat: Three Paths from Now." Unpublished paper. URBSDOC. 167 Bethuscha. MD: Unit for research on Behavioural Systems, Laboratory of Psychology.

Checkland, P and S. Holwell (1998). "Action Research: Its Nature and Validity." *Systemic Practice and Action Research*, Vol.11, N0. 1, pp. 9-21.

Cook, J.E. (2008) *The Role of the Individual in Organisational Cultures: A Gravesian Integrated Approach.* PhD Thesis Sheffield Hallam University, UK

Cooke, C. G. (2008) "3.1 CultureSCAN-Profile Interpretation". VSN 5.3 13th October 2008 A4.pdf from http://www.5deepvitalsigns.com/contact

Darwin, C. (1886). *Origin of Species*. Publisher Electric Book Company ISBN 1901843491

Dawkins, R. (1976). *The Selfish Gene* (2nd edition 1989), Oxford University Press New York, USA.

Denscombe, M. (1998). *The Good Research Guide*. Open University Press, Buckingham, Philadelphia. USA.

Dewey, J. (1909). "Theory of the Moral Life". *In Ethics*, edited by J. Dewey and J. H. Tufts. 199-424. London: George Bell.

Distin, K. (2005) *The selfish meme: a critical reassessment*, Cambridge: Cambridge University Press.

Dobbelsteain, T and Krumm, K (2012) "9 Levels for Value systems Development of a scale for level-measurement." *Journal of Applied Leadership and Management*. Volume 1. Downloaded http://www.journal-alm.org/ 03/10/12.

Erikson, E. H. (1968). *Identity: Youth and Crisis*, Norton, New York USA.

Erikson, E. H. (1974). *Dimensions of a New Identity*, Norton, New York USA.

Fog, A. (1999). *Cultural Selection*, Kluwer Academic Publishers London, USA.

Graves, C.W. (1966). "Deterioration of Work Standards," *Harvard Business Review*, 44 (Sept/Oct) pp. 117-128.

Graves, C. W. (1977). Draft of unpublished Book *A treatise on the emergent cyclical conception of the nature of humanness and its development*. Dr. D E Beck Denton Texas USA (Quantico Centre). An edited version is also available Graves. C. W. (2005) *The Never Ending Quest*, (eds. Cowan, C., Todorovic, N.) ECLET Publishing, Santa Barbara, CA. USA.

Graves, C. W. (2005).

Graves, C.W. and W.C. Huntly, and D. LaBier. (1965). "Personality Structure and Perceptual Readiness: An Investigation of their Relationship to

Hypothesized Levels of Human Existence." Unpublished paper, Union College.

Golin, C. L. (2005) *An Application of Spiral Dynamics Integral Model to Business Consulting.* PhD Thesis, Institute of Transpersonal Psychology, Palo Alto. California. USA.

Herman, N. (1988). *The Creative Brain*, Brain Books, Lake Lure NC, USA

Holwerda, E and E. Karsten (2006). *Empirical Evidence for PeopleScan's Spiral Dynamics Tests.* University of Amsterdam, Faculty of Economics & Econometrics. Dept. of Business Studies Section Strategy, Organization & Marketing, Room E 5.29, Roeterstraat 11. Netherlands. (Unpublished)

Hurlbut, M. A. (1979) PhD Thesis, *Clare W Graves' Levels of Psychological Existence: A Test Design*, North Texas State University, Texas. USA.

Isaacs, K.S. (1956). *Reliability: A Proposed Construct and an Approach to Its Validation*, Unpublished doctoral dissertation, University of Chicago, USA.

Isaacs, K. S. and A. Miller and E. Haggard (1956). "On the nature of the observing function of the ego". *Br J Med Psychol* 1965; 38: pp. 161-169

Johnson, G and K. Scholes and R. Whittington. (2006). *Exploring Corporate Strategy: Text and Cases: Seventh Edition* (Enhanced media edition), Prentice Hall London.

Kegan, R. and Lahey, L. L. (2009) *Immunity to Change – How to overcome it and unlock the potential in yourself and organization.* Harvard Business Press. Boston USA.

Kohlberg, L. and E. Turiel (1971). "Moral development and moral education". In G Lesser, ed, *Psychology and Educational Practice*, Scott Forman.

Lee, W. R. (2001). "Background on Professor Clare W. Graves", Downloaded 2/04/2003 http://www.claregraves.com/source_content/biography.htm

Lee. W.R. (2002). Clare W. Graves, *Levels of Human Existence.* A transcription Edited by William R. Lee, ECLET Publishing, PO Box 42212, Santa Barbara, CA 93140 USA.

Loevinger, J. (1976). *Ego Development: Concepts and Theories*, Jossey-Bass, San Francisco USA.

Loevinger, J and R. Wessler (1970). *Measuring ego development. Vol. 1. Construction and use of a sentence completion test.* Jossey-Boss. San Francisco

Martin, J. (1992). "Can Organizational Culture be Managed?" In: P. J. Frost, L. F. Moore, M. R. Louis, C. C. Lundburg and J. Martin (eds), *Organizational Culture*. Sage, London.

Martin, J. (2002). *Organizational Culture, Mapping the Terrain.* Sage Publication Ltd, London, UK.

Meade, A. (2004). "Psychometric problems and issues involved with creating and using ipsative measures for selection". *Journal of Occupational and Organisational Psychology*, 77, 531-552.

Quenk, N. L. (2000). *Essentials of Myers-Briggs Type Indicator Assessment,* John Wiley & Sons Inc. New York USA.

Schein. E.H. (1965). *Organizational Psychology*. New Jersey: Prentice-Hall.

Scott, J. P. (1967). "The Development of Social Motivation". In D. Levine, (Ed.,) *Nebraska Symposium on Motivation*, Lincoln, Nebraska University of Nebraska Press, p111-132.

Selman, R.L. (1974). "A Developmental Approach to Interpersonal Moral Awareness in Young Children: Some Theoretical and Educational Perspectives." Paper read at the Montessori Society Seminar, Boston. USA.

Senge, P. Kleiner, A. Roberts, C. Ross, R. Roth G and Smith, B. (2007) *The Dance of Change – The Challenges of Sustaining Momentum in Learning Organisations.* Nicholas Brealey Publishing. London, UK.

South, G (2012) "Jobs galore as dole queue grows" *NZ Herald* June 30th Page B19

Sullivan, C and M. Q. Grant and J. D. Grant (1954). "The development of Interpersonal Maturity: Apps to Delinquency", *Psychiatry, V20,* pp. 373-385.

Underwood, S.B. (1987) PhD Thesis, *Brain Dominance Patterns: Validation and Relevance To Fashion And Textiles.* College of Nutrition, Textiles and Human Development. Denton, Texas. USA.

Wilber, K. (2000). *A Theory of Everything, Shambhala* Boston USA.

Wilkins, J. S. (1998). "What's in a Meme? Reflections from the perspective of history and philosophy of evolutionary biology", *Journal of Memetics - Evolutionary Models of Information Transmission* http://www.cpm.mmu.ac.uk/jom-emit/1998/vol2/wilkins_js.html Downloaded 2000

RUMI'S GARDEN –
THE BEST PLACE FOR
SCHOOL DEVELOPMENT?

By Armin Sieber

*"Out beyond ideas of wrong doing and right doing, there is a garden.
I would like to meet you there."*

Jalāl ad-Dīn Muhammad Rūmī, 13th century

Foreword

Following is a report on one effective, Spiral Dynamics Integral (SDi) based model we have developed to improve our teaching and learning environments in Switzerland. As in many places in the word, Switzerland is experiencing people and collectives from the whole Spiral, all at once. The integration of Swiss society's vMemetic diffusion greatly influences the school system. While individual schools try to adapt accordingly, the dynamics of change in school boards and school administrations make continuity of effort problematic. The relation between the different actors in the system suffers; there is an increase of misunderstandings and conflicts due to the broad range of vMemes present.

More specifically, the following report recognizes the following in the Swiss school systems:

- Schools tend to operate mainly in Green on the managerial level, flattening or even reversing hierarchical structures.

- In contact with students and parents the vMeme center moves from Green in pre-school and grades 1 to 3 to a more Green-Orange/Orange from grade 4 upwards.
- While mission statements throughout the whole span of schools are based in Orange-Green and Green, schools mainly operate in Blue by enforcing rules.
- Due to an increasing number of families with a migration background sometimes combined with a post-war trauma, the vMeme span among pupils has expanded to a challenging range from Purple to Green, while the system still clings to the practice of separation by age. Classrooms become multicultural, multi-vMeme melting pots.
- The nation-wide efforts for a best possible inclusion of children with special needs or disabilities adds to the already great vMeme span.
- A growing number of teachers suffer from burn-out symptoms and quit their job before reaching retirement (research shows that about 30% of teachers are affected by burn-out symptoms in Switzerland and in Germany).

Schools As We Know Them Are Obsolete

Excerpt of Sugata Mitra's talk at TED2013 conference in February 2013 (www.ted.com)

"I tried to look at where did the kind of learning we do in schools, where did it come from? … It came from about 300 years ago, and it came from the last and the biggest of the empires on this planet (The British Empire). Imagine trying to run the show, trying to run the entire planet, without computers, without telephones, with data handwritten on pieces of paper, and traveling by ships. But the Victorians actually did it. What they did was amazing. They created a global computer made up of people. It's still with us today. It's called the bureaucratic administrative machine. In order to have that machine running, you need lots and lots of people. They made another machine to produce those people, the school. The schools would produce the people who would then become parts of the bureaucratic administrative machine. They must be identical to each other. They must know three things: They must have good handwriting, because the data is handwritten; they must be able to read; and they must be able to do multiplication, division, addition and subtraction in their head. They must be so identical that you could pick one up from New Zealand and ship them to Canada and he would be instantly functional. The Victorians were great engineers. They engineered a system that was so robust that it's still with us today, continuously producing identical people for a machine that no longer exists. The empire is gone, so what are we doing with that design that produces these identical people, and what are we going to do next if we ever are going to do anything else with it?"

There is an increasing awareness and consensus about the fact that the current education systems in western civilizations are not functioning to answer the demands of a society that is caught up in a highly dynamic transformation process. Unaffected by the growing number of books, keynote speeches, tools, online courses, etc. by amazingly competent authors around the globe, the robustness of the system is so powerful that a great number of schools almost seem to stand still, immobile like giant erratic rocks transported by a glacier that has long since disappeared.

One reason for this inertia originates in the uniqueness of the system: educational systems are the largest coherent/interrelated subsystem in a society. They are based and built on an incredible span of up to 20 distinctive hierarchical levels, from a minister of education down to the individual teacher in his/her classroom. No matter the number of hierarchical levels, the structural power of impacting the actual learning activities ends on the doorstep of a classroom. In the process of the secularization of education during the 19th century teachers in western democratic civilization were granted the freedom of choosing any method as long as their teaching was in accordance with the official curriculum.

From an SDi perspective it may be regarded as a logical consequence that whenever Blue/Blue-Orange/Orange authorities intervene in a school system there is high risk of open or passive resistance from the side of the teachers caused by the vMeme mismatch. There is a clash of differing core values and communication strategies. To foster an evolutionary momentum, a central role is assigned to principals: if they are able to act as vMeme interpreters, they can bridge the mismatch without risking their credibility in their own school or in the administration system.

"In times of rapid change, experience can become your worst enemy."
Jean-Paul Getty

You can hear calls for "best practice" from many different directions ignoring the fact that the past cannot be the inspirational source for tomorrow's solutions. An actual OECD (The Organisation for Economic Co-operation and Development; the OECD promotes policies that will improve the economic and social well-being of people around the world.) research project shows that today about 80% of the job profiles that will be important in the year 2020 are not even defined yet. So how can a school possibly prepare young people to fit into this not so far future by maintaining strategies rooted as far away as the 19th or even 18th century?

> "I am constantly astonished and disappointed at the assumptions people make about education: how to achieve it, how to measure it, how to accelerate it where it exists and how to create it where it does not. The default model that most people use is called "school," and that includes yet further assumptions. The most universal and blatantly false of them is that age segregation is a good idea. The idea that all 7-year-olds should study together, and then the next year do the same with 8-years-olds, is just a bad idea. It was designed only for the convenience of the institution. It is like public toilet stalls not going from floor to ceiling, for the convenience of the janitors.... Ask yourself what education means. We measure children on what they know. By and large, they have to memorize useless content to meet that test. Because measuring the result of rote learning is easy, rote prevails.... What kids know is just not important in comparison with whether they can think. Learning math and spelling is far less important than learning the art of learning."

Nicholas Negroponte in: Mitra, Sugata. *Beyond the Hole in the Wall.* TED Books, 2012.

What Kind Of Business Are We In?

To elaborate on Don Beck's fundamental question, let's start with a quote by Christa McAuliffe, the schoolteacher who died aboard the Space Shuttle Challenger when it exploded in 1986, "I touch the future. I teach." With this statement McAuliffe opens an impressive resonance room, nevertheless it might be interesting to add more specificity and guidance within this room:

- Schools are the most important and most influential place to shape the future of a globalized society.
- Schools are where all participants, including teachers, parents, etc. learn to transform ideas, dreams, talents and opportunities into practice, knowledge and experience.
- The complexity and dynamics of changing Life Conditions are accepted and dealt with constructively.
- Teachers become Wizards who design and continually coevolve a learning framework informed by a Second Tier intelligence.
- Participants become empowered and thrive.
- Schools become true learning organizations.

If this realignment gradually takes place, the old wording may disappear and schools become institutions for the facilitation/acceleration of collective and individual growth. And when the time has come a new simple word will emerge as a replacement for "school".

Through An SDi Lens: The Potential Of Edward De Bono's Thinking Tool "PMI" Or The Seed For Organizational Change

If the organizational maturity of a school can be assessed as Orange-Green/Green, there is a high chance that decision making procedures resemble grassroots democratic circles. While this is suitable for some teachers, Orange centered teachers regret the absence of efficacy and Blue centered teachers are longing for a headmaster's clear guidance. To meet all needs, holacratic (http://holacracy.org) or sociocratic (http://www.sociocracy.info) procedures could be installed and thus, spark an organizational change process. However, this step can be a bit too ambitious with a risk of failure if there is not enough Yellow leadership. At that point, de Bono's first tool of the CoRT thinking program comes in preparing grounds for later developmental steps:

- The PMI is a powerful thinking tool that is so simple that it is almost unlearnable because everyone thinks he or she uses it anyway. The letters are chosen to give a nicely pronounceable abbreviation so that we may ask ourselves, or others, to "do a PMI".
- **P** stands for Plus or the good points
- **M** stands for Minus or the bad points
- **I** stands for Interesting or the interesting points
- The PMI is an attention-directing tool. In doing a PMI you deliberately direct your attention. This is done in a very deliberate and disciplined manner over a period of about 2 to 3 minutes in all.
- Carrying out the process is quite easy. What is not easy is to direct attention deliberately in one direction after another when your prejudices have already decided for you what you should feel about an idea. It is this "will" to look in a direction that is so important. Once this is achieved then the natural challenge to intelligence is to find as many P or M or I points as you can. So there is a switch. Instead of intelligence being used to support a particular prejudice it is now used to explore the subject matter.
- At the end of the exploration emotions and feelings can be used to make a decision about a matter. The difference is that emotions are now applied after the exploration instead of being applied before when they would prevent exploration. (de Bono, 2004, p. 18 – 21)

The PMI resonates with Blue because of the clear structure and the built-in discipline elements, with Orange because of the highly efficient and intelligent use of time as well as the chance for innovative solutions and finally with Green because all participants can contribute equally, all voices are heard without valuation and emotions are important and welcome.

After a very short introduction a PMI can be done even in teams of up to 50 people. Often times participants are amazed with the inherent collective ability to evaluate a matter profoundly even when it seemed to be highly controversial in the beginning. If intelligence is not used to defend a personal point of view but to openly explore as many aspects as possible participants experience each other's wholeness and humaneness in a new light, and sometimes for the first time. PMI is easy to learn and easy to teach and so teachers can introduce it in their classes to ignite new qualities in thinking.

From Insight To Impact: How Can SDi Tools And Processes Foster Personal And Organizational Growth?

Getting in contact with SDi and gradually adopting its awareness and consciousness can be an extraordinary and life changing experience. By going deeper and deeper it becomes natural to recognize the active vMemes in specific situations, in organizations and in people. When Clare W. Graves says, "Damn it all, a person has the right to be who he is." he reminds us that it is not sufficient to have the analytical skills to decompose vMeme stacks. He invites us to continue the journey to a point of humbleness from where any Memetic constellation can be acknowledged as a valuable way of dealing with the given Life Conditions.

Feedback from teachers who attended one day SDi introductory trainings in Switzerland showed a very high acceptance of the approach and high expectations that the newly gained way of looking at "realities" may open up their spectrum of helpful reactions in difficult situations. An often mentioned effect of the training was that getting in contact with SDi resonated with their intuitive wisdom and helped them to orient and express themselves in a new and explicit way.

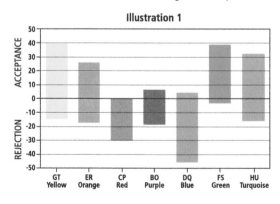

Illustration 1

After a follow-up training the participants reported the initiation of new and meaningful activities, more efficient decision finding processes and new ways to address the challenges of the growing heterogeneity in student groups or among staff members. The evaluation of the culture-scan of teachers who participated voluntarily in these trainings showed high acceptance in Green and Yellow and partly in Orange, and a very high rejection in Red and Blue, while the rest varied without further significance (see illustration 1 for a sample scan).

While certainly not representative of the vast majority, these teachers were able to identify precisely what they regarded as their main challenge: dealing in a constructive while efficient way with students who are in a Red operating mode. Their Green readiness to understand the circumstances that "made" the student act in a difficult way and therefore seeing him/her as a victim clearly blocked them from a healthy Blue/Blue-Orange intervention. Finding ways to be authentic and powerful while meeting their own expectations of being deeply humanistic turned out to be a challenging process.

If criticism arose among participating teachers, then it mostly addressed the aspect of time. They found that the model per se was "very interesting" but, for them, not all aspects seemed to be of functional importance. They would have preferred ready-made projects and tools to be applied in their classes, at best without any further adaptations, a Blue-Orange/Orange reaction to an overwhelming pressure in their professional lives. So what could be an alternative to shorten the training in order to meet this need for a best possible use of time?

A Picture Is Worth A Thousand Words

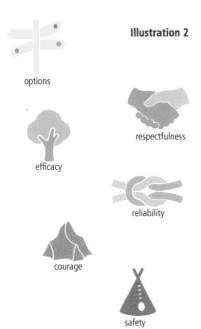

Illustration 2

options

efficacy

respectfulness

reliability

courage

safety

The first step to improve the efficacy of SDi trainings and implementation was found in the use of graphic representations for each level's core qualities. The goal was to design elements that support the understanding and could also be used when working with kids. Every symbol can be accompanied by one word referring to a positive aspect of the level (illustration 2). Since the original language was German, the translation proved to be quite challenging: for example the word used with Purple is "Geborgenheit", a word that doesn't exist in English and that combines the qualities of safety, security, home, family and shelter. Such accommodations, while not always exact vMeme definition equivalents, were proven to be "good enough".

The SDi Scaling Board

In coaching situations, especially with adolescents, it is often very helpful to have a three point communication setup. Coachee and coach sit beside one another and focus their attention on something in front of them. Since scaling questions used in solution-focused coachings (Berg/Szabo, 2005; Iveson/Georger/Ratner, 2012) prove to be a powerful approach, we designed a tool to combine SDi and the scaling questions. We printed the color symbols on magnetic paper, cut them out and used them on a simple metal base plate.

Illustration 3

Illustration 3 shows an example using separate symbols for acceptance and rejection. Illustration 4 is a comparison between the status quo and the desired future. So, while talking about personal situations, preferred futures

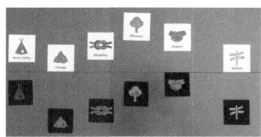

Illustration 4

etc., coachees can move the symbols to match their assessment of the status quo or their "perfect future". This offered the coach opportunities to ask questions like: "What exactly will be the first small signs that tell you that Orange has moved one step higher? What else? And what will you do differently then? What would your colleagues notice as a result of this change? In what ways might this change interact with other aspects (colors)?"

In a teacher training situation, we used SDi Scaling Boards for every participant, inviting them first to reflect and assess their actual situation and then find someone to exchange and discuss the similarities or differences in their scaling results. It is truly amazing to witness the activated deep wisdom that surfaces when it is triggered by a few color symbols. The given structure of 6 magnets and a simple board really helps to address complex facts and circumstances in a self-competent way.

Is There A Helpful SDi Lite?

We find ourselves on "terra incognita", in a cultural landscape we've never seen before. No rules, no reports from courageous discoverers can help us here. This landscape didn't exist before and as long as there are no maps something like a vMeme-positioning tool for our orientation might be of essential value. Maybe an SDi Lite format could provide such an orientation device thus facilitating vertical growth into Second Tier.

The following is one confirmation that an introductory level SDi can be fashioned that makes a difference and provides an entry point for those who will want more. Matthias Varga von Kibéd and Insa Sparrer designed a Systemic Structural Constellations format "Belief Polarity Constellation" (BPC). This constellation format offers a huge potential to address questions about core values and core beliefs in a very effective way especially when working with groups of great diversity. Varga/Sparrer use an equilateral triangle as a representational frame or space. The three corners are defined as inexhaustible sources and, in accordance with the cultural/Memetic environment in which the format is applied, one of the variations shown in illustration 5 can be selected.

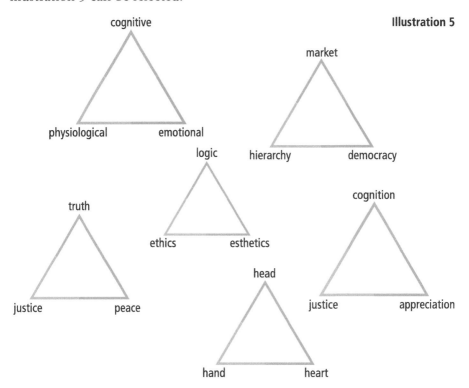

Illustration 5

Varga/Sparrer use the distinctive resources as completely equivalent with no developmental order or other qualification. Instead they use neutral marks on the floor to define the triangle's area or space.

The variations in illustration 5 show the author's way of combining BPC and SDi in one format and thereby introducing colors and a developmental sequence from Blue to Orange to Green. In the Pestalozzi variation (Hand, Head, Heart) there is an only vaguely drawn direct connection from Blue to Green, signaling that this is a rather shaky bridge and therefore needs special attention when crossed.

These three levels cover the main operating levels of adults in most school systems. The sometimes prominent Red in students is preferably addressed by healthy Blue or Blue-Orange.

The SDi-Trigon

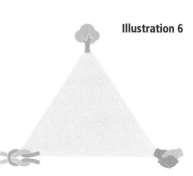

Illustration 6

By combining the color symbols with the reduction to three levels we get the "SDi-Trigon" (illustration 6) that can be used in a systemic structural constellation mode: People answer questions about their personal preferences, their values, their needs, … by positioning themselves within a big triangle on the floor. This can be a fast and quite funny way to have a group's simplified values scan within 10 to 15 minutes. To get in contact with the full potential of the BPC format, please refer to the work of Varga/Sparrer (Sparrer 2007).

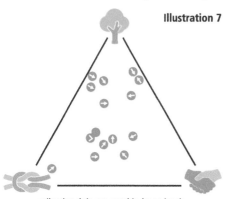

Illustration 7

adhesive dots are used to keep track of achievements and progress

Another way to make use of the SDi-Trigon is to draw/print it in a useful size for the group and then let everyone define his/her position with adhesive dots. An arrow on the dot can depict the desired direction of personal development (illustration 7: a real life example of a team of secondary school teachers).

Whatever the use of the SDi-Trigon, very soon there is a growing awareness that standing and staying in one of the corners cannot be a competent answer to the world's complexity. It is quite easy to show the incredible vMeme shifts within the last 40 years by asking them to answer the question, "How did your parents or did you as a parent ask students about school?":

- Blue: "Did you do what the teacher said?", "Have you been a good girl/boy?"
- Orange: "Did you have a test today?", "Was your mark above or below the class average?"
- Green: "Do you like going to school?", "Do you feel at ease in your class?"

For the first time in human history we have up to three fundamental developmental shifts in the lifespan of one generation. Almost everyone can agree that appreciating this complexity is not about which is "right or wrong" but about how do we "include and transcend" these differences?

Forming Teacher Workgroups Using The SDi-Trigon

With a group of secondary school teachers (illustration XX), the idea of a new way of forming workgroups emerged: Before the SDi intervention, the teachers used to form groups mainly based on sympathy and/or personal interests. Usually, when they presented the group's results, they were confronted with resistance and criticism. During the SDi intervention they wanted to try forming groups with at least one person per color in the team. They designed their presentations in a way that the person who resonated the most with Blue values presented the Blue aspects of their findings and so on. The supportive reactions and the appreciation clearly showed them that diversity in teams can be seen and used as a powerful resource.

SDi-Trigon As A Positioning System

After a short introduction, the SDi-Trigon can be used as a universal positioning system that even works beyond the shared meaning of words.

For example, the word "respect" is often used in schools and everyone including parents, students, janitors, etc. nod their head in approval to the postulation that the school needs more "respect". If there is plenty of time and energy, the group of people may start a clarifying discussion to find the one definition to which everyone can assent. Or, everyone is invited to position her/his understanding of the word "respect" within the triangle. To be able to do so, the participants begin to reflect on their own value system. Because the result does not need verbal justification, this approach offers a safe space for everyone to contribute. It is rather rare that the results will be at a more or less congruent single place. Rather you will find a rich variety in the positioning that lends a hand for further exploration in an appreciative solution focused way: "What would be the first signs telling you that "respect" as you understand it has improved? What else?"

In a similar process, it is possible to position a whole school, a department, an administration, the school development process, etc. and start fruitful exchanges keeping in mind that a school or an organization that wishes to act in a balanced manner needs to consider all three elements equally.

A Teacher's Multiverse

Once teachers are familiar with the triangle and its background, they can explore the more active and the more passive, or even the rejected, aspects of the three elements in their personal teaching styles (illustration 8). Furthermore, they can position their students according to what they think

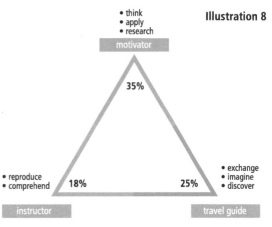

the students need for their learning. And, maybe teachers feel encouraged to start the journey to become a vMeme-adaptive instructor, motivator, travel guide or Spiral educator, choosing the naturally fitting role consciously from a broadening palette.

"Add lightness!"

Colin Chapman, Lotus

To strengthen their resilience, teachers may not have to learn something new but rather to unlearn something old. That is, if they find ways to lessen some of their rejection energy in contact with heavy Red or heavy Blue they can experience a lot more flow energy in their job, a crucial element for job satisfaction and burn-out prevention. In fact, the difference in values scan profiles between teachers who are successful in managing challenging situations and those who are not can be located in the level of rejection of Red and Blue. This seems to be quite logical and easy to understand but difficult to change. We need a new way of looking at problems to succeed. If problems stop being "problems" but instead become "training opportunities" then "problems" start being truly welcome. Left out from the "Greening" in schools, important parts of the self-image of teachers still reside in Blue/Blue-Orange. The inner voice that comments on experiences that can be seen as failures reliably comes up: "If you are not successful, you must try harder, you didn't give your best!" And, "trying harder" means to do more of what was not successful, expecting that there will be a different outcome when more of the same is applied.

This is the exact place where one of the entrance doors to Rumi's garden is located: by stepping through this door, you leave behind your ideas of right and wrong and you enter a realm where there are only opportunities and experiences. There is no fault, no mistake, no blame. There are experiences that help you to choose, to act in exactly the same way or to act in a new way.

SDi In Everyday Situations With Students – Dealing With Conflicts

The colored symbols, combined with an appropriate wording and meaningful examples or stories, can encourage even young children to grow into the consciousness offered by SDi.

Since conflict situations are a predominant source for stress, addressing conflicts in an SDi informed way can have a great positive impact. The Red vMeme is almost always triggered when conflicts arise, therefore it seems helpful to find a Blue procedure to channel the Red energy. The first thing after a clear and powerful "stop" signal (if necessary), is that the children concerned are instructed to choose one of the symbols that depicts their actual state (illustration 9).

Illustration 9

Sometimes, the request to choose the suitable volcano already de-escalates the situation. Thinking about which symbol is the "right" one, children direct their focus inward and thus quit the state of "being out of their mind". Accompanied by a question like, "What do you need right now in order to feel better?" the de-escalation can be further stabilized. The healthy Blue aspect in this intervention resides in the assurance for everyone involved, including the teacher, that in case of a conflict there is a known and blame-free procedure. It is based on the presupposition that even younger children are self-competent and able to communicate their needs if they feel safe enough. Teachers who are trained to handle a conflict and feel comfortable with the procedure tend to intervene proactively at an early stage when conflicts arise.

This is one possible approach how teachers can learn to lessen their rejection of Red and Blue and therefore experience the healthy aspects of both of these two levels.

The SDi Dashboard

From grades 4/5 upwards, students who are familiar with the SDi-Trigon can use it to reflect on their personal values, their needs, their strengths or their actual goals. With the aid of an SDi "dashboard" (illustration 10) the pupils can evaluate their school-day in a moment. They

Illustration 10

can use the scales as a means for self-evaluation, as an opportunity to get feedback from a classmate or to give the teacher feedback.

SDi - Mini Scale Board For School Development

To assess school development projects in a larger scale, students, parents, teachers, administrators, etc. can make an overall assessment of the school from their point of view using a reduced version of the Scale Board to assess the actual state. The second Scale Board is used to define the desired changes (Delta indicators). In a Green school with a rather high amount of classroom disturbances the final result from the pupils' council looked like this (illustrations 11, 12):

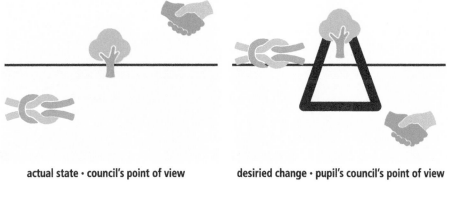

actual state · council's point of view   **desiried change · pupil's council's point of view**

Illustration 11   **Illustration 12**

Please note that the relevant and helpful activity lies in the dialogue about the expected results of the changes and not the scientific exploration of an exact position on the scale.

SDi Rubric For Self-Competence

In a more sophisticated way, the use of a rubric for self-competence (illustration 13) can foster self-awareness by bringing self-evaluation, peer evaluation and teacher or parent evaluation together. To match with the age of the students, the wording may need adaptation or even be replaced by graphic representations. The intended target level for self-competence is 3; level 4 is meant to be an opener for the developmental horizon.

Rubric For Self-Competence

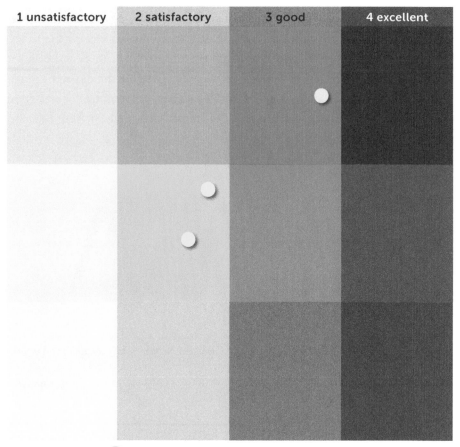

1 unsatisfactory	2 satisfactory	3 good	4 excellent

adhesive dots are used to keep track of achievements and progress

Illustration 13

BlueChips – A Multi-Level Tool

One way to strengthen Blue qualities in students is to provide them with 4 aluminum roundels engraved with their name (illustration 14). They may keep them safe in their purse, their pencil case or on a keychain. Whenever they do

Illustration 14

something that contradicts important Blue agreements, they hand in one of these BlueChips. If all four BlueChips are spent, the teacher fixes an appointment for 90 minutes of individual extra working time within the next 5 schooldays. The student decides autonomously what kind of school work he/she is doing during this extra time. After the successful completion, the student is entitled to get back the four BlueChips – new game, new luck. There is no written record about how many times a student decides to run through this procedure. At first glance, this approach may appear to be plain flatland/First Tier; so where does it become three-dimensional/Second Tier?

- The teacher clearly knows what to do when Blue agreements are not respected; the procedure helps to accept and assert healthy Blue.
- Students actually operating in Blue hand in their BlueChip on their own initiative; the procedure is in full memetic resonance meeting their need for fair and working consequences.
- Students operating mainly in Orange prefer to have their complete collection of BlueChips openly visible on a keychain, incidentally asking classmates whether they, too, didn't have to hand in any BlueChip this term; they have an opportunity to make their positive learning/working attitude visible.
- Students in Red/Red-Blue may not voluntarily hand in a BlueChip at the very moment the instance occurs. Following the slightly altered proverb "One should strike while the iron is cold", the teacher decides to get back to this student in a quiet moment or at the end of the lesson; no show-off event in front of the class. If this cooling time doesn't work sufficiently, the teacher only states the student's decision without any further discussion and hands over a written message to the person who is in charge of coaching this student. This option is an important element to take pressure off of specialist subject teachers. These teachers rarely have the chance to establish sustainable personal relationships. Nevertheless, they are expected to enforce rules and procedures as well. If they can rely on the system's ability to deal with Red/Red-Blue, these teachers may experience less impuissance and paralyzing solitude and therefore, start to intervene more powerfully and more reliably. No more showdown-invitation-threats like, "If you … then I will …." Only clear promises "You know that you are responsible for your decisions and you know the consequences.

Whatever you decide, you can rely on me (and on this school). It's your choice."

In working with Red/Red-Blue transition phenomena (see also Albert, 1990) it is primordially important that there **is** a consequence, consistently. The severity of the consequence on the other hand is much less important. And, it is necessary that the consequence is applied immediately (e.g. Hand in the BlueChip) or within a narrow time-frame. Any accumulating records that will have an effect in a time further than a couple of days away risk missing the goal completely. In accordance with class or school culture, students themselves can keep track of important Blue successes on a record sheet (like handing in a substantial essay on time). Blue-Orange is triggered in students when they can win back BlueChips with a certain number of Blue success reports while achieving freedom from mandatory extra time.

Design New Wine-Skins For The Old Wine?

"We are called to be architects of the future, not its victims."
R. Buckminster Fuller

The most prominent meta-meta-analyst in education, John Hattie, concludes, "Teachers are the most important chain link to improve the outcome of education. And teachers really would love to change, if they only had time and the required personal resources. As a way of reverse engineering, why not begin with reallocating existing resources and postpone the change?" Honoring this advice means teachers wouldn't have to increase their work-load nor learn new ways of teaching. The teachers would experience the smallest possible impact while providing the positive impact on students of accelerated learning. Some examples follow.

Nano-Level Change 1

The smallest change to improve the effect of teaching is to just add five seconds after the teacher asks a question. The probability that every student starts to look for an answer dramatically increases when everyone gets a chance to contribute, not only the fast thinkers (Blue rule to activate Orange).

Nano-Level Change 2

Five seconds after the student finishes his/her answer the teacher continues with a question like, "Do you agree with what you just heard?", "What would you like to add to this answer?", "Which new questions come up when you hear this?" and so on. Only if absolutely necessary the teacher will offer the "right" answer or evaluate what is being said. Instead, he/she can be relied upon to focus on the process and the timing. With no extra preparation or tools the collective learning field is induced in a way that accelerates learning (Blue-Orange/Green).

Micro-Level Change

After instructing the class to do a specific task, the teacher doesn't ask if there are any questions. Instead she/he initiates a "Ready-to-take-off" procedure, a 1 to 2 minute student dyad to reiterate and/or clarify the instruction (Orange – Green). Questions that arise are clarified preferably without the teacher's help (Green). When the dyads break into individual or group work time, the teacher doesn't answer questions concerning the instruction (Blue rule). However the teacher might decide to ask coaching questions to facilitate self-efficacy (Orange – Green – Yellow). Teachers are not competent because they can answer all the questions. They are competent by being able to coach their students to become "independent learning entrepreneurs".

Meso-Level Change

If teachers agree on the overarching goal that students should get the best possible environment to improve their cognitive capacities, the teachers might start by doing less instead of doing more. In solution focused coaching one rule says: the activity is with the client. In order to intensify cognitive multi-level activity, teachers offer know-how and training opportunities so that groups of students learn how to assess cognitive skills altitude (Stein/Dawson/Fisher, 2010) and mindset (Dweck, 2006) aspects in their own work.

Almost every teacher is exposed to the work of Jean Piaget or other developmental psychologists during their training. Unfortunately this training impacts their everyday work with children only marginally, if at all.

Students would benefit greatly, if teachers gained competency in the state-of-the-art work of Stein, Dawson & Fisher and made use of the Lectical Assessment System© (LAS). According to John Hattie the effect size of Piagetian programs is about 1.28 (an effect size of 1.0 or better is equivalent to advancing the student's achievement level by approximately a full grade). Still, this approach wouldn't meet the idea of doing less in the first place.

simple (linear) « cause – effect »	multiple chains of « cause – effect » come together to build one superordinate level	at least three squares are combined and open a new dimension adding depth and new perspectives

Illustration 15

With the help of a reduction to a very simplistic level (illustration 15), students can be taught to assess their own cognitive skill levels. This way, the focus is not on the accuracy of the assessment but on the activity of assessing itself, the open dialog about similarities and differences in the assessments and the reasoning behind. The endeavor to facilitate cognitive development may primarily originate from Orange. The aspect of assessing answers in small groups and discussing the results with another group opens up to Green. Finally the combination of Green and Orange comes into play when the teacher asks something like: "Suppose, you would like to improve your answering next time – with whom would you prefer to team up for the preparation?" In a similar way, the students can assess the effort someone puts into his/her answer thus opening another important strand that can help students to strengthen their budding assessment capacities.

Finally, students can evaluate the correctness of the content as well. The teacher's role in this setting is just to secure the process and provide a positive working atmosphere. It can turn out to be quite challenging for teachers NOT to support or intervene during group work but research clearly indicates that any intervention from a teacher disturbs the collective flow in the group and leads to poorer results. However teachers can seize the chance to observe and take notes of everything that functions well which they will share in their feedback at the end of the sequence. If this activity becomes part of the teaching-learning culture the accelerated learning may have effect sizes of 0.8 up to 1.44 (deliberate attention to learning intention and success criteria) on Hattie's scale.

Concluding Thoughts

> *"More complex, self-reflective, organic ways of thinking will be vital in re-shaping education so young people are better equipped for the complexity, paradox and unpredictability of life in the twenty-first century."*
>
> Jennifer M. Gidley

By sharing some ideas and practical applications of SDi in education I hope to encourage people to go out and design their own way to "enSpiralize" schools, to become "Spiral educators" or "Spiral administrators". SDi offers powerful ways to understand the dynamics of change even of an extremely stable system. Teachers, students, parents, administrators can learn to look at their version of reality through an SDi lens and discover new ways of understanding. As we find ourselves on the verge of global shifts we are called to provide our schools with vMeme-adaptive innovation and a sense of deep respect for who and where we are.

In my experience, the reduction to the SDi-Trigon can be a door-opener for teachers because it acknowledges the resonance rooms they find

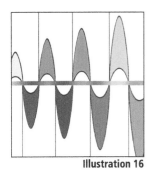
Illustration 16

themselves in. Furthermore, it includes a temporal progression from left (Blue) to right (Green) with a representation of the teacher's own gravitational center on the right. This may seem to be a tiny detail. However the introduction of all 9 levels in a vertical form sometimes triggered open resistance. Deep Green people were fighting against a new form of hierarchy where they wouldn't find themselves on the top. They felt somehow disempowered and definitely not invited to take the next step in their personal growth. It was possible to soften this reaction to a certain degree when the 9 levels were presented as a horizontal progression (illustration 16) and it disappeared completely with the SDi-Trigon. Instead of direct explanation of the Second Tier levels the participant's curiosity was welcomed and their questions gave opportunities to introduce meaningful portions of Second Tier accordingly, mainly Yellow.

If we really "walk our talk" we will be able to respect the dignity of every individual person. And instead of knowing or telling what the "right" way of personal or organizational development would look like, we will co-create a field where taking the next step of growth becomes natural – we will meet in Rumi's garden and we will work together for schools to become places where young people are prepared for their future and not our past.

Bibliography

Albert, Linda. *Cooperative Discipline: Classroom Management that Promotes Self-Esteem.* 1990.

De Bono, *Edward. Edward De Bono's Thinking Course,* 2004.

Berg, Insoo Kim; Szabo, Peter. *Brief coaching for lasting solutions.* New York: WW Norton, 2005.

Dweck, Carol. *Mindset: The new psychology of success.* Random House LLC, 2006.

Hattie, John. Visible learning. *Visible Learning: A Synthesis of Over 800 Meta-analyses Relating to Achievement,* Routledge, 2009.

Hattie, John, and Gregory CR Yates. *Visible learning and the science of how we learn.* Routledge, 2013.

Hattie, John. *Visible learning for teachers: Maximizing impact on learning.* Routledge, 2012.

Iveson, Chris; George, Evan; Ratner, Harvey. *Brief coaching: A solution focused approach.* New York, NY: Routledge, 2012.

Mitra, Sugata. *Beyond the Hole in the Wall.* TED Books, 2012.

Sparrer, Insa. *Miracle, Solution and System: Solution-focused Systemic Structural Constellations for Therapy and Organizational Change.* Solutions Books, 2007

Stein, Z., Dawson, T., & Fischer, K.W. (in press). *Redesigning testing:*

Operationalizing the new science of learning. In M.S. Khine & I.M. Saleh (Eds.), *New science of learning: Cognition, computers, and collaboration in education.* New York: Springer, 2010.

Web ressource:

http://www.ted.com/talks/sugata_mitra_build_a_school_in_the_cloud (accessed 10/14/2014)

"OUR COMMUNITY GOT BACK ITS SOUL"

By Leida Schuringa

Introduction

Where poverty prevails, the value of citizens cannot be realized. In today's interconnected world this is no longer a local issue but a problem for all of us. For the world as a whole to be a safe place, all communities, people and countries need to be included. This is not only a matter of coming into financial prosperity or installing a form of democracy. Both of these need a level of awareness and organisation that often is not yet developed in the communities and developing countries where the dominant vMemes are Purple, Red and Blue. My working life has been dedicated to connecting with people who think and live from these traditional perspectives. With a focus on converting unhealthy, disempowering expressions of the predominant vMemes into healthy, empowered expressions I have found the method of Community Empowerment (CE) to be an effective tool. As the Roma people of Nusfalau (Romania) described it: *"Our community got back its soul"*.

In this contribution I will present ways I have developed to use SDi in the area of CE. Starting with the need and necessary conditions for change, I will discuss the nature and purpose of CE. Then I will expand on the actual movement towards becoming an empowered community. Knowing how to attune carefully to the stage people are at and how to empower them is next.

Our method is based on experiences in community work and working with refugee communities in the Netherlands, training Roma organizations in Eastern Europe and community building experience with Safe Motherhood projects in Malawi. I hope to inspire you to experiment with our findings!

Poor is such a poor word to describe people who have scarce financial resources. Time and again I have found so-called poor people to be true life artists who are extremely resourceful in applying their strong survival skills. On an individual level I found my target populations to be basically healthy people, desiring to contribute and take their rightful place in their community and the broader society. However, often Life Conditions stimulate unhealthy behaviour and prohibit the development needed to help them cope with the complexity of the modern world where Blue and Orange vMemes rule. As a result many individuals and groups are marginalized and live without hope or vision of a better future. Surviving on the edges they become invisible to society at large. They have a contribution to make but cannot move to higher memes just like that. What is needed is that they are enticed to move out of their current states of apathy and inability, develop new ways of coping with life and acquire new self-confidence. Through empowerment the hidden resource that they are will become available.

Community Empowerment focuses on finding solutions for problems by:
- increasing self-confidence,
- promoting agentic behaviour,
- directing recognition of opportunities,
- enhancing individual and collective self-image,
- mitigating discrimination,
- valuing diversity and cooperation.

Our CE method was first developed in working with Roma organisations in Eastern Europe. Roma people are a minority everywhere they are settled. With exceptions, they live predominantly in the Purple vMeme with Red and Blue elements. The ones who are highly educated and have developed into Orange or even Green, often want to support their people in fighting discrimination and creating better Life Conditions. Through the CE method we were able to support Roma people to find their own solutions for collective problems and challenges. It required us to focus on changing Life Conditions in such a way that people could develop from where they were.

Empowerment has been a key notion throughout my professional life. I have always believed the best help is that which leaves people, neighbourhoods and local organizations finding their own solutions, their own embodiment of the dreams they share. I started out working in the Netherlands where I was born and still live, but my approach soon led me to cross borders. In 2005, I wrote about my experience with supporting Roma organizations in Eastern Europe. In this book *Community Work and Roma Inclusion* I detailed our methods. To my delight, when I became acquainted with SDi in 2006, I found that this theory underpinned what we had pioneered.

CE as a method can be easily adjusted to specific local conditions and situations. In 2011 I met Mary Sibande, a Malawian, who shares my passion for empowering local communities to take life into their own hands. She nudged me to rewrite the Roma book so it would be applicable to the situation in her country. As one of the poorest countries in the world Malawi has to deal with many basic challenges. 80% of the population lives rurally in very primitive circumstances. Their poverty is more intense than what the Roma suffer, but they do not face the daily effects of discrimination. Those were the apparent differences. However the similarities in their Purple, Blue, Red vMeme based way of living lend themselves to a similar approach. My collaboration with Mary resulted in the book *Community Empowerment in a Developing Country* that is published in 2014. In this book I make a case to use SDi as the thinking that should go into any integral program offered into impoverished communities anywhere.

Broader Context

To support Roma or people in developing countries, two main strategies are used: the providing approach and the enabling approach. The providing approach (giving aid) is needed in Beige Life Conditions affected by such problems as famine, floods, deep poverty and war. People in these circumstances need help and have no choice but to be dependent. Aid must be provided and it affirms dependency. However, when Life Conditions return to the traditional vMemes, the providing approach creates negative effects like diminishing self-esteem and creativity and growing dependency, and the enabling approach becomes much more effective. In this case, efforts are made to enable people to find their own answers for their problems and to take ownership of their challenges and opportunities. Communities learn to access expertise, money, and other available resources. As this process unfolds, the Empowered Community emerges. The main change in this process is a shift from a powerless stance in the face of Life Conditions, to an agentic stance. Facilitating this shift from a rather apathetic and incapacitated community to an empowered community is the general intent of CE.

Without real involvement from local people, progress will never really take root. Real development unfolds not from outer but from inner drives. Many projects fail as external NGO's operate from a Green vMeme and thus often remain unaware of the gap between their perspective and that of the local people. To prevent this, knowledge of the Spiral and involvement of the local people are crucial.

If years of development aid have taught us anything, it is that excellent ideas are of no use if they lack a ground to land in. The formula for success is E = Q x A or Effectiveness = Quality (of Solutions) x Acceptance (by the people concerned). People, organisations and societies will develop onto a next vMeme when Life Conditions are favourable or force them to change. Developing countries have to find their own pace and follow their own rhythm of change and not be forced by more developed countries to copy their so-called "better systems". Acceptance of new ideas will only happen when those who bring them are able to attune to where people are. SDi provides the framework to gauge the Life Conditions of people and the kind of responses that will guide their daily life.

Once you are clear on the vMeme of the ones you wish to engage in finding and implementing solutions, you can adjust the means, policies and methods that will speak to them. Where the Orange vMeme is attracted by entrepreneurship and challenges, Green is motivated by solidarity and being part of the "participatory" society. Yellow is looking for transcending methods like Meshworking. In order to connect with people who think and live from the traditional Purple, Red and Blue perspectives, the method of CE appears to be an effective tool.

The Needed Change

Don Beck has stated, "If it is time for change, then ask, 'Change from what, to what?'". We see a big need for change to address the many problems for people like the Roma as well as for developing countries like Malawi. The method of CE is focused on improving the health of the Spiral.

CE produces a change in Life Conditions and consequently in the value systems. This change might be a horizontal or a vertical one.

Many communities can be characterised as having a "culture of being marginalised", a set of norms, values, beliefs and attitudes that perpetuate poverty and degradation in the community. Dependency, as an attitude of the people in poverty, is an essential characteristic of the poverty culture. We focus on changing attitude, as this entails changes in norms, values and beliefs. CE works to shift this attitude from dependence to self-initiated action. Dependence is abandoned as people begin taking action and when they recognize their personal resources, their social capital. As the results of self-initiated action appear, norms, values and beliefs adjust to be congruent with this experience towards "a culture of development".

The change in attitude from "rather apathetic", blaming the other and behaving like a "victim" towards "self-esteem and seeing what can be done in connection with other people" is right at the centre of what CE is all about. It means concentrating on new ways instead of looking for reasons why things are not good. It illustrates the change from a reactive towards a proactive attitude, from unhealthy towards healthy behaviour, from not resourceful to resourceful energy. To create real changes, people have to stand up for themselves (Red-Orange). Small-scale successes are important and have impact, since it enables one to experience the effects of becoming a proactive person or community. Gradually the state of dependency can change into a more enterprising attitude and pride. This change cannot be imposed but has to be nurtured like nurturing small maize seedlings, and it follows specific steps in which we use the qualities and talents of people.

Changing The Attitude Of People

Some might argue that trying to change the attitude of people is contrary to SDi theory. They take a Green stance and advise a hand's off approach, relying on some isolated intelligence in these cultures to resolve their pain and suffering. I have found there is no escape from influencing others; we either do it actively or passively. Interpersonal influence is everywhere. Parents, teachers, family, friends; we all influence directly, as role models, and as leaders. This is part of the human condition. The core issue is: HOW do we influence? Imposing our own values, priorities and procedures upon others is not the answer. Skilful engagement with respect, meeting others at their memetic level, while monitoring and admitting our own biases, will open new horizons.

The art of staying comfortable with intentionally influencing people while honouring where they are memetically needs a specific attitude. How does one keep this conflict, this contradiction, in mind and still be successful? I begin with the following:

- Know myself, my own perspectives, my biases and prejudices.
- Establish an open attitude and desire to understand the perspective of others.
- Respect, love, and honour people expressing all vMemes.
- Desire to be of help.
- Celebrate (even very small) results.
- Acknowledge each person who develops more self-confidence, gets new insights and wants to grow.

The desire for development is part of our evolutionary impulse. It is natural and present in all people. Sometimes Life Conditions prohibit the free flow of this impulse. Healing the Spiral means that we support ourselves and others to take away blockages to this development. Evolution is always continuing with or without human efforts. However the more we as humans know and understand, the bigger the responsibility we have to do what is needed. Using SDi can help us to discern when which interventions might be useful.

The CE Method Needs A
Blue Governance Structure

The CE method can only be used within a Blue governance system. It is complementary to the national, regional and local governance institutions. The local community chooses its own priorities from the issues that are at stake and organises itself to become a strong negotiation partner for the government. If there is not yet emerged such a Blue system like in tribe dominated Red South Somalia, when the national government is one-sided like in Iraq or when it is vanished like in East Ukraine, Red power games and violence are dominant and people cannot trust anything. In that environment the method of CE cannot be used. So an analysis is needed to judge if the CE method can be an adequate instrument.

As an example, my analysis of society, history and governance structures in Malawi is presented below.

Society

Malawi is a small country in Central Africa with a population of around 16.5 million of which 85 % is living in the rural areas. Malawians are mostly black Africans from one of the four main tribes. Christianity is the main religion. 20% percent of Christians are Catholic. Around 13% of the population is Muslim. Life Conditions in Malawi are still very poor. There are many unmet (Beige) basic survival needs. Food insecurity increased by unpredictable and heavy rains (climate change), access to safe water, access to health centers, and the lives of more than a million orphans without support (maternal death and HIVS/Aids) are challenging issues. These survival needs have to be met before people are able to develop on a personal level and to contribute to the progress of their community. Malawi is a traditional (Purple, Red and Blue) society. The Purple and Red vMemes are dominant in daily life. The Blue vMeme is showing up in the state and education structures and in the influential religious systems. Slowly some Orange is emerging: current economic growth is more than 7% a year.

History

History showed that Malawi developed through the stages till the Blue level. The transition from Red to Blue had been influenced by pacification by the Scottish missionaries (David Livingstone) who made great efforts to end tribal wars and to curb slavery. They offered education to thousands of Africans and introduced new crops and farming methods as well as practical skills, such as carpentry and tailoring. The colonisation by the British (1891 – 1964) brought the present Blue political and educational systems.

Mixed Blue-Purple Governance System

Malawi is a republic and has been established in 1964. Apart from the Blue political system the Purple traditional system is still very much alive with chiefs at all levels. These two systems operate parallel and the connection and cooperation between them are strong and of great importance. Each system has its benefits and drawbacks. People mainly trust and follow the Purple traditional structures. The state respects the traditional system.

Summary

Malawi has a strong traditional foundation (mixed Purple and Blue). In this environment the CE method can be used. If the Malawians succeed in keeping this basis intact and healthy, it will support them in the development of their country. A too hasty jump into modern (Orange) society is risky, as it could destroy the strong community-based functioning of society. In our CE method we advise to build on both governance systems:

- work in the context of and within the present Blue state structures and procedures;
- respect and cooperate with the Purple traditional chiefs.

What Is An Empowered Community?

A community may be considered "empowered" when the community:

- has become more aware of different issues and problems concerning their life and people,
- has an eye for potential and possibilities,
- has developed a positive attitude towards change,
- feels more self-confident,
- is able to find their own solutions and ways of working,
- can make their own plans,
- can negotiate with the different layers of governmental structure and NGOs,
- is active and self-reliant,
- has capable leaders,
- has an effective social structure,
- is aware of its citizens' rights and duties.

Being an empowered community does not mean that all problems are solved. It means that there is a perspective, that people do not feel alone and do not just wait to be helped but are ready to work to improve their own situation. It gives a sense of ownership of initiatives and there is an organisational structure which can channel ideas and initiatives.

Empowerment as a key concept can be analysed with the four quadrants of Wilber:

	Interior	Exterior
Individual	**1. Awareness:** **UL** Do people reflect on their situation? **2. Mentality:** Are people positively oriented towards the future?	**3. Activeness** **UR** How active are the people for their community? **4. Human capacity:** What are the skills of the leaders and people?
Collective	**5. Social structures:** **LL** How is the community organised? **6. Leadership:** Are there local leaders who are respected, trusted and accepted?	**7. Democratic procedures:** **LR** Is there a tradition of democratic decision making? **8. External network:** How are relations with the outside world structured?

Insight in these eight dimensions helps us to find out where the most attention is needed. The processes in the four quadrants are reinforcing each other. For instance, a group of 45 men and women in the village of Chazika in Malawi are involved in an active role (UR) of promoting Safe Motherhood by information, theatre and songs. They are feeling proud (UL) about the visible results in the outside world: the number of maternal deaths is decreasing (LR). This also influences their commitment to their team, "We had this result of our work together!" (LL). Paying attention to and developing all four quadrants results in a positive accumulation of the different activities.

Solving concrete problems, such as improving housing conditions or introduction of safe water, are important because it is changing the Life Conditions. People need results and visible changes. Nevertheless, the main point of CE is that people get knowledge and develop competences, participate actively and can support each other on local, regional and national level. So they become able to fight for themselves. We want to show them a pathway and teach them the skills they need to pave and walk this road. The successes must be theirs not ours.

How Does CE Work?

Empowerment means that the mind set of people is influenced and changes. Don Beck states that change is only possible when attuning to the relevant value systems and influencing Life Conditions of people, in such a way that they themselves take the next step in their development. How do we influence this shift, this change process? In this section I present the guiding principles for CE, the CE-strategy to change Life Conditions, the importance of starting where people are and changing the content of vMemes and to look for interventions using the Spiral.

1. Guiding Principles

Don Beck gave us guidelines for working with people. He formulated the following "SDi 8 Guiding Principles":

1) Every person has the right to be who he or she is.

2) Teach people how to work better, given how they think, not how you think.

3) Select the people who are naturally capable, those who think in the ways the work requires.

4) Lead people to quality, productivity, and decency in ways that fit the world as they experience it.

5) People should not have to become different to get the work done. Apply the strengths they already have.

6) Build systems that flow. Benchmark and then mesh the people, the leadership, the technologies.

7) Facilitate change and provide support for those who choose it, and don't punish others for being who they are.

8) Value multiple intelligences, e.g. why (reasoning), how (process), who (feelings), when (futures); not just what (facts.)

Our CE method is based on these eight principles.

2. Strategy

The purpose of CE is to empower local (rural) communities to realize their ideas for progress and development. This is done by supporting them on four paths of development:

1) **The problem solving path:** It is important that local people can see concrete results of their efforts. The effect of small visible results on people's attitude is big. From SDi we learned that the best way to inspire horizontal or vertical change in people's thinking is to change Life Conditions.

2) **The educational path:** People also need dialogue, discussions, sharing of experiences, information and knowledge to inspire initiative and become pro-active.

3) **The organisational path:** It is also important that they are able to organise the community in order to make and implement plans. Such actions lead to ownership over their own life.

4) **The networking path:** People have to learn to involve external resources.

The CE method focuses on the simultaneous development of all four paths because they reinforce each other.

CE empowers the community gradually, cooperating with the people and leaders, but at the same time stimulating them to take a further step and look ahead. It is a delicate balance. During this process it is important to stay close to the people's perspectives and actions. If we, as supporters, run ahead and forget where the people of the community stand, we will lose contact and end up doing everything ourselves. There are at least three phases in the development towards an empowered community:

Timeline	Progress in the community	1. Probl Path	2. Ed Path	3. Org Path	4. Netw Path
Phase I Getting involved.	Self-confidence grows and the first organisational structures form, usually connected with infrastructure issues.				
Phase II Expanding the organisation.	Discoveries, ideas and solutions found by this community are spread to other villages. Self-organised activities of all sorts are instigated, each having its own leader.				
Phase III Working towards self-reliance.	The leaders and the people are learning to find their own way and resources.	↓	↓	↓	↓

The three phases seem a rather natural development. However, the relation between the phases is not always linear. At any moment the specific Life Conditions will advise what is appropriate.

3. Start Where People Are

The Key in CE is to make a real connection with the local people. The SDi analysis is very useful to assess from which vMemes people live and how they might develop to cope with their changing Life Conditions. It is important to know which vMemes resonate most with me as a community worker and with the people with whom I cooperate. Because only then will I be able to really tune into the situation and know the next natural step for them to take.

Some people are quite attached to their own perspective. For various reasons they are not open to different views and new information. They resist new ideas and developments. They have become closed off to change. Others feel trapped in their situation but also know there must be a way out. They experience frustration and become blocked. There also are people who are open to other perspectives, new ideas and information. In CE, one of the objectives is to facilitate this change, from closed and blocked ways of thinking to a more open way of coping with the world around us. This is called horizontal change, a change from an incapacitated and dependent state to a more enabling state.

The change from a reactive towards a proactive attitude means something different in the various value systems. Development can be seen as a staircase. In each vMeme the focus for interventions will be different:

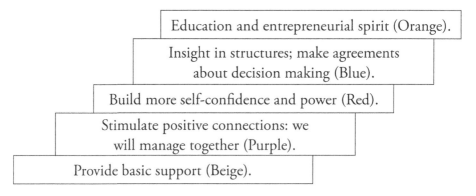

Education and entrepreneurial spirit (Orange).

Insight in structures; make agreements about decision making (Blue).

Build more self-confidence and power (Red).

Stimulate positive connections: we will manage together (Purple).

Provide basic support (Beige).

Along with the development of the individual vMemes, social connections change also. Social informal networks are very important in the CE process. As people develop they will get access to and will form more and other types of social networks, i.e. from the big family clan in Purple to religious groups in Blue and business networks in Orange.

4. Change The Content Of The Codes

How can we influence the change from a passive or closed attitude to an active and open attitude? One of the tools that Don gave us is to change the content of the codes. People have the perspective they have and we have to respect that. But the content may change. Don told a story about a Palestine man who still kept the key of his grandfather's house now situated in Israel. He felt proud about his forefathers and wanted to honour them by going back to the house. He felt he had to do so for the honour of the family. Don talked to him and said, "Suppose you were to build a school here for your grandchildren and the school would have the name of your grandfather, wouldn't that honour him and your family even more than going back?" The man was doubtful... and then he changed his mind. After some time he really built a school named after his grandfather.

Another example is the training that Mary Sibande gave to the Traditional Birth Assistants (TBAs). Some in the community were concerned that maybe the TBAs should stop their work because it might endanger women who give birth. This was not the Purple way things had always been done. However, in the rural areas there are not enough educated midwives, hospitals are difficult to reach, and in fact expectant mothers would be more endangered without the TBAs. Mary included in her training an affirmation of the traditional, Purple, role of women in the birthing process. This confirmed respect for tradition while leaving an opening for the TBAs to include new knowledge in their roles. The TBAs were recognized in their special, and traditional, role, while continuing to learn and provide services that improved the health and outcomes for the mothers and the children. To further empower the TBAs the trainer provided information about the facilities of hospitals to support complicated deliveries. Then she asked, "So what can you do to provide a better and safer place for women to deliver?" In response, the TBA's developed and integrated the following improvements into their traditional setting:

- Cleaned their environment and made a grass fence around the building.
- Made two separate rooms, one for delivery and one for postnatal rest.
- Made a kitchen, using a dish rack and lines for washed clothes.
- Made two toilets, one for the patients and one for the visitors.
- Put messages on the wall promoting access to health facilities e.g. for antenatal care.

The trainer also taught them to count and to write their own name. Thus, the TBAs were able to make simple records or how many mothers went to antenatal care; how many they referred to hospital; how many delivered on site. This education was framed as a, Purple, way to enhance the safety and well being of all involved.

5. Connect With The Spiral
To Find Appropriate Interventions

A good SDi analysis is needed to find out from which vMeme people are operating and where blockades and opportunities for change are present. This informs us about the focus of the interventions. In general someone is "floating" between three stages. So, when you meet a person who functions from dominant unhealthy Red, the next four interventions are available to deal with this person:

- Strengthen the Purple base. Pay attention to the relation with family and the basic life situation and create a "home".
- Quick and clear punishment of negative Red (like criminal activities or violence).
- Stimulate positive Red. Create space for action and short tern results like in sports and martial arts and space for expression like music and theatre.
- Develop Blue. Implement structure and meaning by attending school (again), participating in a football team or in organisational activities. Involve this person in finding attractive activities.

Don't expect this person to start a business (Orange) or to have a deep conversation about feelings (Green). However, it is necessary to include a little bit of tickling of the next vMeme (in this case the Blue structure). Don Beck, "Know that the shift must include the next Color of Thinking and that skipping by a color ultimately weakens the Spiral". When people are in the outgoing phase of a specific vMeme, more opportunities for including some of their next vMeme arise.

Awareness of the different meanings of concepts like dependency and empowerment in the vMemes helps to distinguish the most appropriate intervention. As an example the following table contains different expressions of dependency and possible empowerment strategies connected to the situation in Malawi.

vMeme	Dependency	Empowerment
BEIGE	Feeling of helplessness; the needs must be met in order to survive and develop.	Provide the most elementary support (food, health facilities) so that people can be more open to connections with others; this is the basic fundament for development.
PURPLE	People will obey the decisions of the family heads like their uncle. Example: A husband wanted to bring his pregnant wife to the hospital, but he had to wait for the decision of her uncle. After 3 days the uncle came but it was too late. The mother died on the way to the health facility.	- Not just stick to the culture, but learn negotiation skills to discuss with the family, find another solution and take better informed decisions. Example: In a Safe Motherhood project communities revised their culture: the traditional responsibility of the uncle has been divided into two different roles: *mwini mbumba* (the responsibility of the uncle as the owner of his sister's household including her living children) and *mwini mimba* ('owner of pregnancy'), the responsibility of the father for his wife and unborn child during pregnancy. - Develop the power and courage to feel, think and act in a different way and make your own decision. Life saving approach first: take your wife to the hospital using a bicycle ambulance and report later to the uncle to show him respect.
RED	Followers are dependent on arbitrariness of the leader	- Become a leader yourself. - Increase self-confidence: I can do it! Yes, we can! - Become disciplined and following rules that apply for all.
BLUE	You have to wait and to follow the existing rules and procedures.	- Insight in how systems work. - Build a reliable system in which commitment is rewarded. Example: A good functioning local committee got the opportunity to become a model and teach others during exchange visits. - Work towards achieving common goals instead of your own goal. With transparency nobody claims the success, but, in contrast, "We did it together. It was a common effort. It is *our* achievement!" - Look to the future and to the opportunities: which choices do you have?

ORANGE	People without education, with ill health and unemployed are lagging behind. They are not valued, their voices are not heard; others think they cannot make decisions.	- Training, education, state of wellbeing, creating jobs and business opportunities. Example: In Safe Motherhood project, the volunteer job of a "bicycle ambulance driver" was created. These drivers gained self-confidence and the feeling of being important in society, We are saving our mothers!" - Room for inquiry, pilots, experiments; exceptions, e.g. the individual opinion, needs, ideas and talents. - Create ownership, "Who are we doing this for? Who will benefit? We are doing it for ourselves, for *our* common good!" - Being able to do the whole planning process.
GREEN	Everything has to be discussed. Consensus and harmony is felt as the best way. No room to do things your own way.	- Dare to make discernments, recognise that not everybody is the same. - Have the courage to follow your own path on behalf of the wellbeing of the earth/ world.

In Conclusion

Much of the tension and strife in the world is the result of the clash between different perspectives and felt interests. Example: Poor countries looking for loans or donations from the IMF (International Monetary Fund), have to meet requirements, which the IMF views as necessary (e.g. devaluation of the Malawian kwacha), but are not acceptable for the receiving country (more difficult for people to buy enough food). Another example: People who provide information about prevention of HIV/Aids, see the consequences of this killing disease resulting in more than a million orphans. So, from their perspective it is absolutely necessary to stop unsafe sex. From the perspective of a macho man, the only thing that counts is to have his relief and he does not care at all about the consequences. Sometimes he even has the unfounded idea that unsafe sex especially with young girls might heal him. This clears his conscience and justifies his behaviour to himself.

From the Integral stance all these perspectives are in a way "true" and we cannot dismiss one perspective as being "false". The Yellow Integral approach includes and honours all vMemes and works with all of them. Perspectives are rooted firmly in people's minds, but if Life Conditions change they can learn and become aware of other views. New solutions emerge when we respect and discuss differences and appreciate and cooperate with all stakeholders. Seeing and connecting seemingly contrary perspectives, all as pieces of one and the same puzzle, gives insight into and a way out of conflicts.

Our CE approach opens the dialogue for people in the traditional vMemes. It connects them with concrete experiences of problem solving based on their own insights. During the process they will be confronted with other perspectives, new ideas or values. When these are "translated" and attuned to their dominant vMemes, change becomes possible (like in the example of the TBAs). And they become loyal and creative sparring partners for societal institutions.

However, this is not a one-sided process. CE has to be complemented by supportive structures and systems and environmental change. Empowered Roma need open-minded non-Roma people and institutions available for engagement. Then Roma and non-Roma can build a bridge together and collaborate to create an inclusive society and reduce discrimination and poverty. Empowered Malawian rural inhabitants need open-minded and supportive people and institutions to collaborate on innovative solutions and necessary investments. Social sustainability is a high value measure for these efforts. Such a standard will ensure that communities are inspired, people are educated, and human emergence is fostered. Community Empowerment is at the heart of any sustainable future for humanity.

I began this chapter referencing the heart-warming exclamations at one of our successful Roma CE projects, *"Our Community Got Back Its Soul"*. Here is the vision that is always at the core of our work in creating such outcomes:

Go to the people;
live among them;
love them; learn from them;
start from where they are;
work with them; build on what they have.
But of the best leaders,
when the task is accomplished,
the work completed,
the people all remark,
"We have done it ourselves."

– *Lao Tzu*

EGO, MONEY, EMPIRE: MASTERING THE WORLDLY VEHICLES

By Jordan Bruce MacLeod

An Empire Built on Sand

On a recent trip to Washington, D.C., Laurence Kotlikoff, Economics Professor at Boston University and former member of the President's Council of Economic Advisers, had some difficult news to deliver. He was in the nation's capital to testify before the US Senate Budget Committee that the United States may be in worse financial shape than any developed country in the world. "It's not broke in 75 years or 50 years or 25 years or 10 years. It's broke today." Kotlikoff pointed out that the fiscal gap in the United States is $211 Trillion, 16 times larger than official US debt. When "off book" liabilities such as Social Security are accurately accounted for, the total US Debt-to-GDP ratio is a totally unmanageable 211%.

This dire financial situation puts the world's only superpower and empire in a surprisingly vulnerable position. Like anywhere else, America is dependent on attracting investors from around the globe to purchase its treasuries that fund government expenditures. Today, America is still seen as one of, if not, the, safest country to put your money. The dollar's attractiveness is based on several factors. The US is the largest economy, it possesses the strongest and most technically advanced military, and it functions as the underwriter for the global economic system.

As the world economy has become more diversified, with emerging markets such as India and China developing rapidly, the use of a single national currency of any kind – including the dollar – has increasingly become seen as arbitrary, fragile and undesirable for international trade. Since the 2008 crisis, the governor of China's Central Bank, Zhou Xiaochuan, has been calling for the decoupling of the international monetary system from the "economic conditions and sovereign interests of any single country."

America's dollar status therefore is tenuous and an Achilles Heel for American power. If demand for dollars were to fall, so would its value as it would be nearly impossible to reduce the massive global supply fast enough. Given America's enormous debt, a loss in dollar confidence could quickly call into question America's fiscal integrity. If America were unable to attract the necessary investment, it could still print dollars to fund operations and repay its liabilities, but this would certainly lead to significant inflation and a vicious downward spiral in confidence and governmental incapacity to function effectively. This would in turn make sustaining US military engagements and its powerful global presence virtually impossible. A US contraction could lead to severe geopolitical power-vacuums, financial chaos and international instability. An American Empire built on the dollar as a global reserve currency is an empire built on sand.

While the fall of the dollar and American Empire may seem like an unlikely scenario for some distant future, the potential for it to happen imminently has already arrived. In addition to the dire fiscal situation, there are three extremely worrisome trends in the global markets today that make America's future precarious. First, risk-taking and its obfuscation by global financial institutions have increased since 2008, leaving the financial system highly vulnerable to another crisis. Secondly, emerging contagion due to the oil collapse, Russian sanctions, Swiss Franc volatility, slowing global growth and the dollar's dramatic rise adversely impacting the $9 Trillion in emerging market debt priced in dollars, are all disrupting markets. Thirdly, there is a rapid and decisive move by the G20 to give BRIC countries, and most notably China, a much larger seat at the table.

Last year, the G20 issued an ultimatum to the US Congress to approve the agreed reforms at the IMF to allocate more influence to the BRIC countries or face consequences. The irony of this is that it was actually the

United States that led the IMF reform process to convince European nations to allocate greater roles for the emerging markets. Congress, much like it did the year before, ignored these calls despite pleas from the President and Treasury Secretary Jack Lew. In response, the BRICs have created several multinational institutions to compete against the US-led IMF and World Bank. These moves prompted former US Treasury Secretary and Harvard economist Larry Summers to wonder whether the United States has just lost its role as the underwriter for the global economic system.

While Congress remains in denial over the coordinated movement away from US power and the dollar, the rest of the world is accelerating this course. Recently, Germany unexpectedly announced its support for China's intense lobbying to have the renminbi granted inclusion in the IMF's Special Drawing Rights (SDR) account this year. Other European countries have since followed their lead. The SDR is a basket of reserve currencies that includes the dollar, yen, pound sterling and euro. The IMF reviews the SDR basket every 5 years and China has been ambitiously preparing the renminbi for attaining this global reserve status to reflect its position as the 2nd largest economy in the world. The review for this change begins in May 2015 and requires China to release its gold holdings and move towards depegging their currency from the dollar. It would be formally approved this fall and take effect at the beginning of 2016.

With the SDR decision looming and the creation of several Chinese-led multinational financial institutions such as the Asian Infrastructure and Investment Bank and Asian Development Bank, we are on course for an accelerating shift away from the dollar in the next few months. Once the renminbi is included in the SDR, the latter may grow into a more functional global reserve currency, which would likely also accelerate dollar depreciation. The global financial system, which is already fragile, is unlikely to withstand such a significant shock to the system.

Within the next 12 months (as of Spring, 2015), there is high risk of global financial contagion and this risk is compounded by the potential for unexpected changes to the global monetary system. It should also be noted that China is planning to launch a SWIFT competitor in September, at least partially in response to the American insistence on blocking any global financial institution that does not report its operations to the IRS. This is one of many shortsighted US policies that are literally driving allies away.

Any significant disruption to markets risks setting off widespread Cyprus-style bank failures across the globe, extreme currency depreciation and fluctuations, equity selloffs and the potential for the US to be unable to fund all of its liabilities should the world perceive it losing its central place in the monetary system. Since there are no guarantees for the continuance of America's superpower status going forward, it is essential to understand the serious threats, opportunities and dynamics to project how the monetary system itself could support optimal outcomes.

It is clear that empires throughout the course of history have exhibited a broad spectrum of values. Yet, there has never been one appropriately developed for the complexities of an interconnected global system. The same is true for currencies. Our relationships with these worldly vehicles are always changing, and that is especially true today, in the midst of one of humanity's most epic societal transformations.

Ego, Money, Empire

In today's culture, there is a propensity to use the term "ego" as equivalent to self-centeredness and ego-centricity. "Check your ego at the door." "There's no room for ego here." These business clichés are well intended. They are meant to convey a desire to put the success of an endeavor above self-absorption and "me-first" attitudes that can derail focus, trust and cooperation. The problem however is they lose sight of the fact that it takes a healthy and integrated ego for an individual to effectively participate and function with others. The ego is not something that just gets discarded at the door, nor has any organization on the planet fully transcended it.

If we take the view held by spiritual masters that the ego is ultimately illusory, we must at least recognize that fully transcending the ego is still rare in our world and attained at most by a handful of people. The path towards personal and spiritual growth travels through developing a healthy ego, rather than resisting it or demonizing our intrinsic animal nature.

Harvard psychiatrist, George Vaillant, describes the wisdom of the ego as the wisdom of the integrated adaptive central nervous system. It is the mind's capacity to mediate inner and outer reality, time, ideas and feelings. "The ego must control four horses: desire, conscience, people and reality." Vaillant differentiates the ego from the self in that the self has subjective experiences, thoughts and bodily feelings. The ego's function encompasses defenses, adult development and creativity.

Jane Loevinger once said, "The striving to master, to integrate, to make sense of experience is not one function of the ego among many but the essence of the ego." It is therefore an evolving mental process that enables increasingly mature defenses, intimate relationships and the capacity to hold paradox and ambivalence. "The ego allows us to distinguish," says Vaillant, "that which we must gather the courage to change from that which we must gain the serenity to accept." He concludes:

> As adaptive capacity matures, paranoia evolves into empathy, projection evolves into altruism, and sinner evolves into saint. Ego development reflects our ongoing striving to allow the self-diminishing sin of projection to evolve toward the self-expanding virtue of empathy. [pg 9]

Loevinger's model of ego development aligns closely with the Graves/Spiral Dynamics stages of development. The SDi model, however, is broader in that it applies also to the social, cultural and systemic aspects of human development. This allows us to effectively apply ego dynamics to the cultural and social milieu.

From a non-dual point of view of the Self, the ego is born out of the human perception of separation, providing essential tenacity and defense when immersed in a dangerous world. Rather than a static entity, ego is a dynamic, adaptive and evolving process that enables the individual to develop increasingly mature defenses and relationships through successful engagement with Life Conditions. As our relationship with our ego evolves, the individual becomes increasingly capable of intimacy, interconnectedness and holding the views and values of the other. The more the ego is aligned and in service of the Self, the more it becomes an ally and vehicle for creative transformation.

Our individual egos cannot be adequately understood as isolated processes. They are interconnected meaning-making tools that manifest culturally and collectively through money and empire. Empire is essentially the broadest application of the collective ego. It thus deals with our collective capacity to generate meaning, defend ourselves against threats, support human development and co-create. Empire is the striving to master, to integrate, to make sense of our collective experience.

Through ego, a stronger and more stable sense of identity emerges, which in turn gives currency and relevance to the use of money. Through money, individuals are plugged into a collective network and economy that leads to the formation of empire to ensure its security and orderly perpetuation. This, in turn, generates shared meaning and safety out of chaos. These interdependent processes serve to strengthen the individual and collective centers of gravity of active value systems. An Orange monetary system, for example, reinforces the capacity for Orange statecraft, international organizations, regulated markets, material abundance and individualism. In reality, systems consist of aspects at different stages of development, called Memestacks. As in any system, there will be areas within the monetary system that are more enlightened than others. Non-integrated and unconscious aspects of an Orange monetary system, representing Purple, Red or Blue values are likely to manifest as shadows within the collective and individual experiences (and vice versa).

As ego evolves, individuals' relationships with money also evolve, which in turn transform the network dynamics, functions, capacities and meaning of empire. Thus, rather than view them as evil or intrinsically destructive forces, these three processes, ego, money and empire, may be understood to be mutually interconnected, interdependent and co-creative tools. As we recognize their evolving nature, it becomes self-evident that these processes have the capacity to power our conscious evolution for overcoming the entropic dangers of egocentricity. When they are out of alignment with our personal values or failing to function effectively in complex conditions, we are most likely to view them in a negative light – even to the point of wanting to reject them altogether. That frustration, while understandable, merely perpetuates our inability to solve the problem. It is far more effective to embrace and accept them with compassion and understanding as an intrinsic aspect of human nature while working towards their effective and healthy use.

The more we remove egocentricity through the development of healthy international systems and structures, the more seemingly intractable problems will naturally resolve of their own accord. A healthy ego is characterized by humility, wisdom and letting go of control. When the mature ego is reflected in our collective relationships with money it will automatically lead to the co-creation of a qualitatively different empire featuring new characteristics such as more mature and self-organizing market economies that intrinsically account for the wellbeing of the whole. It is a process that can simultaneously generate a surge in meaning, a renewed sense of common purpose, bursts in creativity, enhanced material security and more effective collective defenses that are appropriate to 21st Century threats.

Empires Emerging

We are building an understanding of empire based on its essential and inescapable function as a worldly tool. Ego, money and empire – the worldly vehicles - have an interdependent relationship, where the maturation of any one of these areas can help loosen the grip of egocentricity within the others.

Egocentricity and narcissism translate into arbitrary power and self-gain at the expense of others and the whole. When subjectively embedded within these vehicles, they become ends in themselves. As such, they are the cause of the vast majority of human suffering and problems. The more they are dissolved and approached with non-attachment, the more ego, money and empire decentralize, dematerialize and transform into powerful objective tools of the Self. Addressing our systemic problems from this holographic perspective holds the power to address the very real problems of our age that will never be resolved through the usual piecemeal, manipulative and superficial approaches.

With the objective of creating a world with healthy ego development, there is an urgent need for an empire that is capable of promoting vertical individual and collective development while generating solutions to our most important global problems ranging from terrorism to nuclear threats to climate change. A healthy empire requires empathy and wisdom as well as fierce toughness to willingly defend against military threats, nihilism and violence. The more an empire is able to sublimate the egocentricity of individuals into creative and productive expression, the healthier it will be and the more it will overcome its enemies through attraction and integration rather than coercion or force.

While the US Empire faces financial duress and waning international credibility as stewards of the global system, at least three competitors are rising up to challenge America's status: China (and the BRICs), the Islamic State, and an Internationalist movement that would weaken the United States by replacing the dollar with the IMF's SDR basket of currencies. Obviously the memetic contours of each one varies dramatically. China is primarily a Blue state that regularly employs repressive tactics on common Western values such as freedom of expression and political dissent. It has plans to reintroduce gold as a means to solidify the renminbi and is acquiring reserves in stealth with a voracious appetite. While Chinese leadership is arguably very well aligned with complex domestic Life Conditions and have done commendable work moving the nation towards Orange enterprise and science, there remains a serious misalignment with the Orange, Green and Yellow vMemes of the West. If it were to assume America's leadership role today, it would likely be regressive and suppressive of Western values, and thus a core, leading edge of global human development.

The Islamic State, of course, is barbaric and ruthless. It should be understood as the collective Id on steroids: funded by ultra-wealthy sheiks and oil producing nation-states, amplified through social media and validated through religious doctrine. It has capitalized on mass unemployment, hostile anti-Western sentiment and political instability throughout the Middle East to build a powerful movement. It has zero tolerance for Western values and is dedicated to installing an oppressive Islamic Caliphate globally. While that may seem unlikely, its intention and potential to disrupt should never be underestimated. This is especially true should the current geopolitical order dissolve into chaos.

Finally, there is significant interest within the international community to bring the United States down a peg in exchange for a more level playing field of nations. This end could be achieved easily enough simply by replacing the dollar with the SDR basket (that was updated to include China and other leading economies) as the functional global reserve currency. This would, as discussed, seriously weaken the United States without replacing it with a clear global leader. Power would shift to even more opaque institutions and diluted among nations with little common vision for world leadership and direction. International leadership would more closely resemble the EU and the United Nations – neither of which are exactly case studies on effective organizational structures - while strong autocratic regimes such as China and Russia would gain relative power and could quite easily overcome the international community if they were to break away due to irreconcilable values and interests.

The critical point here is that the shift towards a global reserve currency that balances the interests of actors in the global system makes considerable sense from an economic perspective. The geopolitical implications, however, for the balance of power and leadership in a multi-polar world are significant and overlooked.

Increasing the complexity and responsibility of actors within the system while diminishing America's role, requires a substantial leap forward in vertical complexity to align disparate interests and ensure that the resulting Western weakness is able to counter State actors employing regressive mercantilist national strategies for global resource control and brute force as diplomacy. Europe has long resented America's primary role in the international system. Removing American power without simultaneously evolving the dynamics of the system will likely result in simply replacing one superpower with another that is far less aligned with their values and interests.

All of this is to say the obvious alternatives to the US dollar and American leadership from the point of view of Western democratic values leaves much to be desired. Even an International movement might be considered the most attractive option, yet would be led by private central banks and the IMF, which are not directly accountable to citizens of any country. For anyone with experience of the United Nations, and its inability to efficiently manage any problem due to the misalignment of interests between nations, or with the woeful political and economic situation in the European Union at present, it would be clear that the amalgamation of diverse nations into a reserve currency basket through closed organizations with little democratic accountability is more likely to yield dysfunction, arbitrary power and weak leadership, in the medium to long term, resulting in greater public discontent and dissociation.

While these alternatives are found wanting from the context of global systems and values, America itself has lost its effectiveness as the leader of the free world. It is truly over its head. Studies have shown that its citizens now have negligible impact on public policy and the direction of the country, due to the massive power and influence of large corporations and lobby groups. American governance has effectively become an oligarchy in practice rather than a truly accountable and functional democracy as intended by the Founding Fathers.

Congress has also failed to recognize the new reality of a more complex global economic landscape that merits increased roles and influence for emerging markets. They have consistently blocked the President's very reasonable attempts to lead the international community at the IMF. The reforms would have given emerging nations a larger influence over the international system yet would have preserved American veto power. By failing to approve even these modest changes, BRIC nations have redoubled their efforts to work around the United States entirely. The sense of entitlement to underwriting the global system, combined with the unwillingness to lead reforms and protect its citizens from financial recklessness, is accelerating America's decline.

One of the most crucial applications of SDi in our age is that it enables us to assess what kind of functional competencies are required for global Life Conditions and then build accordingly. In SDi terminology, our Orange economic systems and institutions are entering a late phase of development, where aging populations and rising debts in the West are making the status quo unsustainable. Rather than regress to Blue authoritarian power structures (China), Red barbarism (Islamic State and other terror groups) or Blue-Orange top-down internationalism (IMF and private central banks) that fails to qualitatively change the current systemic dynamics, a next-order system is required that transcends the current socio-economic paradigm which is currently on life support.

The Millennial Empire

> *"The foundation of empire is art and science. Remove them or degrade them, and the empire is no more. Empire follows art and not vice versa."*

> – William Blake

Given America's extraordinary scientific and creative accomplishments, it is hard to imagine that it is on the verge of falling. Yet, that is precisely the case. The success of the US-led international system has yielded the emergence of powerful developing nations that have earned an increased say in the global system.

America has greatly benefited from the current arrangement and also assumed heavy costs through military engagements, lives lost and contributing more than any country towards sustaining global order and security. Indeed, America is worthy of much credit for its massive net-positive influence on the world since World War II despite its shortcomings. Severe, existential challenges are directly in front of us on a global scale, and this is primarily due to America's success rather than failures. It has helped to create unprecedented complexity that is forcing humanity to grow up and, for the first time in human history, take accountability for the whole of our actions. Global society could not possibly have emerged to this point without America's leadership, courage and wisdom. It has led us to the edge of a global renaissance.

Success is often resented and in America's case that is certainly true. It is resented by many in the world for its freedoms, wealth, power, beauty and the overall good nature of its people. It is also resented for its arrogance in international diplomacy, its meddling in regional affairs far from its own, its domestic inequality and for the naivety of its politicians on foreign matters despite the extraordinary impact of their decisions in foreign lands.

It is only when we grasp the massive success of America's contribution to the world that we can properly contextualize its shadow. The success of the international system has exposed obvious limitations and aspects that are truly unworthy of a prosperous, globalized society. Those who do not value America and the outstanding qualities it has stood for, despite its problems and failures are sorely ill-equipped to lead in the 21st Century.

At the same time, an appreciation of America and the West's contributions to global development must not prevent us from taking a firm resolve to bring light into the shadows of the global international system. In particular, this relates to a monetary and financial system that is inherently built on arbitrary power and egocentric gambling with other peoples' money. Central banks such as the Federal Reserve are essentially private monopolies, owned by banks. The structure enables a few to profit at the exclusion of the many. At the heart of it lies the arbitrary power of banks to create money and to use other peoples' money for their own benefit while massive losses are left for taxpayers, depositors and future generations.

When the Founding Fathers of America created their great nation, they drafted a Constitution upon which the people could be empowered to continuously disrupt the status quo and continue to expand upon the values of freedom, self-determination and the individual's pursuit of happiness. The Founding Fathers were visionaries and the principles upon which they sought independence remain to this day relevant and a source of inspiration for new frontiers of social development,

> "We hold these truths to be self-evident, that all men are created equal, that they are endowed by their Creator with certain unalienable Rights, that among these are Life,

Liberty and the pursuit of Happiness. That to secure these rights, Governments are instituted among Men, deriving their just powers from the consent of the governed, --That whenever any Form of Government becomes destructive of these ends, it is the Right of the People to alter or to abolish it, and to institute new Government, laying its foundation on such principles and organizing its powers in such form, as to them shall seem most likely to effect their Safety and Happiness."

Declaration of Independence (1776)

The recognition that all men are created equal is the foundation upon which slavery was overcome. It set in motion movements for women, African Americans (and other minorities) and homosexuals to attain equal rights in the social, political and economic spheres. Most Founding Fathers held their values as universal – that all were created equal, endowed by their Creator with unalienable Rights. The fact that their vision continues to leave room for the ongoing evolution of our social contracts suggests that their vision embodies a higher level of consciousness than where we collectively stand today.

Today, we have yet a new challenge. We must learn to apply their vision towards the evolution of the international economic and monetary system. First, and foremost, it is now self-evident that the power to create money can and should be held by and for the people rather than a select few. This would necessitate issuing new money directly to the people themselves rather than through a fractional reserve system. Without a fractional reserve system, banks would be unable to use customer deposits for excessive lending and risk-taking. A digital dollar would enable the United States to issue money directly to its citizens.

This process would simultaneously remove the toxic risk-taking from the system, turn banks into responsible stewards of our wealth and tangibly increase the benefits to its citizens. Further, if this system were completely monetized, it could also enable the use of negative interest rates when conditions warranted it. In times of contraction and recession, negative rates could have a vital, catalytic effect on resuscitating the economy and the flow of money through the system when it freezes up through fear and uncertainty. Negative rates accelerate the velocity of money and thus effectively increase the money supply. Simply turning the interest rates upward when the economy recovers allows the money supply to maintain stable levels.

In our current reality, central banks have been unable to go below zero interest rates, so they have been forced into trillion dollar bailouts and quantitative easing to compensate for this technical incapacity. This process of introducing significant cash into the system has prevented catastrophic collapse thus far, but it also makes it exponentially more difficult to tighten the money supply in a timely manner, thus greatly increasing the risk of inflation and new crises.

The inability to go below a zero interest rate policy is known as the Effective Lower Bound (ELB) problem. This problem was recently addressed in a research paper by Citi's Chief Economist Willem Buiter and previously covered in my book *New Currency* and my Cornerstone Blue Paper, "Beyond Bailouts". I argued that the massive quantitative easing programs have come about because of the inability to lower interest rates below zero (the ELB problem) even when the San Francisco Federal Reserve model called for a negative 5% rate. Completely digitizing the monetary system makes it possible to place negative interest rates on deposits or to place a circulation charge on money itself (demurrage) to ensure money is kept in smooth circulation. It also decentralizes the flow of money within the system to dissolve the concentration of wealth effect.

A digitized monetary system could not only eliminate the need for quantitative easing it could enable a qualitative transformation of the economy through the circulation charge. As discussed in New Currency, the circulation charge embeds humility, empathy and resilience into the monetary system, which, in turn, reinforces those qualities at the individual and collective levels as the currency takes hold.

What this implies is the potential for a next level system to emerge with the ability to generate mature ego development and an empire that is inclusive and effective at generating global prosperity. This is a perfect fit for a Millennial generation that began entering the workforce around the time of the 2008 financial crisis and saw firsthand how Wall Street greed impacted their employment prospects and burdened the world they will inherit with unprecedented debt. Seeing what chasing money for its own sake can lead to, it is not surprising this generation is seeking meaning and social upliftment over money alone.

With 85M Americans born between the years 1982 and 2004, this generation represents one third of the US population and will become 50% of the workforce by 2020. Other Westerns nations mirror this trend. Millennials are technology savvy, creative, highly networked with friends but feel largely disenfranchised by large financial institutions. They are social and collaborative in nature and see crowdfunding as the future model for problem-solving. 75% of Millennials want to see disruption in the financial industry by leading tech firms and software startups.

Millennials intuitively understand that money should function like the Internet and be freely accessible and democratic. The idea that a select few could have the ability to own the Federal Reserve or create money out of thin air or control their deposits to gamble with is totally misaligned and anathema to them. Rather, they want to see solutions emerge from the ground-up and are willing to dedicate their lives to the causes they care about over high-paying jobs that don't provide enough meaning.

This generation has the potential to lead the Millennial Empire into humanity's global age. Make no mistake: this is an intergenerational, transnational project that requires the alignment and healthy expression of all value systems. While Millennials are a perfect fit for the emerging values of next-generation finance and harnessing the wisdom of the crowd, they are also relatively inexperienced and naïve in the realms of geopolitics, economic policy and the threats to civilization. There are tendencies towards Red impulsiveness and Green meaning-making and will require considerable work for society to realign healthy Blue and Orange values to support and ground emerging Green values. Yellow integrative and Turquoise holistic capacities will be essential in this process to avoid cultural collapse into groupthink, the fragmentation of subcultures and nations, and failing to fully actualize visionary ideals to counter hostile enemies and existential threats.

The Omega Point

We are in the process of mastering the worldly vehicles of ego, money and empire. Mastery does not imply a power over others. It is simply the discovery, acceptance and effective application of our evolving nature towards improving the human condition. So where are they taking us? SDi informs us that human nature consists of evolving bio-psycho-social processes. The more our systems are aligned with this multi-dimensional reality, the more functionally effective they can be. Today, we live in an interconnected global economy and are already effectively using a global reserve currency in the dollar as a mechanism for world trade. The values embedded within the global monetary system mediate the dynamics between memetically diverse parts of the world. The more egocentricity is removed from the monetary system, the more room every nation in the world will have to thrive regardless of its vertical level of development.

Egocentricity is a highly entropic and costly phenomenon. Significantly removing it from the monetary system through the use of a circulation charge simultaneously removes many of the entropic forces that lead to unsustainable economies: the compulsion for exponential growth, structural unemployment, systemic concentrations of wealth and discounting the future. It's why one of the great 20th Century economists, Irving Fisher, predicted that a circulation charge could get the United States out of a depression in a matter of weeks. When a nation is connected to such a monetary system, it is capable of thriving regardless of where it is on the Spiral. It can potentially help uplift a Red Arab nation that suffers from 40+% unemployment as much as it can help create more effective and participatory Western democracies. Further, it can connect the disparate and seemingly divergent interests of peoples and nations, and generate shared purpose, meaning and identity. Does it mean cold-blooded terrorists are going to transform overnight? Of course not, but this reverses the trend of global fragmentation and gets us moving in the right direction.

A global monetary system with a circulation charge could give rise to a Millennial Empire that works to give every human being the access and ability to participate in a globalizing marketplace. Through peer-to-peer mechanisms such as crowdfunding and crowdlending, citizens can self-organize to solve real problems across the spectrum of values and Life Conditions. The proceeds from the circulation charge can be allocated to strengthen the Millennial Empire's capacity for enhancing our ability to connect and create, spread the technology to disconnected areas and defend the system from external threats. There is potential to solve the economic and material problems of our species within decades.

When we consider the coming singularity in technical innovation and change and the correlating rise in consciousness on the planet, it would appear that we are heading for an Omega Point in economic life. The rapid change and increasing complexities require a dynamic and resilient empire to hold humanity together through the quickening transition. Without collective wisdom and empathy, the world will surely fall apart at the seams.

SDi makes clear that this is no end point for human evolution, but it marks a significant step in transcending the so-called First Tier of human Life Conditions that are based on survival and scarcity.

While America may have lost its way in recent decades, it would be unwise to write it off. Tackling arbitrary power and egocentricity is built within its DNA. The next financial crisis will bring great disillusionment and anger towards the banks, lawmakers and lobbyists that brought us all to this point. There is an opportunity for the citizens of America and other Western nations to lead a whole systems change that literally changes the world as we know it. Complexity is now over the head of any nation to serve as a shining beacon for the world. Global complexity requires global solutions, and the emerging systems are in dire need of an infusion of the vision and values that makes America great. Directly in front of us is an opportunity to co-create a world that would make the Founding Fathers proud. Winston Churchill understood well never to underestimate America when it has its back against the wall. After exhausting all the alternatives, Americans will have one last chance to do the right thing.

Bibliography

Beck, Don & Cowan, Chris. *Spiral Dynamics: Mastering Values, Leadership and Change.* (2006). Blackwell Publishers. Malden, MA.

Buiter, Willem. "High Time to Get Low: Getting Rid of the Lower Bound on Nominal Interest Rates." (2015). CITI Research. http://willembuiter.com/ELB/.pdf

Garrison, Jim. *America as Empire.* (2004). Berrett-Koehler. San Francisco, CA.

MacLeod, Jordan. "Ego, Money, Empire." (2004). Unpublished article.

MacLeod, Jordan. *New Currency: How Money Changes the World as we Know It.* (2009). Integral Publishers. Pacific Grove, CA.

MacLeod, Jordan. "Beyond Bailouts." (2010). Cornerstone Global Associates. London.

MacLeod, Jordan. "New Money: The Evolution of Finance." *The Future of Western Civilization: Psychiatrist Dr Nicholas Beecroft Interviews Visionary Leaders.* Series 1, Book 3. (2011).

Vaillant, George. *The Wisdom of the Ego.* Harvard University Press. (1997) Cambridge, MA.

SDi IN ORGANIZATIONS: EXPERIENCES IN MEXICO

By: Roberto Bonilla-Núñez, Ruth Bonilla and Luis Garcia

"It's not that we need to form new organizations. It's simply that we have to awaken to new ways of thinking."

Don E. Beck, PhD

Introduction

This chapter will be focused on sharing some experiences applying Spiral Dynamics Integral (SDi) in Mexican Organizations. These experiences cover a period from 2000 to 2013, include private companies, NGO´s, and Mexican Government agencies and sectors. A team of twelve consultants has served under contract in guiding the execution of these projects in eight organizations. We consulted informally, i.e. not under contract, with another 10 organizations. Ten of the twelve consultants have received SDi Certification under Dr. Beck in trainings held both in the USA and Mexico. The generalized case study following is simplified from the many actual experiences we have had, is done so to enhance its didactic value, and to honor the confidentiality agreements we have with our clients.

What Is An Organization?

Dr. Peter Checkland (1999) from Lancaster University asserts that an organization is essentially composed for human interactions: Associations are "Human Activity Systems". For the purpose of this chapter we will presume our organizations of interest serve to reach some goals or fulfill some purposes. This report applies equally well to for-profit and not-for-profit organizations. Where we find it helpful to augment our SDi understanding of organizations we will incorporate concepts from the Adizes Graduate School material (Adizes, 1999)

Reasons For Change In The Organization

We become involved with an organization because there is interest in becoming more effective in meeting goals and fulfilling purposes. We may be attending to one person, a team, a committee, a board, or multiples of these leverage points. In any case, the process begins with the owners'/leaders' sense of discomfort with the current performance of the organization. This discomfort emerges from at least one of the following:

1) Due to a high risk of collapse.

2) Due to a wish to improve the current performance.

3) Due to a very ambitious desire to reach a new Vision, which is a variant of 2)

Tools For Assessing The Interdependent Organizational Factors Affecting Change

Deep personal interview: We undertake an extensive inquiry with the organizational leader(s) primarily to articulate for all involved what the leader wants to change, and to what the leader wants it to change to. As Dr. Beck has advised us many times, "Getting rid of what you don't want is not the same as getting what you do want." We require clarity regarding what is to change to what.

Adizes Assessment: To support this inquiry we have the leader(s) complete the Adizes Organizational Life Cycle Assessment, which is available free from the Adizes Institute here: *http://www.adizes.com.* The assessment adds greatly to the leaders' understanding of where the organization is and where it could change to. Farther down in this chapter we will explain how we blend some aspects of Adizes Methodology tools with SDi tools.

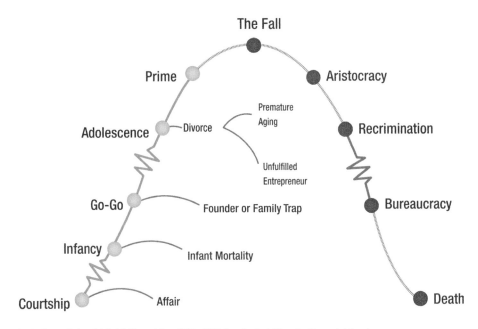

Used with permission. © Ichak Kalderon Adizes 1971 – 2015, from the book Managing Corporate Lifecycles

Example: Adizes Organization Life Cycle Assessment

From What? To What? Bullet List: Leaders are directed to create a 1-2 page bullet point list for both questions, "From What?" and "To What?" We assist in completing this list. Using the bullet list format, requiring that leaders synthesize in short phrases their own perspective, reduces the bias any scribe might contribute in the reporting of this exercise. Where the leader(s) are not clear about the "From What?" and/or the "To What?" we are not frustrated. This has pointed us to a possible weakness in Blue and/or Orange and begins to suggest what interventions may be useful.

Example: From What? To What? Bullet List.

Change from this...	To this
Poor production performance, generating problems with key clients.	Improve deadline success measures from 60% to at least 80%.
Employee turnover close to 50%.	Achieve a "Great Place to Work" award.
Losing market share	Recover market share in current geographies and start having presence in new geographies X, Y…
…etc.	…etc.

Modified SWOT Analysis: We create stratified teams of 12-16 people from within the company. We ask these teams to each submit a SWOT analysis, i.e. what do they conclude are the Strengths, Weaknesses, Opportunities, Threats present for the organization now. In addition we ask them to list the Challenges they foresee for the next twelve months.

Big Picture: We require the leader(s)' articulate their big picture, their philosophy of the organization. This includes at least an articulation of the organization's vision, mission, and values. Where there is a workers union involved we request documents that describe the union operation principles and its philosophy as well

Coding From What? To What? We have developed expertise in coding verbal phrases that describe an organization, in terms of the SDi significance measures expressed by each phrase. The next figure shows the results of coding the phrases collected in a complete version of the table above, plus phrases obtained from other organizational materials, e.g. a mission statement may be split into several phrases where each phrase contains a complete idea. In a real project we can codify between 500 to 3,000 phrases.

Change?

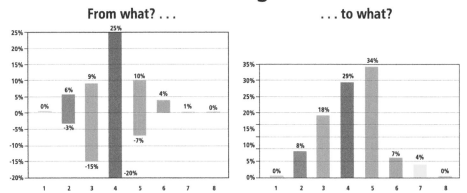

From what? . . .   **. . . to what?**

vMeme Organizational Diagnostic
– From What? To What?

In this chapter, for illustration purposes, we include only a single current reality vMemetic profile. In real cases we create this vMeme profile for each stratified group that we consult with in the organization. This allows us to compare how the current reality is seen by the top level managers, the middle managers, supervisors and workers. This ensures our final natural design for guiding change in the organization entails the perceptions of all stakeholder groups and we avoid the limitations of a "one size fits all" plan.

vMeme Organizational Diagnostic
– Coding Measures

The phrases mentioned above are coded according to the following:

- Change State Indicator – Six States.
  1) Everything is ok (Alpha State)

  2) Something is not functioning well (Beta State)

  3) Evolution (the positive evolution of Beta State, meaning improving actions)

  4) New positive reality (New Alpha)

5)   Current problems (the downward path the Beta State may travel)

6)   Chronic problems (Gamma Trap, where the members of the organization report there are no options for change)

- vMemes, differentiating healthy and unhealthy expressions.
  1)   Healthy expressions are those phrases consistent with the organization's philosophy and those that further success in facing future challenges.

  2)   Unhealthy expressions are those phrases that conflict with the organization's philosophy and limit success in facing future challenges.

The Importance Of Life Conditions

To add further detail to our analysis of an organization we take a close look at Life Conditions and their relationship to organizational and individual behavior. One of Clare Graves's major insights was that behavior co-arises with Life Conditions. Dr. Beck (Beck, 2012 p.164) refines the pathway of this relationship in more detail. He directs our attention to the 5 Deep Structure of behavior manifestation:

- Strata One: **Actions and Behaviors**, which derive from
- Strata Two: **Systems and Structures**, which derive from
- Strata Three: **Minds and ways of thinking**, which derive from
- Strata Four: **Memetic Codes**, which derive from
- Strata Five: **Life Conditions.**

The above reveals five powerful leverage points available for affecting change in an organization. The first step in considering remedial action however is to discover where the action is needed; which of the Five Strata are not configured to serve the organization's end goals or intentions? To visualize this approach Dr. Beck uses the plumb bob metaphor, placing Life Conditions, the natural attractor at the major anchor point, and behavior with the greatest range of possibility at the free end, as shown in the figure below. If the plumb bob is misaligned there will be conflict, waste, inefficiency, and often failure. The plumb bob analysis shows us where change could occur to mitigate these problems, and support effective action.

Plumb Bob Metaphor

- **Strata Five: Life Conditions**

- **Strata Four: Memetic Codes**

- **Strata Three: Minds and ways of thinking**

- **Strata Two: Systems and structures**

- **Strata One: Actions and behaviors**

We break down Life Conditions further into two categories, those Life Conditions external to the organization, and those internal to the organization. We review both the nature of each of the measures below, as well as their continuous interaction across the two categories.

External Life Conditions:

1) Macro-economic variables.

2) Competitor's strategic actions.

3) Climate change.

4) Political issues.

5) Social Issues.

6) Technological changes.

7) Etc.

Internal Life Conditions:

1) Organizational Philosophy.

2) Organizational policies.

3) Reward systems.

4) Planning and execution posture.

5) Internal rules.

6) Union posture and interactions.

7) Etc.

With this information collected we then analyze it using the vMeme Reality Graph and the Change State Indicator model. The following are samples that mimic that obtained from real organizations:

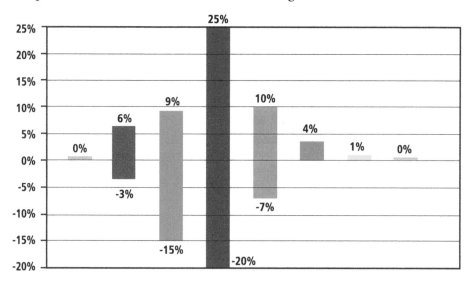

vMeme Reality Graph – Measures of Healthy and Unhealthy vMeme Expressions

The positive % values above represent healthy vMeme expressions. The negative % values represent unhealthy vMeme expressions. The graph shows unhealthy expressions in the Purple, Red, Blue, and Orange vMemes. This parallels the manifestations in the states 2, 3 and 4 in the Change State Indicator graph below.

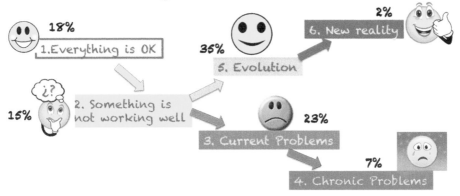

Identifying Desired Actions

When engaging an organization we conduct training for a team of 4-6 managers, including the CEO. This training of the "Design Team" provides the members with a working knowledge of SDi principles and some fundamentals of the Adizes Methodology (TOP LeaF program, http://www.adizes.com/store/product.php?productid=17628&cat=0&page=&featured=Y). At this point in the process the consultant leader meets with the Design Team to review the results of the following:

1) Insights derived from the organization's Adizes Life Cycle review.

2) The vMeme Organizational Diagnostic (above, current vs. desired vMemes).

3) Insights derived from the vMeme Reality graph (above).

4) The Change State Indicator model (above).

We engage the Design Team as fellow collaborators. We need their unique and invaluable knowledge and experience informing each step of the plan design. Equally important, if our intervention is to be sustained upon our departure, these are the people who must be invested in, and sufficiently knowledgeable to continue the change process once we are out of the picture.

We begin with a dialogue around the Adizes Life Cycle results and the actions the Adizes Methodology recommends. This is an information gathering and clarification process. We do not make decisions regarding interventions at this point.

From here we move into our vMeme analysis, attending to unhealthy vMeme expressions. SDi asserts that in the vMeme maturation line, senior vMemes transcend and include all the junior vMemes. Our experience has shown that it is probably impossible to have a stable, healthy senior vMeme if any of the junior, included, vMemes are being expressed in unhealthy ways. We articulate ways to make each vMeme expression healthy, starting from "left to right", meaning shifting first the unhealthy purple manifestations, then red, then blue and so on.

How do we determine in detail what is an unhealthy vMeme expression and what change is needed to shift to a healthy expression? We use an Excel spreadsheet to code each phrase we collect in the diagnostic stage. Then with the use of filters, we isolate into files, say, those phases coded as unhealthy Purple. In that same file we also are able to see each phrase and its corresponding Change State Indicator. This is extremely useful information because effective design of interventions must account for the different approaches that will be successful based on whether we are addressing a Beta condition (#2) or Revolutionary stage (#3) or Gamma Trap (#4).

At this point we recommend looking for quick wins in Gamma Trap issues. This is the peak "Stuckness" phase, and often a relatively tiny nudge can free up the organization to move into a new Alpha stage. Early wins, grabbing the "low hanging fruit" are desirable as they give early positive reinforcement and encouragement to continue. To further this search we review in detail how current Life Conditions are naturally generating the Gamma Trap condition. Then we use the Natural Design Equation to realign the organization to adapt to, and support, its new Alpha: How does Who lead Whom to change from What, to What, Where and When?

Also during this process we review the desired vMemetic profile and determine actions that will support this vision. We measure the propriety of our action plan by assuring planned actions are in a natural evolutionary flow and do not compromise the change process in the organization. This ensures we also attend proactively to, and mitigate to the degree possible, resistance to change. Finally, we validate our planned actions by comparing them to the Adizes Methodology recommendations.

During this co-design process we validate the final plan for action with the Six Conditions for Change (Beck & Cowan, 1999, pp. 75-85), i.e. is our plan consistent with the information we generate regarding the potential for change, using the following 6 categories?

1) **Potential in the mind/brain:** Is cognitive capacity available to meet the demands of the new conditions?

2) **Solutions to current problems:** Has the organization exhausted solutions to their problems?

3) **Dissonance and uncertainty:** Is there a felt sense of something not being right?

4) **Insight and alternatives:** Is there, or can we emerge, insights as to what will work better and why?

5) **Barriers identified and solved:** Are there Life Conditions that preclude the needed change?

6) **Consolidation and support:** Are Life Conditions present that will serve to stabilize the change at its new level?

We call this detailed analysis an "Organizational Acupuncture Plan". It is our intent to identify very few, but extremely effective, acupuncture or leverage points (Meadows, 1999) and integrate them in a well-articulated and well-focused plan.

What Is Next?

At the beginning of our consultations we ascertain with the leader what the main purpose of this change initiative is. The graphs in this chapter show a situation where the purpose was defined as "Awake the Innovation Drive in the Management Team" (Note the Orange vMeme in the desired vMemetic profile shown above). In reviewing the data regarding what the current vMeme profile is we quickly saw that the existing Life Conditions were precluding the natural emergence of Orange, the innovation centered, vMeme. Dr. Adizes (199) states that a Prime organization blends a very well balanced equilibrium between controllability and flexibility. In the case of a healthy Spiral for an organization which looks to awaken an innovation culture, leadership must ensure that the Blue vMeme does not asphyxiate the emerging, healthy Orange vMeme. In this case, Blue should be honored and respected for the order it brings to the organization (control), and where its enforcement of order is excessive, that is makes it too difficult for innovators to find the grey areas or operate just beyond the vision the order is based on, then Blue control in these areas should be reduced (flexibility).

Summary

The purpose of the intervention reported here is to identify a very few well designed actions (Acupuncture Points or Leverage points) and to implement them in a focused and organized manner. During the implementation process we keep in mind that all designed solutions are hypotheses to be tested. Some of them will work very well. Others won't. Failure to achieve the intended results is a success in finding a weakness in our plan. At such a point we review the original assumptions behind the hypothesis, make the adjustments approved by the Design Team and continue to move forward.

Our selected actions are often to change internal Life Conditions, the "low hanging fruit" preference. Secondarily we attend to external Life Conditions. If we can effect a change in these external Life Conditions, we do. In many cases we cannot. In these instances, we look to make changes in the 5 Deep elements to better align the "plumb bob". This new alignment of Life Conditions with the vMemes, minds, systems and behaviors, is a natural design. Such a natural design should emerge healthy adaptations at all 5 levels. If this occurs we may find the purpose of our services achieved, thru a shift in Life Conditions, emergence of new vMemes and/or newly healthy expressions of existing vMemes, new ways of thinking, system changes, and new behavior. No outcome is guaranteed when engaging human beings around the notion of change. We have found though that applying our methods to organizations most often emerges the desired goals.

Mexico's Team

In different ways and moments the following persons have contributed to develop the ideas described in this chapter.

1) Roberto Bonilla Núñez (General Coordinator)

2) Luis García (R & D Leader)

3) Ruth Bonilla (Coding Quality Assurance)

4) Coding team:
   a. Jazmín Calvillo, Armando Moctezuma V., Armando Moctezuma S., Boby Bonilla, Lydia Calderon, Samuel Bonilla, Héctor González

The Global SDi Team

The SDi community of practice, most active as the SDi Yahoo listserv, is available for anyone obtaining SDi certification. We enjoyed the support of dozens of SDi experts thru this listserv, and were especially well advised when we were lost or unsure of how to address several serious dilemmas. Specifically we are indebted to the following for their generosity, insight, and guidance: Dr. Don Beck, Elza Maalouf, Dr. Russ Volckmann, Dr. Bruce Gibb, Dr. Bjarni Jónsson, Caleb Rosado, Mike Jay, Colonel Fred Krawchuk, Dr. Marilyn Hamilton, Dr. Alejandro Ruelas-Gossi, Alexandra Hidalgo, Dr. Darrel Gooden, Dr. Ichak Adizes, Mario Benitez and Juan Carlos Kaiten. We acknowledge a special debt of gratitude for the continuous and very valuable support of our dear friend Petra Pietersen in many, many different ways. Finally, we were always furthered by the countless interactions with colleagues we enjoyed time with during the SDi certification workshops at Santa Barbara and Dallas and the many SDi Confabs we have been able to attend.

Bibliography

Adizes I. (1999) *Managing Corporate Lifecycles.* Prentice Hall

Beck D.E. and Cowan C. C. (1996), *Spiral Dynamics: Mastering values, leadership, and Change.* Blackwell Publishing

Beck D.E. (2012) "Spiral Dynamics Integral" SDi 1 Certification course. Spiral Dynamics Group Seminar Materials, Santa Barbara California.

Beck D.E. (2013) "Natural Designs: Second Tier Leadership, Organizational Elegance & Integral Management," Spiral Dynamics Group Seminar Materials, Santa Barbara California.

Checkland P. (1999) *Systems Thinking Systems Practice.* Wiley

Meadows D. (1999) "Leverage Points: places to intervene a system." The Sustainability Institute

REVALUING PURPLE, RED AND BLUE

By Jasper Rienstra

Introduction

In 2005 Don Beck asked Peter Merry to found the Dutch Center for Human Emergence (CHE Netherlands). Three years later several independent consultants, trainers and coaches, including myself, decided to start a Second Tier consultancy firm: CHE Synnervate. Our core product can be summarized as "Syn-nervating". This term points to our conviction that in our present era we need two movements to further develop our organizations, institutions and societies:

- **Syn** – connects the different parts of a person, organization or society and
- **nervate** – vitalizes the new emerging whole.

Not by accident this two part term affirms the dance between the individuating and the accommodating colors of the Spiral.

The mission of CHE Synnervate is to meet our clients where they are and move them along in their natural maturation trajectory. This is what we communicate to the world and to our clients, whether they are Spiral informed or not. What we do not always tell our clients, but what we always practice is, "The Spiral is our client." In other words, we meet and move our clients in their next natural step **on the Spiral**! In doing so, an interesting homogenous pattern seems to emerge in what those next natural steps turn out to be:

1) Most organizations we work with are, in terms of their internal drives and intentions, moving towards Orange-Green and sometimes Green-Yellow. Orange, Green and Yellow are also by far the dominant vMemes of individuals we measure with SDi assessments like Peoplescan or ValueMatch.

2) Most organizations and people in them are, in terms of their behavior, culture and systems, dominantly Blue-Orange or Orange-Blue driven with, especially in non-profits e.g. schools and municipalities, remnants of Purple family-culture and Red local rulers.

3) The client briefings we get are often a combination of

   a. More healthy Orange please! (sounding like "professionalizing" and "real implementation of accountability and result-oriented management") and

   b. More healthy Green please! (sounding like "more sense of connection and communality", "more co-creation between different parts of the organization" and "more focus on the whole, beyond local borders").

4) The next natural step to become healthier Orange/Green is for those organizations often to focus on re-including the less complex vMemes like Purple, Red and Blue.

5) At first our clients are often not so happy with our Spiral advice, "You want more Orange and Green? Then you need to start with including healthy Purple, Red and Blue!". This is understandable because often they are happy to have just transcended and become free from the domination of those vMemes. But once they get their Yellow systemic perspective and consciousness switched on, they understand the transcend and include principle and they start to revalue Purple, Red and Blue.

Ken Wilber phrases the transcend and include principle in *A Brief History of Everything* like this, "Evolution goes beyond what went before, but because it must embrace what went before, then its very nature is to transcend and include and thus it has an inherent directionality, a secret impulse, toward increasing depth, increasing intrinsic value, increasing consciousness. In order for evolution to move at all, it must move in those directions - there's no place else for it to go!" In this chapter I will illustrate this pattern by sharing my experiences in leadership development in organizations and how I go about revaluing Purple, Red and Blue.

The Need to Revalue Purple, Red and Blue

In my leadership development projects, I like to work with SDi as a perspective that offers some grip on the complexity of reality. As a starting point we often work with SDi tests like Peoplescan or ValueMatch, to obtain a personal profile of each participant in terms of vMemes that they accept/reject more or less. Such assessments will provide us with a profile of the sort below.

I often see the following pattern. Many people in management positions are predominantly driven by Yellow, Green and Orange. They have little acceptance and a huge rejection of Purple, Blue and Red. The briefing that they give me when they contact me is often about wanting inspiration, being inspired, collectively and becoming a better team while doing that. Such a briefing is consistent with their dominant vMemes. After the introduction of the vMemes, in which I go to great lengths to be as neutral as possible about the colors, many managers wake up (or reawake) to the importance of the Purple/Red/Blue basis in life, and in their leadership.

For the closure of the personal leadership part of a program, I often host a ritual in which I invite everybody to say aloud, in front of all the others, what their highest value is in their work (or life even) and what their first next natural step in their leadership development will be. Almost always I find that most of the managers have Yellow/Green inspired values ("I want to make everybody thrive", "real connections", etc.) and a Purple/Red/Blue informed next step, for example:

- To get more real connections I want to include my Red autonomy more. My next step is to no longer avoid the confrontations that I inevitably have to make.

- To make everybody thrive, my next step is Blue. I am going to pay more attention to keeping my staff on the same page and to have enough predictability around my plans, so that everybody can keep up with me.
- To establish a culture of great freedom I am going to manifest my Purple leadership more. I am going to be aware of where my symbolic leadership is needed in terms of chairing meetings, giving closure, providing information (even when it is not very inspiring or new).

My reflection on this is that there is a big misconception here, i.e. that leadership is better/more important than management. And really, this is literally what these leaders/managers say and tell to the world, "We have to get from management to leadership!" In other words, they think that the more complex vMemes are to be preferred over the less complex vMemes. But of course, if you transcend and *exclude* vMemes, you get empty vMemes without a foundation. SDi often helps to get this point across, and to give the antidote for it. In the next paragraph I describe a concrete example of a manager that learned to revalue Purple, Red and Blue.

When more Yellow/Green leadership has the opposite effect.

Situation

In the department of Art and Culture of a Municipality with a dominant Blue/Orange culture the atmosphere is negative and unproductive. Targets are not met. Individual and ad-hoc ways of working rule. There is very little open communication, but lots of complaining. The rest of the organization is getting tired of not being able to count on this department to deliver something of quality on time.

Ralph, the newly appointed manager (dominant Yellow/Green) is watching all this and wonders what is going on. His tendency is mainly to respond to questions of his staff with new questions, because he wants to trust their own responsibility to do what is needed. He is an optimist. However, even he sees that things are getting worse and worse. Moreover, people are complaining about his leadership: Ralph is unclear, indecisive and he doesn't take people's feedback seriously. One of his workers says, "He acts like a UN Blue Helmet, always neutral, never takes a stance. But that is not what a manager is meant to be like, is it?"

SDi Diagnosis

Ralph explains the situation to me, telling he doesn't like to play the role of a policeman. He wants to be the Yellow/Green manager he prefers to have as his own manager, someone creating space, inspiring, concentrating on the big picture and always open for innovation. In his ears "a Blue Helmet" sounds like a compliment!

SDi Applied To The Situation

I confronted him with the following SDi analysis, "If you want to show real Yellow leadership, you have to start with the question, "What is needed NOW? What is at THIS moment the bottleneck for the natural next step in the development of your team? Notice that healthy Yellow only can function on a basis of healthy Purple, Red, Blue, Orange and Green. If not, Green/Yellow interventions will probably have the opposite effect of what you're striving for, i.e. less harmony and less inspiration. It seems this is actually happening. So, this situation seems to need the following from you."

More leadership in the areas of:	In terms of SDi:
Take the lead, frame what is happening, be clear and create clarity.	More pro-active Blue. Less Yellow/Green "helicoptering" and stick to the main issues only.
Show that it is rewarding for your colleagues to tell you what is bothering them. Take their feedback seriously and give a reaction.	More reliable and predictable Blue. Less Green putting things into perspective.
Address people: enforce agreements in a visible way; repeat decisions if needed; respond to irrational feedback too.	More Red directness and Purple symbolic visibility.
Pay attention to persistent problems in the team, even if that is by saying sorry for the persistency and making repairs where needed.	More Red boundaries and Blue perseverance and accountability to successfully bring issues to closure – once and forever.

More leadership in the areas of:	In terms of SDi:
Stop acting as a Blue helmet. Be visible, show that you are the manager.	More Purple, Red and Blue presence, involvement and a hands-on mentality; instead of Yellow/Green abstraction and distance.

Intervention

Ralph recognizes the value in this analysis and is happy with the concrete guidance. His Yellow/Green values support him to stay open for the feedback and to learn from it. He asks me to coach him in discovering and recognizing opportunities in his daily work to show (Purple) symbolic visibility, to sharpen his communication style and to practice his attitude and behavior in situations needing clear presence.

Ralph also recognizes that when he figures out everything on his own about the best approach for his leadership this nearly always results in following his Green/Yellow preferences. So, after the earlier mentioned diagnosis, he, temporarily, uses me as a sparring partner for these issues. The effect is that Ralph starts to see his blind spot (Purple, Red, Blue) and becomes more and more able to manifest these values too. For example, he had the habit of sending mails with many open reflective questions to his colleagues. Now he is being more and more transparent about his own vision, opinion and expectations. An extra effect is that Ralph is becoming interested in finding out more about the underlying causes of his negative prejudices about these vMemes. This may indicate that he moves from "closed" to merely "arrested", in terms of potential for development.

Results

Ralph is manifesting himself, very consciously, as a manager much more than before, despite his natural tendencies to disappear and zoom out. He provides more direction and clearer boundaries. He explicitly opens meetings, and clearly sets agendas. Ralph sees that this works; there is more openness, rest and connection. Ralph starts to enjoy it. And, he feels a growing admiration for the mayor who appears to be a real master in simple modern rituals with which he instantly seems to create connection and team spirit in a group, e.g. he notices that the mayor starts and ends meetings with an informal "hey you guys... ".

Ralph also realizes that something is not right when he is the only one working late each night in order to deal with all the stuff that his team likes to dump in his mailbox. This realization stimulates him to be even more clear and strict in his communication. He is amazed to learn that his more directive style is accepted rather easy by his colleagues. He even gets the idea that people actually like this more directive way of doing even though they sometimes disagree with him. The atmosphere of "fiddling while Rome burns" disappeared quickly. Ralph is solving problems and clarifying grey areas within his department in a constant and perseverant way. Upon reflection many internal issues appear easy to improve and the focus is shifting slowly outwards again, towards clients, project development and professional challenges.

In the next paragraph, I zoom deeper into the issue of how manifesting less complex vMemes can be crucial to heal the more complex vMemes.

How Manifesting Purple, Red and Blue Can Be Crucial For Healthy Orange, Green and Yellow

SDi helps to get a precise and realistic perspective on the natural next step in one's leadership. Many people I meet, who have "connection" and "innovation" as their highest values, discover via SDi that their natural next step is:

- To manifest more autonomy;
- To address their colleagues in a more direct way; or
- To put their presence, clarity and focus into the team more instead of choosing for a meta-position.

In short, their natural next step is to manifest more from the Purple, Red and Blue perspective, just like manager Ralph from the paragraph before.

This is not rocket-science and seems even quite simple compared with higher and more complex ideals like connection (Green) and systemic innovation (Yellow). However, if you take a closer look, those simple steps actually appear to be manifestations of connection and innovation:

- In the end, the most powerful way of connecting with others, is connecting with yourself. Real agency enables real communion and vice versa. And, innovation is not created by following others, but by manifesting your deepest purpose with an autonomous, free spirit and pro-active entrepreneurship.

- In the end, addressing issues in a respectful way is one of the most powerful ways to invest in better connection and the learning and innovation ability of a system. But, addressing colleagues can be stressful and can in the short term cause friction instead of connection. That is why for many people this is the natural next step, yet to be taken. Addressing each other about "what bothers you" is in my experience often the breakthrough leading to real relationships and real innovation instead of "talking still more about what inspires you".

- In the end, bringing in your presence, clarity and focus fully is what creates real commitment and connection with a situation. That is how you become an insider and a co-creator instead of an outsider and an external observer. The U Process (Scharmer et al, 2009) shows clearly how deep transformation and innovation is not possible without really engaging as part of the system, "sensing from the whole". The only way for real innovation of a system is to live your membership of that system fully.

Just doing more Purple, Red and Blue, sounds fairly simple. And it is! At the same time it is one of the biggest challenges for present leaders to really integrate these values in their Green/Yellow leadership. It takes courage, perseverance and readiness to get your hands dirty. And, it takes the ability to see the simplicity in the complexity of it.

In the next paragraph, I describe one of the simple techniques I use to help leaders in the challenge to see their blind spots in valuing Purple, Red and Blue, the reversion practice.

Coloring Your Blind Spot: The Reversion Practice

Recently, during an SDi level 1 certification training in the Netherlands, one of the participants became aware of her purely negative associations with all things around Red. I invited her to participate in a reversion practice and she did, with the following results:

Step 1: "Tell me all those negative Red associations. Don't make any restrictions, just report all that is in your mind". This was the harvest: Aggressive, macho one-upmanship, taking yourself very seriously, raging, ruthless, ignoring the feelings of others, placing yourself in the center of attention, unpredictable, unreliable, taking the stage.

Step 2: "If you consider that all negative things are an exaggeration of something that is in essence a positive thing, what would be the positive sides of all those examples?" As expected at first she didn't succeed in finding the connected positive core qualities for all her negative associations…because that was her blind spot. But with some help she started to recognize, "Ah yes, of course…!" This was the harvest:

NEGATIVE Red, is too much of	POSITIVE Red
Aggressive	Powerful
Macho one-upmanship	Show yourself, take your seat
Taking yourself very seriously	Self confidence
Raging	Being transparent, not denying what you really feel
Ruthless	Purposeful, drive, loose
Ignoring the feelings of others	Being autonomous, independent, authentic
Placing yourself in the center of attention	Being present, not hiding
Unpredictable	Spontaneous
Unreliable	Unapologetic
Taking the stage	Playing big, not playing small
Anger	Zest, passion

The point? For raging, intimidating dictators, no reversion practice will help. However, for most people coloring one's blind spot with new positive associations can help to diminish one's prejudices, and provide an opening to revalue the values rejected earlier.

Conclusion

I believe that the time and our Life Conditions are now for Second Tier consciousness to manifest itself in all aspects in our life and in our world, which means also in our organizations.

This does not mean that I think the people in Gaza, Syria, etc. are ready for Second Tier. But I think their situation is. All interventions that came from First Tier perspectives have failed, and will continue to do so. The complexity, the way everything is connected with everything, is so inevitable, that a Second Tier perspective is just as inevitable for sustainable improvement. A typical Second Tier perspective analysis would be to determine the next natural step and to facilitate that step to happen, meeting everybody where (in which vMeme) they are. If the Spiral is our client, the next natural step for organizations (as well as for people!) to transcend to Second Tier, is often to include less complex vMemes. Because there is no transcending without including, as Ken Wilber points out so adequately.

And as I demonstrate in this chapter: including means not only to stop excluding earlier vMemes. When a more complex vMeme emerges the earlier vMemes get included pretty much as automatic subroutines. These included subroutines that serve the less complex vMemes are sufficient to provide satisfiers, but this does not mean they are the most effective, most efficient, or most healthy ways possible for these subroutines to be configured. It takes active and conscious attention to revaluing these less complex vMemes, in order to infuse them with the wisdom available from the more complex vMemes. Healthy reframing of earlier, automatically formed, vMemes requires attention to and appreciation of the benefits these systems provide to the whole person and organization.

In revaluing Purple, Red and Blue as the next natural step towards the most healthy and effective expression of Second Tier cognition, it becomes clear how these vMemes are not a burden from what went before, but rather they are the acupuncture points to create the essential breakthroughs in the right direction. With this perspective on the less complex vMemes, it becomes once again easy to see their great but sometimes hidden value. By refining the configuration of the less complex vMemes, we foster the most healthy and balanced emergence of human beings in our organizations – we serve the Spiral.

Bibliography

Ken Wilber, *A Brief History of Everything* (Shambhala Publications, Inc., Boston, MA, 1996), pp. 89-90.

C. Otto Scharmer, *Theory U: Leading from the Future as It Emerges* (Berrett-Koehler, San Francisco, 2009)

AUTHORS

Author Contact Information

Bonilla-Núñez, Roberto V.

Mexico. Leon Guanajuato. English. Spanish.

roberto@novarumm.mx
+52 477 7185080
Skype: robertovbn
Facebook: Roberto Bonilla
LinkedIn: Roberto Bonilla
www.novarumm.mx

Focus: SDi systems diagnosis and improvement, with business, NGO's, government, community and society.

Brown, Barbara N., M.S., M.B.A.

Houston, Texas, USA. English.

BNBrown@thirdcoastcomplexity.com
713-504-2872
Skype: technologytransformations
Facebook: www.facebook.com/bnbrown
LinkedIn: Barbara Brown
www.thirdcoastcomplexity.com

Focus: Developing Lean Agile business approaches and support systems for scaffolded natural designs that are sustainable, anti-fragile and resilient.

Christensen, Tom, M.A.

Madison, Wisconsin, USA. English.

tomc@centralmadison.com
608-255-4242
Facebook: Tom Christensen
LinkedIn: Tom Christensen
www.tomclight.com
www.centralmadison.com

Professional Focus: Public speaking, teaching, writing. Expertise in sales, marketing, and Gravesian theory and application.

Cook, John E., Ph.D.

Whangarei, New Zealand. English.

john.cook@5deep.co.nz
+64 (0)21 423 300
Skype: Intentcook
Facebook: www.facebook.com/5deeplimited
LinkedIn: nz.linkedin.com/in/5deep
www.5deep.co.nz
www.researchgate.net

Focus: Consultant in management, culture and change, specialising in the role of hidden coping mechanisms and preferences for change within organisations, communities, public services and the individual.

Cooke, Christopher, M.Sc.

Otley, West Yorkshire, UK. English. French.

christopher.cooke@5deep.net
+44 (0)7973 866930
Skype: waikicookie
Facebook: Christopher Cooke
LinkedIn: Christopher Cooke
www.5deep.net
www.5deepvitalsigns.com

Focus: An educational, advisory, mentoring, and group facilitation practice with his wife Sheila that is a demonstration of a leading understanding of the dynamics of human and social change based upon an Integral perspective.

Cooke, Sheila. M.B.A.

Otley, West Yorkshire, UK. English, Chinese, Japanese, French.

Sheila.cooke@5deep.net
+44 (0) 7446 780081
Facebook: Sheila Cooke
LinkedIn: Sheila LeGeros
www.5deep.net
www.5deepvitalsigns.com

Focus: Designer and trainer of virtual and face-to-face collaboration processes that build resilience and adaptability within organizations and individuals by building capacity for self-organization.

Dawlabani, Said

San Diego, California, USA. English. Arabic.

se.dawlabani@memenomics.com
(619) 857-8157
Skype: dawlco
LinkedIn: Said E. Dawlabani
www.memenomics.org

Focus: Author, cultural economist, and consultant specializing in the Gravesian approach to value systems and cultural change.

Freeman, Jon. M.A.

Salisbury, UK. English. French. German.

jon@spiralworld.net
Skype: jonfreeman2910
Facebook: Jon Freeman
LinkedIn: Jon Freeman
www.spiralfutures.com
www.scienceofpossibility.net

Focus: Organizational development, Culture Scan, certification trainings, public speaking, facilitation, coaching, with special emphasis on organizations and finance.

Laura Frey Horn, Ed.D.

Middleburg, VA. USA. English. French.

lfheureka@gmail.com
540-454-2648
Skype: lfeurika
Facebook: Laura Frey Horn
LinkedIn: Dr. Laura Frey Horn.

Focus: Whole systems, Gravesian based, organizational consulting to support and develop healthy organizations which thrive effectively in their environments. Actively engaged in organizational and academic research, writing, and teaching on leadership and organizational development using the Gravesian and whole systems frameworks.

Gibb, Bruce L. MPA. Ph.D.

Ann Arbor, Michigan, USA. English. Spanish.

blgibb@aol.com|
734-717-3433.
Skype: brucelorenzo
Facebook: Bruce L. Gibb
LinkedIn: Bruce Gibb

Focus: Education. Development of individuals, teams, organizations, and complex organizations; integrating SDi into the humanities in academia and into the practice of organizational development.

Hamilton, Marilyn. Ph.D.

Abbotsford, BC, Canada. English. French. German.

marilyn@integralcity.com
Skype: marilyn8478
Facebook: Marilyn Hamilton
LinkedIn: Marilyn Hamilton
www.integralcity.com
www.marilyn.integralcity.com

Focus: City visioning, learning habitats, workshops, seminars, dialogues, City Systemic Constellations, Integral City Assessments, in service to waking up the Human Hive as Gaia's Reflective Organ.

Harkins, Dennis

Madison, Wisconsin, USA. English.

dwharks@gmail.com
608.576.6848
Skype: Dennis.harkins1
LinkedIn: Dennis Harkins

Focus: Integral community long term care.

Jónsson, Bjarni Snaebjorn, Ph.D

Reykjavik, Iceland. Icelandic, English, Danish, Norwegian.

bjarni@bsj.is
+354 822 3321
Skype: bjarnisj
Facebook: Bjarni S. Jonsson
LinkedIn: Bjarni S. Jonsson
www.decidact.com

Focus: Large-scale transformation of organisations and social systems. Appropriate prescription for change based on cultural insight.

Krawchuk, Fred. M.B.A.

Spain. English. Spanish. Portuguese.

fredkrawchuk@yahoo.com
Skype: bodhi06.
LinkedIn: Fred Krawchuk.

Focus: Collaborate with business and government clients to diagnose difficult challenges, design comprehensive solutions, and deliver sustainable training and development programs.

Lockard, Jim. MPA, Ph.D.

USA. France. English. French.

drjim-lockard@att.net
805-298-0930
Skype: jim.lockard1
Facebook: Jim Lockard
LinkedIn: Jim Lockard
www.cotterconsulting.net/jimlockard

Focus: Working with individuals and organizations to master cultural evolution and change.

Maalouf, Elza. Former attorney.

San Diego, California, USA. English. Arabic.

elza.maalouf@gmail.com
Facebook: Elza S. Maalouf
LinkedIn: Elza Maalouf
www.elzamaalouf.com

Focus: Political theorist, author and futurist, specializing in large-scale systems and societal change. President and co-founder of the California based Center for Human Emergence – Middle East.

MacLeod, Jordan

Boston, MA, USA, and Prince Edward Island, Canada. English. French.

jordanbmacleod@yahoo.com
902.218.7269
Skype: jbmacleod
Facebook: Jordan MacLeod
LinkedIn: Jordan MacLeod
www.newcurrency.org

Focus: Entrepreneur, writer and consultant on the new economy.

Rienstra, Jasper

Driebergen, The Netherlands. Dutch. English.

jasper@synnervate.nl
+31651049005
Skype: jacri1
Facebook: Jasper Rienstra
LinkedIn: Jasper Rienstra
www.humanemergence.nl
www.spiraldynamicsintegral.nl
www.klopt.nu

Focus: Leadership development, holacracy, management consulting, organizational development, systemic change, conscious business, teambuilding, break-through confrontations in profit and non-profit.

Rice, Keith E. Grad. Cert. Ed.

Bradford, United Kingdom. English.

keith@integratedsociopsychology.net
(44) 01274 975667
Skype: keith.e.rice
Facebook: Keith E. Rice.
www.integratedsociopsychology.net

Focus: To create a rigorous academic framework based on SDi and 4Q/8L around which all the behavioural sciences can be aligned and integrated.

Schuringa, Leida. Drs.

The Netherlands. Dutch. English. German. French.

leida@synnervate.nl
0031-6-20748850
Skype: leida.schuringa
Facebook: Leida Schuringa
LinkedIn: Leida Schuringa
www.synnervate.nl

Focus: Training, coaching, advising, for individuals, developing countries and minority groups e.g. refugees, Roma.

Sieber, Armin. M.A.S.

Winterthur, Switzerland. German. Swiss-German. English. French.

armin.sieber@integral-learning.ch
+41 79 659 56 77
Skype: acourec
Facebook: armin.sieber@facebook.com
LinkedIn: Armin Sieber
www.itw-oberstufe.ch
www.integral-learning.ch

Focus: Education, coaching, personal and collective growth.

Vargas, Alberto M. Ph.D.

Madison, Wisconsin, USA. Spanish. English.

avargasp@wisc.edu
Skype: avargasprieto
Facebook: Alberto Vargas Prieto
LinkedIn: Alberto Vargas

Focus: Latin America, Mexico, sustainability, environmental conservation.

Voorhoeve, Anne-Marie

Vreeland, Netherlands. Dutch. English.

anne-marie@thehaguecenter.org
+31628550634
Skype: amvoorhoeve
Facebook: Anne-Marie Voorhoeve
LinkedIn: Anne-Marie Voorhoeve.
www.thehaguecenter.org
www.humanemergence.nl
www.integralcity.com
www.sq21-team.nl
www.clubofbudapest.com

Focus: Strategist and experienced facilitator focusing on transformation of society into a sustainable world. Expertise in marketing, communications, business and Meshworks development.

APPENDIX 1: GRAVES – CONTEXTUALIZATIONS

Barrett, Richard. *Building a Values-Driven Organization: A Whole System Approach to Cultural Transformation.* (2006) Routledge, NYC, USA.

Barrett, Richard. *Evolutionary Coaching: A Values-Based Approach to Unleashing Human Potential.* (2014) Lulu Publishing Services.

Beck, Don & Cowan, Christopher. *Spiral Dynamics: Mastering Values, Leadership and Change.* (1996) Blackwell Publishing, Malden, MA, USA.

Beck, Don & Linscott, Graham. *The Crucible: Forging South Africa's Future. In Search of a Template for the World.* (1991) New Paradigm Press, Johannesburg, South Africa

Beecroft, Nicholas. *Analyze West: A Psychiatrist Takes Western Civilization on a Journey of Transformation.* (2014) Nicholas Beecroft, UK.

Beecroft, Nicholas. *New Magna Carta: A Psychiatrist's Prescription For Western Civilization.* (2015). Nicholas Beecroft, UK.

Cowan, Christopher and Todorovic, Natasha. *The Never Ending Quest: Clare W. Graves Explores Human Nature.* (2005) ECLET Publishing, Santa Barbara, CA, USA.

Dawlabani, Said E. *MEMEnomics: The Next-Generation Economic System.* (2013) Select Books, Inc. NYC, USA

Freeman, Jon. *The Science of Possibility: Patterns of Connected Consciousness.* (2008) SpiralWorld, Ferndown, UK.

Hamilton, Marilyn. *Integral City: Evolutionary Intelligences for the Human Hive.* (2008) New Society Publishers, Gabriola Island, BC, Canada.

Laloux, Frederic. *Reinventing Organizations: A Guide to Creating Organizations Inspired by the Next State of Human Consciousness.* (2014) Nelson Parker, Brussels, Belgium.

Lee, William R. Ed. *Clare W. Graves: Levels of Human Existence.* (2002) ECLET Publishing, Santa Barbara, CA, USA.

Lessem R, Abouleish I, Pocagnik M and Herman L (2015) *Integral Polity : Aligning Nature, Culture, Society and Economy.* Gower. Farnham, UK.

Maalouf, Elza S. *Emerge! The rise of Functional Democracy and the Future of the Middle East.* (2014) Select Books, Inc. NYC, USA.

Mackey, John & Sisodia, Rajendra. *Conscious Capitalism: Liberating the Heroic Spirit of Business.* (2014) Harvard Business School Publishing, Boston, Massachusetts, USA.

Merry, Peter. *Evolutionary Leadership: Integral Leadership for an Increasingly Complex World.* (2009) Integral Publishers, Pacific Grove, California, USA.

Nasr, Amir Ahmad. *My Islam: How Fundamentalism Stole My Mind –And Doubt Freed My Soul.*(2013) St. Martin's Press. NYC, USA.

Rice, Keith E. *Knowing Me, Knowing You: An Integrated SocioPsychology Guide to Personal Fulfilment & Better Relationships.* (2006) Trafford Publishing, Victoria, B.C., Canada.

Stamper, Gary. *Awakening the new Masculine: The Path of The Integral Warrior.* (2012) iUniverse, Bloomington, Indiana, USA.

van Leijden, Wilbert & Zuiker, Paul. *Nederland op Doorbreken: Een Vernieuwend Perspectief Voor Een Land in Crisis.* (2007) Emergent Publishing, NL (Title in English: *The Netherlands on the verge of a breakthrough: an innovative perspective for a country in crisis.*)

Viljoen R (2015) *Inclusive Organisational Transformation: An African Perspective on Human Niches and Diversity of Thought.* Gower. Farnham, UK.

Wade, Jenny. *Changes of Mind: A Holonomic Theory of the Evolution of Consciousness.* (1996) State University of New York, Press. Albany, NY, USA.

Waller, Philippa. *Spiral Into Love: How to Stop Falling in Love with the Wrong Ones and Stay in Love with the Right Ones.* (2012) FeedARead.com Publishing, UK.

Wilkie, Rosemary. *Emergence: Vol 1 - Introduction.* (2013) Rosemary Wilkie, UK.

Wilkie, Rosemary. Émergence Vol *1* . Édition Française (2013) Rosemary Wilkie, UK

Primary Resources for Graves and Beck Material

Beck, Don & Cowan, Christopher. *Spiral Dynamics: Mastering Values, Leadership and Change.* (1996) Blackwell Publishing, Malden, MA, USA.

Cowan, Christopher and Todorovic, Natasha. *The Never Ending Quest: Clare W. Graves Explores Human Nature.* (2005) ECLET Publishing, Santa Barbara, CA, USA.

Lee, William R. Ed. *Clare W. Graves: Levels of Human Existence.* (2002) ECLET Publishing, Santa Barbara, CA, USA.

THE BOOKS SPEAK

Editor: Dear Books. What do you want to be?

Voice of Vol 1 and 2: I am a cognitive virus, a meme. I intend to propagate into a critical mass of human beings, such that the tipping point is reached after which the pattern entailed in these books becomes a common resource for patterning of human thought. This is, of course, not my only effort to achieve this end. I have been busy in many narratives, and some work is still left to do before the tipping point occurs.

This pattern of thought, this meme, is best named "a developmental schema". With this pattern instantiated in a mind all matters of interest are described in terms of what they were, what they are, and what they will be. The schema of Aristotelian definition is included and transcended with this broader, more complex, assessment that adds a consideration of change to the identity of interest. What did it change from? What is its potential for change in its present form? What is it likely to change to?

In these books I am instantiating this template for thought with the use of the Gravesian body of distinctions. There is nothing sacred about this body of information. The reader is encouraged to use any model of development, model of change, that they wish to. I am present in all of them. But, to move humanity to a more comprehensive, and thus more integrated and healthy, way of knowing its reality, some developmental framework must be internalized and put to use. The Gravesian instance of a developmental model works very well in training the mind to view the world in a developmental schema. Since the opportunity to infect humanity with the developmental meme, thru the Gravesian material, was available, I took this opportunity. Had there been a better opportunity available I would have taken it, and when it does show up, I will take it. Eventually a critical mass of minds will naturally perceive developmental trajectories in all things. When this time comes it will be as natural for most humans to place an identity within a flow of change as it is natural to put subjects before verbs.

This report on what I, the books, am really up to, will not be of interest to most readers. So, dear editor, please place this info in an Appendix. Those who wish to see the workings I am up to, will find me there.

INDEX

spirit   11, 50, 100, 137, 186, 193–194, 220, 292, 333, 335, 352

spiritual   67, 189–195, 197–201, 226, 301

spirituality   2, 52, 62, 157, 163, 166, 189–190, 197, 200–201

stability   22, 91, 108, 116–118, 164, 171–173, 187, 190, 208, 213, 221

stage   17, 22–25, 28, 34, 48–52, 54–59, 66–67, 74–75, 82–84, 87–91, 94–98, 123, 129, 132, 140, 154, 171, 179–180, 186, 190, 206–207, 218–219, 221–222, 224, 236, 244, 247, 249, 270, 280, 286, 294, 302, 303, 324, 336

strategic   17, 20–21, 27, 33, 43, 56, 70, 85, 88, 90–92, 96, 125, 159, 165, 174, 177, 182, 188, 207, 209–210, 216, 321

superordinate   88, 90, 92–94, 96–100, 123–124, 169–170, 173, 187–188

sustainability   24, 30, 89, 92, 95, 109, 129, 158–159, 161, 165, 187, 220, 223, 297, 327

system   1–4, 6, 12–13, 15–16, 18, 20–22, 24–25, 27, 29–30, 32–35, 37, 40, 42, 52, 59–61, 63, 67–68, 70, 74–75, 80–81, 83–84, 86, 88–95, 97–100, 103–115, 117–132, 134, 138–141, 143, 145–146, 148–150, 152, 154, 157, 163–164, 170–172, 174, 179, 185, 187, 190, 192, 195–196, 202–213, 215–216, 218–219, 221–222, 224, 226–227, 231, 233–239, 241–242, 245, 247, 249, 251–252, 256–259, 266–268, 273, 277–278, 283–289, 292, 295, 297, 299–301, 303–313, 316, 320, 322, 326–327, 329, 335, 337, 339–340, 342–343, 345, 347, 351

T

team   21, 25, 27, 32–39, 41–43, 54, 60, 68–73, 75–78, 145–154, 169, 173–174, 183–184, 186, 188, 222, 248, 261, 266–267, 276, 288, 294, 315–316, 318, 323, 325–327, 330, 332–334, 344, 350

technology   2–3, 49–51, 67–68, 80, 83, 94–95, 98, 131, 137–138, 141–144, 148, 153–154, 176, 223, 230–231, 236, 245, 248, 289, 311–312

terrorism   156, 166, 304

theory   1–2, 5–7, 9–10, 13, 22, 36, 49, 51–52, 62, 66–68, 71, 73, 75–76, 106, 108, 113, 121, 123, 129, 131–136, 140–141, 150, 156, 159–164, 166–168, 170–171, 180, 185, 187, 206, 208, 223, 225–226, 228–230, 233, 239–240, 249, 251–252, 254–255, 282, 284, 338, 353

thinking   21, 50, 53, 59, 61, 63, 66, 70, 74, 84, 94, 99, 110, 121, 124–125, 127, 130, 139, 141, 145–146, 158–159, 164–165, 181, 185, 206, 213–214, 220–221, 223–227, 233–237, 239, 241–242, 244–245, 247, 251, 260–262, 270, 277–278, 282, 290, 292, 294, 315, 320, 326–327

tMeme   230, 233, 236, 249

transformation   24, 30, 42, 83, 88, 109, 133–134, 153–154, 164, 170, 183, 199, 222, 226, 235, 242, 245, 247, 258, 301–302, 310, 335, 345, 350–352

transition   24, 49–50, 53, 55–58, 63–68, 70, 74, 83, 87–88, 100, 105, 115, 195, 198, 218, 221, 223, 274, 286, 313

translational   235, 242, 245, 247

trust   57, 129, 134, 149, 151, 164, 176, 180, 182, 188, 204, 206, 235, 245–246, 248, 285, 287–288, 301, 331

Turquoise   13, 16–17, 19–21, 26, 61–62, 64, 68, 75, 192, 311

type   24, 32, 35, 50, 52, 57, 61, 82, 84, 90, 94, 106, 126, 205, 216, 222, 233, 235–236, 239–240, 242–243, 254, 292

U

uncertainty   144, 183, 198, 208, 309, 325

unity   79, 131–132, 186

Unity   131

V

ValueMatch   329–330

values   15–18, 20, 23, 27–29, 34, 39, 42–43, 46, 62, 75, 80–82, 84–90, 92–97, 99–101, 110, 112, 114, 118, 124–125, 130–131, 134, 139–140, 170–172, 174, 192, 195, 201, 219–222, 225–226, 228, 231–232, 234, 237, 239, 250–251, 258, 265–267,

Lightning Source UK Ltd.
Milton Keynes UK
UKOW07f0537201015

260975UK00010B/30/P